The Earl of Rochester

The Works of
The Earl of Rochester

*Edited by David M. Vieth,
with an Introduction and Bibliography*

Wordsworth Poetry Library

First published by Yale University Press, New Haven, USA.

This edition published 1995 by Wordsworth Editions Ltd,
Cumberland House, Crib Street, Ware, Hertfordshire SG12 9ET.

Copyright © Yale University 1968.

ISBN 1-85326-441-5

Printed and bound in Denmark by Nørhaven.

The paper in this book is produced from pure wood
pulp, without the use of chlorine or any other substance
harmful to the environment. The energy used in its
production consists almost entirely of hydroelectricity
and heat generated from waste materials, thereby
conserving fossil fuels and contributing little to the
greenhouse effect.

Preface

The plan for this edition of Rochester's poetry originated in 1959, during the preparation of my book *Attribution in Restoration Poetry: A Study of Rochester's "Poems" of 1680* (Yale University Press, 1963). At that time it became evident that although a critical edition of the complete works was still far from feasible, Rochester scholarship had reached a point where a less ambitious edition of his poems could be produced which would be superior to anything then available. Such a volume, it seemed, would have value for three types of readers: students in advanced university courses in Restoration and eighteenth-century English literature, for whom it could serve as a text-book; specialists in the period, who lacked a reliable text for quotations from Rochester's poetry; and perhaps a broader audience with less professional interests. Subsequently, some aspects of the task were facilitated by the unexpected opportunity to collaborate with Professor Bror Danielsson on *The Gyldenstolpe Manuscript Miscellany of Poems. by John Wilmot, Earl of Rochester, and other Restoration Authors* (Almqvist & Wiksell, 1967), which involved further investigation of the Rochester text and canon. Meanwhile, the reappearance of the

Muses' Library *Poems by John Wilmot, Earl of Rochester* in a slightly revised second edition (Routledge and Kegan Paul, Harvard University Press, 1953, 1964) offered assurance of increasing need for the kind of volume I proposed.

Excluding Rochester's prose and dramatic works, which hold less interest for the general reader, this edition attempts to assemble every scrap of the nondramatic verse on which his fame as a poet chiefly rests. The omitted prose consists of his very readable letters, Alexander Bendo's bill, and a fragment of a prose comedy surviving in his handwriting. Besides this fragment, the dramatic works omitted are his adaptation of Fletcher's *Valentinian* and the scene he wrote for Sir Robert Howard's *The Conquest of China. Sodom*, I assume, is spurious. Printed with the poems, however, are Rochester's one prologue and two epilogues, which are akin to the nondramatic verse in style and subject.

In deference to the readers for whom this edition is designed, the explanatory material needed to understand each poem is conveniently placed with its text, in headnotes or footnotes; information of concern only to specialists is relegated to the Notes at the back of the volume. Even these Notes avoid extended analysis of the authorship of the poems, directing the reader, whenever possible, to the detailed discussions in my two earlier books and elsewhere. For easy reference, the Table of Contents and the First-Line Index give page numbers for both the text and the Notes on the Texts, Authorship, and Dates of the Poems. At the head of each textual note, a marginal page reference locates the poem in the text. Since the poems are printed in approximately their order of composition, the account of Rochester's life in the Introduction provides a necessary biographical framework, especially for readers who have little familiarity with Restoration literature. The list of Rochester Studies 1925–1967 furnishes a research tool unavailable elsewhere. Not intended primarily for the specialist, it emphasizes central contributions to Rochester studies instead of trying to be exhaustive. Brief annotations, descriptive rather than evaluative, indicate the contents of most items in the list.

To Southern Illinois University, and above all to its late chairman of the Department of English, Robert D. Faner, I am grateful for various kinds of aid, especially the released time from my teaching duties which made possible the completion of this edition. Similar obligations are owed to the University of Kansas and the former chairman of its English department, William P. Albrecht, who arranged the released time in the spring of 1962 during which the volume was begun. Arthur Mizener and Richard C. Boys responded repeatedly with data from their first-line index to poems in miscellanies. John Harold Wilson furnished information and suggestions resulting in substantial improvements in at least a dozen of the explanatory notes. Sister Scholastica Mandeville contributed material to the explanatory notes for one poem. Paul Arthur Schilpp offered useful comments relating to Section 3 of the Introduction. To the staff of Morris Library of Southern Illinois University at Carbondale, particularly its Humanities Librarian, Alan M. Cohn, I am indebted for many acts of assistance. Also notably helpful were the staffs of the University of Illinois, Newberry, and Yale University libraries.

The Duke of Portland granted permission to reproduce several poems from the holographs of Rochester and his wife at the University of Nottingham (Portland MS. PwV 31). James M. Osborn and Robert H. Taylor generously allowed publication from early poetical manuscripts in their possession. The Carl H. Pforzheimer Library supplied a microfilm of its apparently unique copy of one of the Rochester editions of 1680 (A-1680-PF). For assistance in connection with unpublished

manuscript materials in their collections, I wish to thank the
following: British Museum; Victoria and Albert Museum;
Lambeth Palace Library; Bodleian Library; All Souls College,
Oxford; Merton College, Oxford; Worcester College, Oxford;
Cambridge University Library; University of Nottingham Li-
brary; County Archives, Maidstone, Kent; Chetham's Library,
Hunt's Bank, Manchester; National Library of Scotland; Uni-
versity of Edinburgh Library; Österreichische Nationalbiblio-
thek, Vienna; Harvard University Library; Yale University
Library; Princeton University Library; Ohio State University
Library; University of Illinois Library; University of Chicago
Library; Folger Shakespeare Library; Henry E. Huntington
Library.

D. M. V.

Southern Illinois University, Carbondale
June 1968

Contents

EARLY MATURITY (1672–1673)

POEMS POSSIBLY BY ROCHESTER

The Imperfect Enjoyment

By ye E. of R.

Naked she lay, claspt in my longing Armes,
I fill'd wth Love, & she all over Charmes!
Both equally inspir'd wth eager fire,
Melting through kindnesse, flameing in desire!
Wth Armes, Leggs, Lipps, close cinging to embrace
She clips me to her Breast, & sucks me to her face.
The nimble Tongue (Loves lesser Lightning) play'd
Wthin my Mouth, & to my thoughts conveyd,
Swift Orders, that I shou'd prepare to throw
The all-dissolving Thunder-Bolt ~~~~~~~
My fluttring Soule, ~~~~~~~~~~~~~~~
Hangs hovering o're ~~~~~~~~~~~~~~~

B.

P.62 of Yale Manuscript 'Songs and Verses upon Severall Occasions',
reproduced by permission of the Yale University Library.

Introduction

1. Rochester's Life

No man was ever more typical of his age than John Wilmot, second Earl of Rochester. The legend that sees him as the darling of the polished, profligate Court of Charles II is true as far as it goes, although somewhat simplified. Etherege's Dorimant may well be a fictional copy of Rochester, as is generally assumed, but the question need hardly be raised: since both epitomize the same fashionable Restoration society, one on the stage and one in real life, generic resemblances are inevitable.

In an age when the English aristocracy was still politically, socially, and culturally supreme, Rochester was socially and culturally potent. The erratic brilliance of a Shaftesbury or a Buckingham shone also in him. In an age when skill in writing verses was a practical asset to a courtier, Rochester became the second-ranking poet, excelled only by Dryden. In a decade when the most significant literature was being written for the stage, he was patron to several important playwrights, served as model for countless witty young rakes in Restoration comedy, and wrote some dramatic pieces himself—in addition to numerous nondramatic poems which influenced the drama and were influenced by it. As a contemporary of Descartes, Hobbes, Locke, and the Royal Society, he was a skeptic, and he even dabbled in chemistry, as did Buckingham and King Charles. In an age when the average man was still pious, he died devout. His death in 1680 at the young age of thirty-three is peculiarly appropriate, for the way of life he represented had, in a sense, already expired in the Popish Plot terror. Yet Rochester was never more typical of his age than in his ability to step outside it, sardonically viewing it and himself *sub specie aeternitatis,* or at least in terms of one or more of the several dozen creeds that are a heritage of Western civilization.

He was born on the first day of April, 1647, at his mother's manor house at Ditchley in Oxfordshire, the sole surviving child of what was a second marriage for both his father and his mother. His parentage mirrored the political and religious forces that were tearing England apart. His mother, Anne, the daughter of Sir John St. John, came from a prominent Puritan family and seems to have been a sober, strong-minded, shrewd woman, well able to manage a household. His father, Henry Wilmot, Baron Wilmot of Adderbury in Oxfordshire, was a royalist general under Charles I and a veteran of countless military actions. Witty, a good companion though occasionally cantankerous, and almost quixotically fearless and tireless, Lord Wilmot was a popular commander with his officers and men. After the death of Charles I, he became one of the new king's chief advisers. He accompanied Charles II to Scotland in 1650 and fought in the disastrous conflict at Worcester in 1651, after which he played a major part in effecting the King's escape. In reward for his services, he was created Earl of Rochester on 13 December 1652. Thereafter Charles employed him in many diplomatic missions on the continent, as well as in leading the abortive royalist insurrection in Yorkshire in 1655. He died at Ghent on 19 February 1657/8, a relic of the old breed of bluff, extroverted Cavaliers. John Wilmot's relationship with a father he saw rarely, if ever, may partly explain his later distrust of father-figures like Charles II, whose true greatness as king he seems not to have understood.

The young Earl of Rochester was necessarily brought up by his mother. After being tutored at home by her chaplain, Francis Giffard, he was sent for more formal training to Burford Grammar School. There he is reported to have been "an extraordinary Proficient at his Book," acquiring the knowledge of Latin which reveals itself in his later translations and adaptations from Ovid, Horace, Lucretius, Petronius, and Seneca. On 18 January 1659/60 he matriculated as a fellow commoner at Wadham College, Oxford. Wadham at that time was a center of the intellectual group which was to become the Royal Society, although one may doubt that a boy not yet in his teens could have been much influenced.

At Oxford, Rochester undoubtedly shared in the jubilation which greeted the Restoration of Charles II. His tutor was Phineas Bury, a capable mathematician, but he is said to have been instructed in poetry and debauchery by Robert Whitehall, a fellow of Merton College. Under Rochester's name were published some congratulatory lines on Charles II's return in 1660 and two consolatory poems, in Latin and English, on the death of the Princess of Orange in midwinter of 1660–61 (printed on pp. 155–58). Probably Whitehall wrote these verses for the thirteen-year-old Earl, whose father's career would render such offerings fitting. The ironic circumstance that Rochester was destined to be an important English poet could scarcely have been foreseen.

King Charles was not a man to forget Henry Wilmot's son. He granted Rochester a pension of 500 pounds a year in February 1660/1, retroactive to the preceding spring. At a convo-

cation at Oxford on 9 September 1661, the strait-laced old Earl
of Clarendon, Lord Chancellor of England and Chancellor of
the University, conferred the courtesy degree of M.A. on the
young Earl with a kiss on the left cheek. Having seen to Rochester's formal education, King Charles next sent him on the
Grand Tour. As his tutor the King appointed Sir Andrew Balfour, a distinguished Scottish physician and scholar who succeeded in imbuing the boy with a love of knowledge. Leaving
England on 21 November 1661, Balfour and his charge traveled
through France and Italy for four years. They reached Venice
before 1 October 1664, and at Padua on 26 October Rochester
signed the register at the university. Back in England, Rochester
appeared at Court on Christmas day 1664, bearing a letter to
the King from his sister "Madame," the Duchess of Orleans.

The seventeen-year-old nobleman who now arrived on the
Court scene was easy and witty in conversation, graceful in person and manner, handsome, and tall, but with a slenderness
betraying his lack of a robust constitution. Although several
years younger than Sedley, Buckhurst (later Earl of Middle-
sex and Dorset), Etherege, Buckingham, and others who were
already at Court, Rochester was soon setting the pace for the
coterie of fashionable wits who surrounded the King. Probably
he began to write verses about this date, and he launched into
a series of wild but still rather conventional exploits. In view
of the sulphurous atmosphere which enveloped his reputation in
following centuries, it is well to recollect Rochester's relative
youth and the fact that comparable high jinks are not unknown
on twentieth-century college campuses.

Continuing to act *in loco parentis*, King Charles determined
to find a wife for Rochester. The royal choice was Elizabeth
Malet, the daughter of John Malet of Enmore in Somersetshire, who came up to London in the spring of 1665 with her
grandfather, Sir Francis Hawley. Described by Pepys as "the

great beauty and fortune of the North" and by Grammont as the "melancholy heiress," she was also sought in marriage by Lord John Butler, son of the powerful Duke of Ormonde; William, Lord Herbert, heir to the Earl of Pembroke; Lord Hinchingbrooke, eldest son of the Earl of Sandwich; a son of Lord Desmond; and Sir Francis Popham. Miss Malet's money-hungry relatives opposed a marriage to Rochester, who had no property except the scanty paternal acres at Adderbury, no income except his pension from the King (perpetually in arrears), and few prospects. Taking matters into his own hands, Rochester attempted on the night of 26 May 1665 to abduct the heiress. As Lord Hawley was returning with his grand-daughter by coach after supping with "la belle Stuart" at White-hall Palace, she was forcibly taken from him at Charing Cross and spirited out of town in a coach-and-six with two female attendants. Rochester was promptly apprehended at Uxbridge and sent to the Tower, while Miss Malet was restored to her family. Several weeks later, on 19 June, Rochester was freed after submitting a contrite petition to the King.

Balked temporarily in matrimony, Rochester redeemed himself by volunteering for the Second Dutch War, which had begun early in June with the English naval victory off Lowestoft. On 15 July 1665 he joined the fleet, commanded by the Earl of Sandwich, as it sailed on its ill-judged attempt to capture the rich Dutch East India ships in Bergen harbor. Serving on board Sir Thomas Teddiman's flagship the *Revenge,* Rochester was in the thick of the enemy bombardment on 2 August, two friends being cut down beside him by a single cannon ball. The next day he penned a charmingly boyish account of the battle in a letter to his mother. On 9 September he was still with the fleet when several East Indiamen were captured, and by 16 September, with the Great Plague at its height in London, he was back at Court giving King Charles a personal account of the action.

Pleased with his gallantry, Charles rewarded him on 31 October with a free gift of 750 pounds, and on 21 March 1665/6 he was sworn in as a Gentleman of the Bedchamber to the King—although he did not assume the post until 14 March 1666/7, and his pension of 1000 pounds a year was not authorized until 2 October 1667. During the summer of 1666, Rochester briefly rejoined the fleet, coming on board Sir Edward Spragge's ship on 20 July. In St. James's Fight on 25 July, he distinguished himself by delivering an important message in an open boat under heavy fire. Also in July, he was given command of a troop of horse.

In London, the Great Fire came and went in September while Elizabeth Malet, Penelope-like, playfully mystified her many suitors. On 29 January 1666/7, she defied her family and surprised everyone by marrying Rochester, whom apparently she preferred from the start. She was appointed Groom of the Stole to the Duchess of York. At this time, too, for reasons which remain obscure, she was converted to Roman Catholicism partly at Rochester's instigation, remaining a Catholic until a few weeks before her husband's death in 1680. Early in her marriage she was probably the excuse, if not the inspiration, for a number of Rochester's love lyrics. She was herself literary, as is shown by some of her poems that have survived in her own handwriting (one is printed on p. 10).

Over against the occasional hints of homosexuality in Rochester's poems and elsewhere, if these were introduced for more than their shock value, should be placed the evidence that Rochester and his wife enjoyed an unusually happy marriage. An affectionate record of their relationship is preserved in their letters—which, however, reveal that Lady Rochester suffered from mother-in-law troubles. Four children resulted from the marriage. The eldest daughter, Anne, baptized on 30 August 1669, was married first to Henry Baynton of Bromham, Wilt-

shire, and second to Francis Greville, by whom she became an-
cestress of the Earls of Warwick. Rochester's only son, Charles,
baptized on 2 January 1670/1 (Dorset and Sedley were god-
fathers), succeeded him in 1680 as third Earl. Elizabeth, baptized on 13 July 1674, married Edward Montagu, third Earl
of Sandwich, the son of the Lord Hinchingbrooke who had
wooed her mother in vain. Said to have inherited much of her
father's wit, she died in Paris in 1757. The youngest daughter,
Malet, baptized on 6 January 1675/6, married John Vaughan,
second Viscount Lisburne.

Difficult to understand in terms of post-Victorian morality is
the custom among Restoration aristocrats of keeping a mistress,
which should perhaps be regarded as polygamy or concubinage
rather than adultery. Not counting miscellaneous wenches of
an evening, only two of Rochester's mistresses have been au-
thenticated: Jane Roberts, a minor mistress of the King who
died in the summer of 1679, and Elizabeth Barry, whom Rochester is reported to have trained for the stage. Although she
failed in her first trial with the Duke's Company about 1675,
Elizabeth Barry vindicated Rochester's confidence by returning
to a long career as the greatest actress of the age. In December
1677 she bore Rochester an illegitimate daughter, named Elizabeth Clerke, who died when twelve or thirteen years old. Rochester acted as trustee and adviser for Nell Gwyn during the
late 1670s but is not known to have been her lover.

On 10 October 1667 Rochester took his seat in the House of
Lords along with John Sheffield, Earl of Mulgrave, although
both were underage and the Lords protested. Rochester's record
of attendance at meetings of the House is far from exemplary,
but it improved near the end of his life as he became more seriously interested in politics. On 28 February 1667/8 he was appointed Gamekeeper for the County of Oxford.

The notorious group of young blades known as the "Ballers,"

to which Rochester belonged, had been formed by 1668. On 2
December 1668, Pepys heard "the silly discourse of the King,
with his people about him, telling a story of my Lord Rochester's having of his clothes stole, while he was with a wench;
and his gold all gone, but his clothes found afterwards stuffed
into a feather bed by the wench that stole them." More dangerous, at a banquet at the Dutch Ambassador's on 16 February
1668/9, Rochester reacted to some objectionable remarks of the
elder Thomas Killigrew by boxing his ears in the King's presence, a serious offense. Although the King pardoned the affront,
public indignation made it advisable to send Rochester to Paris
on 12 March bearing a note from Charles to the Duchess of Orleans. He was in the entourage when Ralph Montagu was for-
mally installed as English Ambassador on 15 April, and he may
have been among the Ambassador's gentlemen who were introduced to Louis XIV the next day. It was probably on one of
these occasions that King Louis refused to receive the Earl at
the French Court, asserting that his crime against monarchy itself was too great to be forgiven. Rochester's response to the
French king may be preserved in a scornful distich that he allegedly scrawled on a public monument (p. 21).

On the night of 19 April, while crossing the Pont Rouge in
Paris in a sedan chair, Rochester was set upon by six armed
men and robbed of his money, cloak, watch, and a very fine
periwig. Two months later, on 21 June, as Rochester was sitting
on the stage at the Paris opera with William, Lord Cavendish
(later Earl and Duke of Devonshire), one of a group of drunken
French officers began to insult Cavendish, who thereupon struck
the Frenchman in the face. Swords were quickly out of their
sheaths, and Cavendish, badly outnumbered, found himself
backed against the side scenes with several severe wounds. He
was saved by a Swiss servant of Montagu, the new English Ambassador, who seized him and threw him into the pit. Roch-

ester's behavior during this melee is less fully recorded (he may have been slightly wounded while endeavoring to aid his companion), but the episode was widely remembered to Cavendish's credit. Rochester returned to England early in July.[1]

A near-duel occurred in late November 1669 with the Earl of Mulgrave, who was led to challenge Rochester by a false report of some malicious remarks. As Mulgrave told the tale many years afterward, Rochester kept the appointment on the field of honor but excused himself from fighting because of illness, thereby giving rise to accusations of cowardice. The more reliable records of the House of Lords suggest, however, that Rochester was only too anxious to fight. When an officer of the guards was dispatched to his lodgings to arrest him, he promised not to escape but then vanished out a back door, presumably to meet his antagonist. Mulgrave, who thereafter was Rochester's inveterate enemy, impressed many contemporaries as a narrow-minded prig with an inflated opinion of his abilities as soldier, lover, and by the late 1670s, poet. Rochester subsequently pilloried him in "A Very Heroical Epistle in Answer to Ephelia" (summer of 1675), "My Lord All-Pride" (late 1670s), and "An Epistolary Essay from M. G. to O. B." (end of 1679). Mulgrave included a venomous portrait of Rochester in "An Essay upon Satyr" (November 1679).

In the seventeenth century, gentlemen wore swords and were expected to use them with courage and skill. On 21 March 1672/3, a duel between Rochester and Viscount Dunbar was barely stopped by the intervention of the Earl Marshal of England. In December 1674, when his friend Henry Savile was challenged by Mulgrave, Rochester offered to act as second.

1. All dates are Old Style. Although my account of Rochester's life is generally limited to facts available in the standard biographies, some details of his sojourn in Paris are drawn from unpublished documents in the British Museum and the Public Record Office which were transcribed for me by Professor George H. Jones of the Department of History, Eastern Illinois University.

In early March 1679/80, a duel between Rochester and Edward Seymour, former Speaker of the House of Commons, was averted when Seymour backed down.

From 1670 through 1675, the real story of Rochester's life becomes increasingly the story of his gradual development as a poet. He was no child prodigy. During the winter of 1671–72 his first genuine poems to be published, two rather amateurish Ovidian imitations (pp. 17, 18), were printed anonymously by Hobart Kemp in a miscellany of verses composed mostly by various Court wits. By spring of 1673, however, he produced the more impressive satires "A Ramble in St. James's Park" (p. 40) and "On the Women about Town" (p. 46), and by the end of the year the hilarious "Signior Dildo" (p. 54). Most of his best poems followed in 1674 and 1675, after his twenty-seventh birthday.

During the summer and autumn of 1670 Rochester was in service in London, where on 24 November John Evelyn met him at dinner with the Lord Treasurer and pronounced him "a very prophane Wit." The decade began in relative serenity as Rochester apparently tried to settle into the quiet routine of a country landowner. According to John Aubrey, "he was wont to say that when he came to Brentford the devill entred into him and never left him till he came into the country again to Adderbury or Woodstock." In midwinter of 1670–71 he was at Adderbury for the christening of his son. Back in London during the spring and summer of 1671, in September he departed suddenly for the country suffering from eye trouble. Although the Third Dutch War was waged from early 1672 through early 1674, he not only shunned it but ridiculed it lightheartedly in his poems. In late spring and summer of 1672 he alternated between his wife's estate at Enmore and his own at Adderbury, where in June a friend's birthday occasioned some elaborate merrymaking. On 31 October he was appointed a Deputy Lieutenant of Somerset.

In early January of 1673/4, however, an inadvertent but scandalous prank forced Rochester to flee from the Court. Probably in a state of drunken befuddlement, he intended to give King Charles a lampoon on some ladies ("Signior Dildo"?) but handed him by mistake the coarse lines on the King himself beginning "I' th' isle of Britain long since famous grown" (p. 60). Charles's displeasure cannot have been serious, for on 27 February 1673/4 and 2 May 1674 Rochester secured the coveted offices of Ranger and Keeper of Woodstock Park, which entitled him to reside at the fine old High Lodge. In October and November 1677, Woodstock was the scene of a notable gathering of Rochester's cronies, including Buckingham, Dorset, and others.

To Burnet, Rochester later confessed that "for five years together he was continually Drunk: not all the while under the visible effects of it, but his blood was so inflamed, that he was not in all that time cool enough to be perfectly Master of himself." Another mad prank occurred at Whitehall on 25 June 1675. Bursting into the Privy Garden after a night's revelry, Rochester, Dorset, Fleetwood Shepherd, and several other gentlemen-wits suddenly found themselves confronted by the King's sundial, an elaborate confection of glass spheres arranged in a phallic shape. Seized by an alcoholic inspiration, Rochester shouted, "What! Dost thou stand here to —— time?" and in a moment he had demolished the offending instrument. Whether he was banished from Court for this escapade is not known, but it may have been during a period of disgrace in 1675 or 1676 that Rochester masqueraded as the quack doctor Alexander Bendo, setting up practice on Tower Hill and issuing a mock mountebank bill which has survived in several texts.

The spring of 1676 marks a subtle yet definite change in the direction of Rochester's life. In some respects this was a season of triumph. March 1676 was the month of Rochester's apotheosis as the half-angelic, half-diabolical Dorimant in Etherege's

The Man of Mode. By this date most of Rochester's best poetry had already been written and was, if anything, being overpraised by contemporaries. "Timon" and "Tunbridge Wells" had been composed in the spring of 1674, "A Satyr against Reason and Mankind" was in existence by 23 March 1675/6, and "An Allusion to Horace" was a product of the winter of 1675–76. In 1676 and 1677 an increasing number of Rochester's lyrics were printed in songbooks and miscellanies.

On the other hand, Rochester's career now begins a slow downward spiral. The mood of pessimistic probing which lent tragic maturity to many of his poems of 1674 and 1675 was deepening into the misanthropy which partly explains the lessening literary activity of his remaining four years of life and which led finally to his dramatic deathbed repentance. In late summer of 1675, having offended the Duchess of Portsmouth, the King's mistress, in some way which was initially puzzling to him and remains a mystery to us, he suffered a prolonged banishment from Court that caused him much mental anguish, as his letters show. During the winter, a lawsuit by some of his mother's relatives even deprived him of the reversion of the Rangership of Woodstock Park.

An affair occurred at Epsom in late spring of 1676 which Rochester's enemies never allowed him to forget. On the night of Saturday, 17 June, a crew of gentlemen-rakes, including Rochester, Etherege, George Bridges, a certain Captain Downs, and possibly William Jephson, were amusing themselves by tossing in a blanket some fiddlers who refused to play for them. A barber, hearing the noise, came to investigate, whereupon the revelers seized him instead. To escape a blanketing, he cannily offered to show them the house of the handsomest woman in town—which, unknown to them, was actually the house of the constable. Learning that the rakes wanted a whore, the constable understandably declined to admit them. They broke down the doors and proceeded to beat him unmercifully, but he escaped at last and returned in short order with the watch.

Probably outnumbered by now, the rioters sobered up temporarily and Etherege made a speech promising an end to the disturbance. The watch had begun to disperse when Rochester, prompted by some mysterious impulse, suddenly drew his sword upon the constable. Downs grabbed hold of Rochester to prevent his pass, the constable shouted "Murder!" and the watch came running back. Misinterpreting the situation, one of the watch dashed behind Downs and gave him a crashing blow on the head. As the other gentlemen fled, Downs vainly defended himself with a stick until he was run through the side with a half-pike. Ten days later he died of his wounds.

Amid talk of bringing Rochester to trial, Rochester, Etherege, and Bridges went into hiding. Nothing further came of the matter, but thereafter the public was only too willing to think the worst of Rochester's actions. On 4 June 1677, when a cook was stabbed at a tavern in the Mall where Rochester happened to be dining, the Earl was gratuitously assumed to have wielded the knife. In October, lurid rumors described how Rochester and his guests were cavorting stark naked in Woodstock Park. They were merely trying to dry off after swimming in the river, Rochester explained in a letter to Henry Savile, terming himself melodramatically "a Man whom it is the great Mode to hate."

The winter of 1675–76 also brought a drastic realignment of Rochester's literary friendships, for which a key document is his satire "An Allusion to Horace." The two factions which emerged probably originated in personal relationships, but later, with a few changes of sides, they formed the basis for the dichotomy between Whig and Tory writers. "An Allusion to Horace" is primarily an attack on Dryden, with whom Rochester had earlier been friendly. In the spring of 1673 Dryden had dedicated his comedy *Marriage À-la-Mode* to Rochester and had written the Earl an obsequious letter. By late 1675, however, Dryden accepted as his patron the Earl of Mulgrave, Rochester's enemy. Dryden retorted to "An Allusion to Horace" in his Preface to *All for Love* in March 1678. Concurrently, Thomas Shadwell, with whom Dryden had been quarreling since 1668 and whom Rochester scorned in poems written up to May 1675, receives high praise in "An Allusion" as a comic dramatist and literary critic. Between mid-1676 and late 1677, Dryden satirized Shadwell in *Mac Flecknoe*.

Other dramatists tended to line up with either the Rochester-Shadwell or the Dryden-Mulgrave axis. Nathaniel Lee had dedicated his first play, *Nero*, to Rochester in late spring of 1675 but is roundly damned in "An Allusion to Horace." By 1677 he had joined Dryden, with whom he proceeded to collaborate on several plays. Shortly after Rochester's death, nevertheless, Lee paid him tribute as Count Rosidore in *The Princess of Cleve*. Thomas Otway followed an opposite path. After ridiculing Otway's first play, *Alcibiades*, in "An Allusion," Rochester took pains during the spring of 1676 to insure the success of the dramatist's second effort, *Don Carlos*. Otway's preface to the printed play is hostile to Dryden and friendly to Rochester and Shadwell. Early in 1677, Otway dedicated to Rochester his third play, *Titus and Berenice* with the *Cheats of Scapin*. By the winter of 1679–80, however, Rochester and Otway were at odds, perhaps because of political differences (see p. 148). John Crowne, who in 1672 had dedicated his *History of Charles the Eighth* to Rochester, may have remained clandestinely amicable with the Earl even though he receives unfavorable notice in "An Allusion." Etherege was Rochester's close friend at this time, and Wycherley is praised alongside Shadwell in "An Allusion," but these gentlemen-authors also maintained close ties with the Dryden-Mulgrave faction. Sir Francis Fane, who dedicated his comedy *Love in the Dark* to Rochester in late spring of 1675, was too minor a figure for his allegiance to carry much weight.

A special case is Sir Carr Scroope, a foppish young baronet with literary pretensions. Attacked in a three-line passage in "An Allusion to Horace" although he contributed a song flattering Rochester to *The Man of Mode,* Scroope replied about the summer of 1676 with a somewhat longer passage on the Earl in his "In Defence of Satyr." Rochester retaliated with "On the Supposed Author of a Late Poem in Defence of Satyr," to which Scroope responded with a deft epigram (see pp. 132–33). Rochester later satirized Scroope in "On Poet Ninny" (p. 141) and perhaps in "The Mock Song" (p. 136). Rochester's example was followed by numerous other satirists, mostly unidentified, who poured forth their own libels on Scroope. By early 1677, probably in self-defense, Scroope drifted into the Mulgrave-Dryden-Lee camp.

The last four years of Rochester's life were characterized by prolonged illness, depressed spirits, an increasing seriousness of intention, and a poetical output that dwindled appreciably in quantity and quality. He read history and turned to politics, hobnobbing with Whig and Whig-leaning lords like Buckingham and Dorset. In 1677, when Buckingham and three other leaders of the Country party were sent to the Tower for insisting that Parliament had been automatically dissolved, Rochester, Dorset, and other members of the "merry gang" procured his release. That summer Buckingham was frequently at Rochester's lodgings in Whitehall, and in autumn he visited Woodstock. During 1679, parliamentary records show Rochester voting consistently with the Whig leaders. In London in April 1678, Rochester impressed at least two letter-writers with his penitence. During the winter of 1678–79 and again in February 1679/80, he engaged in philosophical discussions with the young deist

Charles Blount, to whom he sent his eloquent lines on death translated from Seneca's *Troades* (p. 150). Beginning in October 1679 and continuing through early spring, Rochester entered into the famous conversations with Gilbert Burnet, a rising Scottish clergyman and historian, which were to prove instrumental in gathering the Earl into the Anglican fold.

During the latter part of March 1680, Rochester attended the races at Newmarket with the King. Returning to London, he felt well enough in early April to ride post to his wife's estate in Somersetshire. The exertion induced such a state of collapse that he could hardly be brought by coach to Woodstock, where he arrived in late May wasted in body, filled with remorse for his past life, and virtually certain that he must soon die. At his bedside were his wife, whom he now reconverted from Catholicism, his mother, his children, and several physicians and clergymen. What happened next can be judged only as a matter in the privacy of a man's soul. While his mother's chaplain, Robert Parsons, was reading aloud the messianic verses of Isaiah, Chapter 53, Rochester felt overcome (as Burnet wrote) "by a power which did so effectually constrain him, that he did ever after as firmly believe in his Saviour, as if he had seen him in the Clouds." Burnet, sent for by letter on 25 June, delayed coming to Woodstock until 20 July. Contrary to Rochester's wish, he slipped away again early on the 24th without taking leave. Hearing some hours later of Burnet's departure, Rochester murmured, "Has my friend left me? Then I shall die shortly." At two o'clock in the early morning of 26 July, his restless, inquiring spirit passed quietly away. He was buried in Spelsbury Church under a plain stone with no inscription.

Rochester's sensational repentance and death called forth more than a half-dozen elegies and a spate of pious publications, including the funeral sermon preached by Parsons and Burnet's *Some Passages*. His wife died in late July 1681, followed about the middle of November by his son Charles, the third Earl, whereupon the title became extinct in the Wilmot family. Rochester's mother lived on until 1696, when she was interred at Spelsbury with her two husbands. Within weeks after Rochester's death, probably in September 1680, what purported to be a volume of his poems was published surreptitiously—the first of some fifty editions of his works which appeared before 1800. With that, Rochester passes out of the realms of biography and history and becomes a task for the bibliographer and textual critic.

2. *Rochester's Poetry*

The purpose of this volume is not to provide comprehensive criticism of Rochester's poetry, but to make such criticism for the first time possible. Nevertheless, when his genuine poems are arranged in approximately their order of composition in good texts, some new conclusions are bound to result. Rochester's poems possess value in three directions which are difficult to separate in discussion: historically, as a crucial contribution to the shaping of the new literary idiom which was brought to perfection by Swift, Pope, and their contemporaries; biographically, as part of a life-story so compelling that it constantly threatens to overwhelm his poetry; and artistically, as unique formulations of universal human experiences.

The peculiar temper of the best literature of the Restoration, differentiating it from both the early seventeenth and early eighteenth centuries, grows out of the often-noted circumstance that this period was an intellectual crossroads. The rich array of predominantly aristocratic attitudes inherited from past centuries was increasingly tested under the pressure of new ideas, such as those of the rising middle class. The Restoration combines maximum awareness of the many traditional value-systems which might be brought to bear upon the human condition with an inability to accept any one of them fully or to the exclusion of the others. It suspends judgment; it questions, though it does not doubt; it wishes to believe, but is not sure it can. Analytical rather than synthetic, it nevertheless opens up possibilities for syntheses such as those of Swift and Pope. Although intensely revolutionary, it is reluctantly so. The Restoration temper is most sensitively reflected in the pyrrhonistic skepticism of Etherege's comedies, the almost mystical ambiguity of Wycherley in *The Country-Wife* and *The Plain-Dealer,* or the tragic agnosticism of Otway's *The Orphan* and *Venice Preserv'd.* Less clearly articulated, it can also be recognized in the inductive method of the new science; in the philosophies of Descartes, Hobbes, and Locke; in economics, in the transition to a money economy from the feudal theory based on ownership of land; and in politics, in the question of sovereignty which is debated so poignantly in lines 759–810 of *Absalom and Achitophel.*

Within the Restoration context, Rochester's special emphasis is his striving for *immediacy* of experience—as in his startling statement that pleasure may be an illusion, "but pain can ne'er deceive" (p. 88). Just here, however, readers of later centuries must guard against a serious misunderstanding. The Restoration temper should be carefully distinguished from superficially similar mental stances such as those of the French Revolution and the *Lyrical Ballads,* the "roaring twenties" (which initiated the twentieth-century interest in Rochester), or the rebellious youth of the 1960s with their disengagement from society, antiwar demonstrations, extravagant garb, and drug-taking. Rochester's demand for immediacy of experience obviously includes sensual gratification, but it is not limited to appetites which could be satiated by a night in a tavern or stews. Despite the "dissociation of sensibility" that is said to have taken place in the late seventeenth century, experience could still derive almost as directly from an abstract idea, a code of conduct (e.g. morality, honor), a tradition, a literary convention (like formal satire), an emotion, or a belief (for instance, that Christ is one's Savior). Even Dryden's heroic drama, that most-misjudged of Restoration literary genres, is a partially successful attempt to render a firsthand contact with the intangible concepts that were assumed to guide human behavior.

Rochester's distinctive technique as a poet involves the simultaneous manipulation of several conflicting levels or planes of experience. The point at which two or more such planes intersect is the poem, and the name of the resulting effect is irony. To be sure, something resembling "Rochesterian irony," as it may be called, can be found in other Restoration poets and might even be considered an essential element in all good poetry. Nevertheless, Rochester's special way of structuring a poem, especially as he had devised it by 1674, can best be grasped in these terms. For example, in "Upon His Leaving His Mistress" (p. 81) there are three intersecting planes of experience: masculine "heroic" honor in war, requiring the conquest of thousands of victims; feminine honor in love, which is more defensive and discriminating; and the fertility of nature, of which the human is and is not a part. In the song "By all love's soft, yet mighty powers" (p. 139), the key phrase advising Phyllis to "take to cleanly sinning" brings together the planes of morality and hygiene. "The Disabled Debauchee" (p. 116) turns upon an unstable equation of debauchery and heroic warfare, with a further wry twist in the concluding stanza. In the translation from Seneca's *Troades* (p. 150), the line "God's everlasting fiery jails" forces the pagan classical context to accommodate a Christian meaning that is alien to it (with the last word importing a humorous suggestion of the local lockup). Similar but much more complex effects are achieved in some of Rochester's other translations and adaptations from Latin literature, particularly the formal satires. Rochester's discovery of the way to link discontinuous modes of experience in a poem may have been his great gift to the new literary sensibility as it developed from 1670 to 1675.

Rochester's poems fall into four rather well-defined chronological groupings, which I have designated Prentice Work (1665–1671), Early Maturity (1672–1673), Tragic Maturity (1674–1675), and Disillusionment and Death (1676–1680). If the work in the earliest group seems immature and trivial, this is because the planes of experience are rigidly segregated into sharply different types of poetry instead of being ironically yoked in the same poem. At one extreme are the self-consciously conventional poems, including pastoral dialogues, Ovidian imitations, and lyrics incorporating features of the general courtly love and Petrarchan traditions (pp. 3–19). Life in these verses resembles an elaborate ritual or game, strangely removed from reality, as in a painting by Watteau or Fragonard. Among these set pieces, however, are a few of Rochester's most celebrated songs, notably those beginning "My dear mistress has a heart" (p. 12) and "While on those lovely looks I gaze" (p. 12). At the opposite extreme is a series of personal poems (pp. 20–24), so directly in contact with raw flesh and blood that they have little formal structure and were even, in some cases, composed extemporaneously. The fact that not one of these verses was published before 1700 suggests that they were regarded as ephemera and that a much larger quantity of the same kind may have perished. Rochester's later penchant for satire begins to assert itself in these personal poems as a scorn for specific people, be they Louis XIV or an anonymous psalm-singing clerk.

Some foreshadowing of later developments can be found in this earliest group. The extemporaneous verse letter to Rochester's wife includes a little mocking of conventional gallantry—the posy for the ring, "low-made legs," and "sugared speeches"

(p. 23). In the lampoon on Miss Price and in "The Platonic Lady" (pp. 24, 25), Rochester employs a woman as persona or speaker, as he was later to do in "A Letter from Artemisia in the Town to Chloe in the Country," "A Song of a Young Lady to Her Ancient Lover," and elsewhere. Moreover, in "The Platonic Lady," which is translated from Petronius, Rochester alters the effect of the original by reversing the sex of the speaker. Even more interesting is the song "Fair Chloris in a pigsty lay" (p. 27), which not only incorporates two planes of experience by being mock-pastoral as well as pastoral, but adds a third through its Freudian elements of wish-fulfillment in a dream and the symbolic cave with a gate at its mouth. Also noteworthy is Rochester's occasional practice of composing poems as pendant pieces. To mention a few obvious instances, the early poems include a pair of pastoral dialogues (pp. 4, 7) and a pair of Ovidian imitations. Later examples are "Timon" and "Tunbridge Wells"; "A Satyr against Reason and Mankind" and "Artemisia to Chloe"; the two songs beginning "Against the charms our ballocks have" and "By all love's soft, yet mighty powers" (pp. 137, 139); and "On Poet Ninny" and "My Lord All-Pride," which satirize Rochester's two enemies, Scroope and Mulgrave, by using complementary metaphors of theater and carnival.

The poems assigned to 1672 and 1673 display a marked improvement in quality, although nothing to equal the achievements of Rochester's full maturity. His skill as a lyrist, already further advanced than his technique as a satirist, approaches its zenith in such songs as "Upon His Drinking a Bowl" (p. 52), one of the few that can be accurately dated. In satire, conspicuous triumphs are "A Ramble in St. James's Park" (apparently a crucial work biographically), "On the Women about Town," the satirical song beginning "Quoth the Duchess of Cleveland to counselor Knight," and especially "Signior Dildo." In the last three of these, Rochester brilliantly taps the comic spirit at its source in the sex relationship. Perhaps it was to gather material for lampoons like "Signior Dildo" that he disguised a footman as a sentinel, with a red coat and musket, and stationed him outside the doors of various Court ladies who were suspected of carrying on amours. In poems written about 1673, Rochester's exploitation of obscenity as a means of inducing immediacy of experience is more prevalent than at any other time in his career. A circumstance that went unnoticed prior to this edition is the impact on Rochester's poetry of the Third Dutch War. Whereas the earlier war with the Dutch prompted him to heroic deeds in 1665 and 1666, the renewed conflict inspired antiwar sentiments in his poems, although his satirical mood remains more high-spirited than it was later to become.

A curious and puzzling fact is that before 1674, Rochester was seemingly unable to write fully successful satires in heroic couplets. Three attempts, including the corrosive lines on King Charles (pp. 33, 34, 60), are fragmentary or loose in structure. His best poems in the iambic pentameter couplet, with its requirements for syllabic quantity deriving partly from French and Latin, still tend to be nonsatirical efforts like the fine translation of Ovid's *Amores*, 2.9 (p. 35). Conversely, the best satires follow native traditions and are written in a native four-stress measure, either iambic tetrameter couplets resembling those of *Hudibras* or anapestic tetrameter that recalls the accentual, alliterative verse of Old English. It is almost as though Rochester, in order to make his contribution to the newly emerging literary sensibility, was condemned to relive the history of English prosody, as a human embryo is said to recapitulate the stages of evolution prior to birth.[2]

During the early months of 1674, Rochester attained his full

2. For a comparable phenomenon in Waller's development, see Alexander Ward Allison, *Toward an Augustan Poetic: Edmund Waller's "Reform" of English Poetry* (Lexington, University of Kentucky Press, 1962), pp. 62–87.

growth as a poet. Perhaps this sudden burgeoning was connected with his banishment from Court for his satire on King Charles; probably, however, the causes go much deeper. In "Timon" and "Tunbridge Wells," Rochester has impressively mastered the writing of heroic couplets for satirical purposes.[3] Two elements entered so profoundly into his final achievement that their ramifications are impossible to trace fully: Roman satire and contemporary English drama. Oddly, the impetus of formal verse satire came, not directly from Horace, Juvenal, and Persius nor by way of earlier English adapters like Donne and Hall, but indirectly through the medium of Boileau, whose third and eighth satires are imitated, respectively, in Rochester's "Timon" and "A Satyr against Reason and Mankind."[4] Although references to contemporary plays and playwrights are virtually absent from Rochester's poems before 1674, a glance at the footnotes will show how frequent they become from that date on. Doubtless this new interest in the drama combined with the sense of the dramatic which was always part of Rochester's nature. Almost incidentally, the lyrics printed on pages 81–90 are the finest of the late seventeenth century and among the best in English literature.

From 1676 through 1680, because a high proportion of the poems can be dated, the decline of Rochester's verse in quantity and quality is well documented. The most ambitious work, "An Epistolary Essay from M. G. to O. B.," is relatively a failure although it repeats the technique that Rochester had used successfully four years earlier in "A Very Heroical Epistle in Answer to Ephelia." As if they were throwbacks to Rochester's

---

3. The heroic-couplet style of "Timon" and "Tunbridge Wells" is briefly analyzed in my *Attribution in Restoration Poetry*, pp. 286–92.

4. For the impact of Boileau on Rochester and its significance in the later history of English satire, see Harold F. Brooks, "The 'Imitation' in English Poetry, Especially in Formal Satire, before the Age of Pope," *Review of English Studies*, 25 (1949), 124–40.

earliest period, other poems of 1676–1680 tend to be short and much simpler in structure, consisting often of a single withering blast of scorn for some individual—Scroope, Mulgrave, Otway, Sue Willis, Cary Frazier, or Rochester himself. Modest though these lampoons are, some of them show that Rochester could still hone his couplets razor-sharp.

Even after Rochester's poems have been placed historically and biographically, they retain a uniqueness that probably accounts for their perennial appeal to readers who care nothing about the seventeenth century and know little about their author. In the best of the poems, an open-ended, Pirandello-like quality makes them seem forever contemporary, especially in the modernized format adopted for this edition. This quality is nowhere more apparent than in Rochester's masterpiece, "A Letter from Artemisia in the Town to Chloe in the Country," whose structure resembles a room full of mirrors endlessly reflecting one another. Which of the poem's many characters represents the truth? It may be the booby squire who dies in serene possession of "the perfect joy of being well deceived." Or it may be the whore Corinna who skillfully dupes him and finally poisons him, or the penetrating "men of wit" such as the one who initially ruined Corinna. Or it may be the "fine lady" who argues so plausibly in favor of fools as lovers—although, as Artemisia observes, she knows "everyone's fault and merit, but her own." Artemisia speaks self-righteously of the traditional spirituality of love, but she proves to be little more than a gossipmonger, powerless against those who reduce love to a mechanical operation of the spirit and who conform so completely to fashion "that with their ears they see." These, in turn, as the violently synesthetic image implies, have foregone the immediacy of experience. Perhaps the norm is suggested by Chloe, Artemisia's correspondent, who may stand for the reader but whose presence is entirely a creation of Artemisia's words. Being analytical rather than synthetic, in the manner of the best Restoration comedy, the poem offers no clear synthesis.

In a sense, the structure of "Artemisia to Chloe" simply illustrates the multiplicity of assumed identities or personae used by Rochester as speakers in his poems, thereby raising the philosophical question of identity which has been such an insistent concern in the twentieth century. Logically, in a literary construct based on intersecting planes of experience, with immediacy of experience a desideratum, there must at the point of intersection be a perceiving or participating consciousness, the "I" of the poem. This inherently unstable identity is defined largely by its relationship to the intersecting planes. Enriching the situation further, Rochester's poems, to the extent that they are a coherent body of expression, acquire a corporate unity as projections of what we imagine to have been his real-life personality. To a greater or lesser degree the "I" of each poem is always Rochester, even when the speaker is a woman.

The male speakers in Rochester's poems can be ranged on a spectrum of identities. At one extreme is the transparent, unindividuated spokesman of the love lyrics and the conventional poems generally. Translated into a satirical context, he becomes the more individualized speaker in "An Allusion to Horace," the idealized man-about-town in "Timon," the irascible voice of "Tunbridge Wells," and perhaps the strident hedonist and Hobbist who declaims most of "A Satyr against Reason and Mankind." At the middle of the spectrum is the identity used most memorably in "The Disabled Debauchee": an experienced roué, but rather obtuse, occasionally frustrated, mildly depraved, and slightly repulsive. An obvious reflection of Rochester's real-life dissipation, he is not presented as admirable, but he is not satirized very directly. Similar speakers appear in "The Imperfect Enjoyment," "A Ramble in St. James's Park," "To the Postboy," and several songs. At the far edge of the spectrum are Bajazet and M. G., who cannot be wholly detached from Rochester's personality despite their primary function as satirical portraits of Mulgrave.[5]

Augmenting this multiplication of identities was the real-life Rochester's practice of disguises. As Burnet relates,

> He took pleasure to disguise himself, as a *Porter*, or as a *Beggar*; sometimes to follow some mean Amours, which, for the variety of them, he affected; At other times, meerly for diversion, he would go about in odd shapes, in which he acted his part so naturally, that even those who were on the secret, and saw him in these shapes, could perceive nothing by which he might be discovered.

The outstanding instance, of course, was the affair of Alexander Bendo, in which "he disguised himself, so that his nearest Friends could not have known him . . . " Interestingly, after the unsuccessful royalist uprising in Yorkshire in 1655, Rochester's father escaped identification through a similar skill in disguises, even though he was arrested.

As literary heirs of Rochester, both Swift and Pope display a highly sophisticated sense of the problems of identity involved in an author's relationship to his work. Ingeniously contrived so as to block any pat answers, *Verses on the Death of Dr. Swift* and the *Epistle to Dr. Arbuthnot* ask, who is the *real* Swift? and who is the *real* Pope? The ambiguous conclusion in each poem is that a fictitious identity may be at least as real as the "real" one.

3. This Edition

The specific aim of this edition is to provide, for the first time,

5. Rochester's "A Very Heroical Epistle in Answer to Ephelia" and "An Epistolary Essay from M. G. to O. B." are analyzed in detail in Chapter 4 of my *Attribution in Restoration Poetry*, pp. 103–36.

reliable texts of all the poems which antecedent scholarly studies have shown are probably authentic. With the text thus taking priority, the explanatory material in headnotes and footnotes is limited to what the intelligent reader needs to know in order to comprehend each poem. No systematic attempt is made to trace sources, analogues, or the later history and reputation of a poem, nor is much space devoted to the rich intellectual background of such a work as "A Satyr against Reason and Mankind"—matters the investigation of which will, it is hoped, be stimulated by this edition. Extensive documentation is avoided. Ordinarily no documentation is given for facts available in multiple sources or in standard works like the *OED*, the *Dictionary of National Biography*, various encyclopedias, the G. E. C. *Complete Peerage*, and even Pepys's and Evelyn's diaries as edited by Henry B. Wheatley and Esmond de Beer.[6] Sources are cited, however, for direct quotations and similar information that is unique or difficult to locate.

For the authorship of most of the seventy-five poems here printed as Rochester's, the Notes on the Texts, Authorship, and Dates at the back of the volume refer the reader to the relevant portions of my *Attribution in Restoration Poetry* (hereafter called *ARP*), to the supplementary information afforded by *The Gyldenstolpe Manuscript Miscellany*, and occasionally to other discussions. Also accepted as authentic are all poems attributed to Rochester in Jacob Tonson's edition of 1691, except for three printed in Poems Possibly by Rochester (pp. 155–58) and two more, evidently by Lady Rochester and Sir Carr Scroope, which have already been considered at length (*ARP*, pp. 209–11, 231–38).

Probably the Rochester canon, which seemed an insoluble puzzle as recently as 1950, has now been established about as securely as those of most authors ever are. Nevertheless, prob-

6. *The Diary of John Evelyn*, ed. E. S. de Beer, 6 vols., Oxford, Clarendon Press, 1955.

lems continue to be posed by the mass of poems, almost all spurious, whose authorship has either not yet been fully investigated or cannot be analyzed within the compass of this edition. Particularly troublesome are a number of poems which, because they are ascribed to Rochester only in early manuscripts, have heretofore remained uninvestigated by Restoration scholars and even unknown. Excluded from the edition are all poems assigned to Rochester on the unsupported testimony of the following sources: all early Rochester editions except those of 1680 and 1691 (see *ARP*, pp. 8–15); all of the *State Poems* miscellanies; *Examen Miscellaneum*, 1702; the second volume of Buckingham's *Miscellaneous Works*, 1705; and Harvard MS. Eng. 636F. Other cases are judged on their individual merits. For genuine poems not already discussed in detail elsewhere, the notes at the back of the volume are perforce restricted to a minimal list of early texts and a brief mention of the evidence favoring Rochester's authorship—not in any case to be construed as a complete presentation.

For most of the eight items in the section of Poems Possibly by Rochester, the evidence for and against authenticity is roughly equal. For each of the 177 items in the First-Line List of Poems Omitted from This Edition, the true authorship is specified if it is known. Whenever possible, the reader is referred to more extensive treatments elsewhere. At a minimum, a brief indication is given of the sources attributing the poem to Rochester (often a list of independently descended early texts) together with a reason for concluding that he did not write it. In many instances a complete list of early texts is not provided, and rarely is there a full statement of the case against Rochester's authorship.

Beyond question, the ideal order in which to print Rochester's genuine poems is the order of their composition. His collected works reveal no large design like that in George Herbert's *The Temple*, for example, nor have previous attempts to arrange his poems by genre, or in terms of the early editions in which they were first printed, proved particularly illuminating. On the other hand, not only does Rochester's chronological development as a poet hold unusual biographical interest, but for the crucial years 1670–1675 it comes perilously close to coinciding with the development of English poetry itself. Waller, another innovator, had already made his contribution; Dryden, whose creative energies were being channeled into the drama, did not write his revolutionary *Mac Flecknoe* until 1676 or 1677; and Dorset, while his impact on the newly developing sensibility was not negligible, remains a lesser figure.

Although precise dates of composition are not forthcoming for the majority of Rochester's poems, the advantages of the chronological arrangement adopted in this edition greatly outweigh the hazards. Within each of the four periods through which Rochester's literary career can be regarded as having passed, poems whose order of composition remains uncertain are arbitrarily grouped on some other basis such as genre, theme, or tone. At the head of each poem, immediately below the title, the date of composition is given to the left between square brackets, with the date of first publication to the right between square brackets and in italics. The reader is cautioned, however, not to assume conclusions about the date of a poem without first checking the more detailed note at the back of the volume.

Punctuation, spelling, and capitalization have been modernized simply because there is virtually no basis for an old-spelling text of Rochester's poems. The chosen copy-texts exhibit a bewildering and largely meaningless variety of treatments of accidentals by different compositors and copyists, ranging from the heavy pointing of the first edition of 1680 to an entire absence of punctuation in some manuscripts. In a number of copy-texts, the accidentals are so unsatisfactory by either seventeenth- or twentieth-century standards that they would in any event have to be revised by an editor. Also, Rochester's verse, especially the heroic couplets used in his mature satires, apparently proved difficult for seventeenth-century scribes and compositors to punctuate, so that an editor would wish to command the full resources of twentieth-century punctuation in order to clarify meaning. Moreover, since the surviving holographs of Rochester's poems show that he himself tended to punctuate lightly, twentieth-century conventions of punctuation may actually be truer to his intentions than the more emphatic styles commonly employed in seventeenth-century printing houses. (Unmodernized versions of Rochester's holograph poems are printed, rather inaccurately, in the Muses' Library edition.)

It has, however, seemed desirable to retain certain linguistic peculiarities of the copy-texts which do not amount to verbal variants. Thus the reading of a copy-text is almost always preferred in decisions between "thy" and "thine," "you" and "ye" (when not a rhyme word), "while" and "whilst," "does" and "doth," "them" and " 'em," "troth" and "truth," "writ" and "wrote," "ev'n" and "e'en," "y' are" and "you're," "th' are" and "they're," and other analogous situations. On grounds that it is a slightly different word, the seventeenth-century form "satyr" is not modernized to "satire." Besides a difference in pronunciation, affecting the scansion of lines of verse, the obsolete spelling preserves the false but significant Renaissance etymology which traced the literary genre back to the rough, hairy creatures of Greek mythology.

Although Rochester scholarship has shown encouraging progress in recent years, its level of accomplishment does not yet warrant incorporating into this edition a complete textual apparatus, including lists of all variants in the independently descended versions of each poem and a detailed account of the procedure, sometimes quite elaborate, by which these variants were used to establish text. Moreover, the discipline of textual criticism is itself currently undergoing such change and uncertainty that basic points of methodology are difficult to settle. Old approaches have been successfully challenged, while newer methods have not yet emerged. Formerly, textual criticism was dominated by genealogical or Lachmannian assumptions, which held that by analyzing the variants in the surviving texts of a work, a logical or mathematical pattern could be discovered which would infallibly yield a stemma or "family tree" illustrating how these texts descended from an archetype. By working backward through the "family tree," one could then decide objectively which variants most nearly approximated what the author wrote.

Decades of practical experience, however, failed in too many cases to bridge the gap between the existing texts of a work and the theory which claimed to explain how they evolved into their observed states. A particular problem is "conflicts," or sets of variants which seem to require incompatible forms of the stemma. Some aspects of textual criticism raise surprisingly philosophical questions, in this instance whether the universe (not to mention the human mind) is fundamentally rational. Impressive attempts have been made to explain the phenomenon of conflicts as forms of convergent variation: that is, conflation or contamination, coincident variation, or separate descent from different author's drafts of a work. Yet even this more sophisticated approach conceals an untested assumption that a full logical explanation is feasible in terms of causality.

For the future, the most promising possibilities may lie in applications of statistical methods or probability calculus that go far beyond anything envisaged when my own principle of "probability" was first formulated.[7] Widely used in most branches of

7. *ARP*, Chapter 2, pp. 29–55. In view of the broader applications of probability which now seem imminent in textual criticism, my principle should be given a more restrictive designation. For a theoretical preview of some of these applications, see Antonín Hrubý, "Statistical Methods in

the sciences, these methods are ways of coping with a universe neither wholly rational nor wholly irrational: if not entirely intelligible, it is at least partially predictable and controllable. A very fundamental example is Heisenberg's principle of indeterminacy in quantum mechanics. To draw a somewhat simplified illustration from subatomic physics, in dealing with particles too small for direct observation, it frequently happens that, for practical purposes, patterns of behavior can be predicted only in large numbers, on a percentage basis. Thus, although one cannot predict with certainty that any specific particle will exhibit a given pattern of behavior, nor explain causally why it must do so, one can nevertheless ascertain a probability that it will follow this pattern. Similarly, in textual criticism, a probability can be achieved that one variant rather than another is original without reconstructing a "family tree" or explaining causally how each surviving text of a poem came to inherit its particular combination of variants.

Lacking more rigorous methods, I have endeavored to establish text for Rochester's poems by using an eclectic blend of recognized procedures—not excluding the genealogical approach, which in many situations still retains varying degrees of value. Essentially, different forms of probability are pitted against one another, with several types of subjective judgments being used as mutual correctives. A rough analogy can be found in physics,

---

Textual Criticism," *General Linguistics*, Vol. V, No. 3 (Supplement, 1962), pp. 75–138, and "A Quantitative Solution of the Ambiguity of Three Texts," *Studies in Bibliography*, *18* (1965), 147–82. Hrubý insists—too strenuously, I believe—that in textual criticism "everything which conflicts with either common sense or reason should be rejected as mere hocus pocus" (*SB*, p. 182) and that the generic relationships of the surviving texts of a work must be known in order to determine which variants are closest to what the author wrote. My procedure in this edition has been perceptibly influenced by a long conversation I had with Professor Hrubý on 28 December 1962 in Washington, D.C., after he read his paper "The Application of Probability Calculus to Textual Criticism" at the annual meeting of the Modern Language Association of America.

where both the wave theory and the corpuscular theory must be invoked to explain the phenomena of light. Aside from special cases such as holograph drafts, a series of six steps (not all of them always applicable) has been rigidly followed for each poem:

Step 1. As a preliminary, all early texts of the poem which are known to have survived are assembled, and all their verbal variants are collated. Then, using my principle of "probability" or some other trustworthy procedure, all texts descended from other extant texts (principally manuscripts and printed texts derived from printed texts) are identified and eliminated from consideration, for they offer no information not available in their sources, and their presence would seriously distort later results. The remaining texts are independently descended and may be used for succeeding steps. Conflated texts with one ancestor no longer extant may be laid aside for future consultation, but they can be accorded no more than secondary status. For many poems in the edition, this preliminary step was already performed in my *Attribution in Restoration Poetry* and *The Gyldenstolpe Manuscript Miscellany.*

Step 2. The old genealogical method is now applied to the independently descended texts in an attempt to reconstruct their "family tree." This step is divided into two separate, successive operations: [8]

(a) Ignoring the question of whether variants are original or corrupt, the texts are grouped on the basis of their shared variants into a *distributional* or nondirectional stemma, conventionally expressed by a horizontal instead of a vertical diagram. The procedure is from smaller groups to larger, or from the

---

8. In stressing the separateness of these two operations in opposition to the "common errors" fallacy, I agree with Vinton A. Dearing, *A Manual of Textual Analysis*, Berkeley and Los Angeles, University of California Press, 1959. For a succinct statement of the point, see my review in *Journal of English and Germanic Philology*, 59 (1960), 553–59, especially p. 557.

periphery of the diagram toward its center. Attention is first given to unique variants, which would indicate that the texts containing them constitute terminal states, at the extremities of the diagram; then to variants shared by two texts against all other texts; then to variants shared by three texts, four, five, six, and so on.

(b) The resulting distributional diagram is erected into a *directional* stemma. Each set of variants is scrutinized for examples which would show the direction of change among the texts, from original readings to corruptions. If this step produces a stemma without major conflicts, succeeding steps tend merely to duplicate its conclusions; if it is a total or partial failure, succeeding steps become absolutely essential.

Step 3. Ignoring the possible bibliographical relationships of the texts, individual sets of variants are analyzed in an attempt to determine which readings are original and which are corrupt. The methods employed are familiar to textual critics: for instance, the principle of the *lectio difficilior,* if applicable; consideration of the types of mechanical scribal error or deliberate change by which one variant might have arisen from another; the question of which variant is most satisfactory in the context; the criterion of esthetic superiority, on grounds that Rochester, a gifted poet, could have produced a better reading than an anonymous copyist or compositor; and the circumstance that, other factors being equal, the majority variant is probably correct, even though unique or minority variants should always be examined for signs of originality.

Using these choices of variants, a tentative reconstructed text of the poem is written out. This process involves less risk than the inexperienced observer might suppose. Normally, at least 80 per cent of all choices of readings involve unique variants which any two people would agree are corrupt. Also, if a small number of wrong choices are made at this step, most or all of them will be rectified in Step 5.

Step 4. Using the tentative reconstructed text as a basis, tabulation is made of the number and seriousness of the departures from this text by each one of the early texts. That early text having the least departures from the tentative text is selected as copy-text for the poem. Notice is also taken of any other early texts which exhibit relatively few departures from the tentative text.

Step 5. The choices of variants made in Step 3 are reconsidered, with greater weight now given to the readings of the copy-text and those of any other early texts which Step 4 has shown to be superior. The reading of the copy-text is retained unless there is substantial reason to substitute a reading from other texts. Conjectural emendations are resisted and, if deemed unavoidable, are always conspicuously enclosed in square brackets. Greater freedom is exercised with titles, however, since these may often be scribal additions (*ARP*, p. 220).

In the special case of poems surviving in a single independently descended text, that text is reproduced without verbal alteration if possible. When there are two independently descended texts, one is reproduced without verbal alteration if possible; otherwise one is chosen as copy-text, with variants substituted from the other only if there is substantial reason.

Step 6. The rudimentary apparatus in the textual notes at the back of the volume can now be prepared. (If the text of the poem has already been analyzed in print, the reader is referred to this analysis.) First the copy-text is identified and, if necessary, described. Then follows a list of "other texts consulted" from which readings have been taken; if the copy-text is reproduced without verbal alteration, no such list need be included. Reference is made to any additional lists of early texts in *Attribution in Restoration Poetry, The Gyldenstolpe Manuscript Miscellany,* or elsewhere.

Departures from the copy-text are recorded in this basic form: line number, lemma followed by a square bracket, followed by the reading of the copy-text or an indication, in italics, of the situation. In citations from the copy-text of whole lines and passages, the lemma is omitted. At the very least, therefore, a reader who is disposed to quarrel with my choices of variants in any poem can reconstruct for himself the verbal readings of one superior early text—which, in the distressingly abstract and controversial field of textual criticism, is about as close as one can come to factual certainty.

4. *Rochester Studies 1925–1967*

(No systematic attempt has been made to include marginal items, e.g. brief passages on Rochester in works on other subjects. A few items published before 1925 are included because of their importance.)

(A) BIBLIOGRAPHIES

Prinz, Johannes. *John Wilmot, Earl of Rochester.* (See under "Biographies.")

Vieth, David M. *Attribution in Restoration Poetry: A Study of Rochester's "Poems" of 1680.* Yale Studies in English 153. New Haven and London, Yale University Press, 1963.

A detailed analysis of the collection of poems which was printed in 1680 as the first edition of Rochester's works. Although problems of authorship are the primary concern, new information is offered on many other aspects of Rochester and of Restoration literature generally. Includes checklists of early Rochester editions, broadsides and pamphlets, manuscripts, and other sources of the Rochester text.

(B) EDITIONS

Danielsson, Bror, and David M. Vieth, eds. *The Gyldenstolpe Manuscript Miscellany of Poems by John Wilmot, Earl of*

Rochester, and other Restoration Authors. Stockholm Studies in English XVII (Acta Universitatis Stockholmiensis). Stockholm, Almqvist & Wiksell, 1967.

An edition of a manuscript transcribed about August 1680, with the text in photographic facsimile and an introduction. Includes notes on the authorship, dates, and other early texts of the 65 poems in the volume.

Duncan, Ronald, ed. *Rochester*. The Pocket Poets. London, Edward Hulton, 1959.

Reprints 24 selections from poems attributed to Rochester.

————, ed. *Selected Lyrics and Satires of John Wilmot, 2nd Earl of Rochester*. London, Forge Press, 1948.

Not a scholarly edition.

Hayward, John, ed. *Collected Works of John Wilmot, Earl of Rochester*. London, Nonesuch Press, 1926.

The earliest twentieth-century attempt to reprint all of Rochester's works.

Johns, Quilter, ed. *The Poetical Works of John Wilmot, Earl of Rochester*. Halifax, Eng., Haworth Press, 1933.

Similar to Hayward's edition, but less useful.

Levin, Harry, ed. *A Satire against Mankind and Other Poems By John Wilmot, Earl of Rochester*. Norfolk, Conn., New Directions, 1942.

Reprints 12 of Rochester's genuine poems from Tonson's edition of 1714.

Needham, Francis, ed. *Welbeck Miscellany No. 2. A Collection of Poems by Several Hands*. Bungay, Suffolk, R. Clay and Sons, 1934.

Prints two poems from Rochester's holograph.

Pinto, Vivian de Sola, ed. *The Famous Pathologist, or The Noble Mountebank, by Thomas Alcock and John Wilmot, Earl of Rochester*. Nottingham University Miscellany No. 1. Nottingham, Sisson and Parker, 1961.

Prints a manuscript text of Alexander Bendo's bill and an account of the mountebank episode written by one of Rochester's servants.

————, ed. *Poems by John Wilmot, Earl of Rochester*. The Muses' Library. London, Routledge and Kegan Paul; Cambridge, Mass., Harvard University Press, 1953. 2d ed. rev., 1964.

The most recent attempt at an edition of Rochester's complete poems.

————, ed. *Restoration Carnival*. London, Folio Society, 1954. Pp. 149–211.

Reprints 18 selections from poems attributed to Rochester with a biographical introduction.

Rochester, Earl of. *Sodom, or The Quintessence of Debauchery*. The Traveller's Companion Series No. 48. Paris, Olympia Press, 1957.

Thorpe, James, ed. *Rochester's "Poems on Several Occasions."* Princeton Studies in English No. 30. Princeton University Press, 1950.

An important contribution to the textual study of Rochester's poems. Thorpe's text is a photographic facsimile of the Huntington edition, the earliest of the "1680" editions, whose interrelationships are analyzed in the introduction. The notes discuss the authorship and list other early texts of the 61 poems in the volume.

von Römer, L. S. A. M., ed. *Rochester's Sodom. Herausgegeben nach dem Hamburger Manuscript*. Paris, H. Welter, 1904.

Wilson, John Harold, ed. *The Rochester-Savile Letters, 1671–1680*. Columbus, Ohio State University Press, 1941.

An admirably annotated edition of the correspondence between Rochester and his friend Henry Savile. The introduction includes what is still, after more than a quarter-century, the most accurate account of Rochester's life.

(c) BIOGRAPHIES

Dobrée, Bonamy. *Rochester: A Conversation between Sir George Etherege and Mr FitzJames*. London, Hogarth Press, 1926.
Fiction.

Kellow, Kathleen. *Rochester—The Mad Earl*. London, Robert Hale, 1957.
Fiction.

Lane, Jane (pseudonym of Elaine Kidner Dakers). "Court Rake." In *Puritan, Rake, and Squire* (London, Evans Brothers, 1950), pp. 74–135.

Murdock, Kenneth B. " 'A Very Profane Wit': John Wilmot, Earl of Rochester, 1647–1680." In *The Sun at Noon: Three Biographical Sketches* (New York, Macmillan, 1939), pp. 269–306.

Norman, Charles. *Rake Rochester*. New York, Crown Publishers, 1954.
Not a scholarly biography.

Pinto, Vivian de Sola. *Enthusiast in Wit: A Portrait of John Wilmot, Earl of Rochester, 1647–1680*. London, Routledge and Kegan Paul; Lincoln, University of Nebraska Press, 1962.
A revised version of Pinto's *Rochester: Portrait of a Restoration Poet*. Although untrustworthy in many respects, this is the fullest available account of Rochester's life.

————. *Rochester: Portrait of a Restoration Poet*. London, John Lane the Bodley Head, 1935.
See *Enthusiast in Wit*, above.

Prinz, Johannes. *John Wilmot, Earl of Rochester: His Life and Writings*. Palaestra 154. Leipzig, Mayer & Müller, 1927.
This is the pioneer twentieth-century study of Rochester's life and works. Besides a biography, it includes criticism, a survey of problems of the canon, an edition of some of Rochester's

letters, and a bibliography of early editions.

Williams, Charles. *Rochester*. London, Arthur Barker, 1935.

A serious biography which does not, however, contribute new documentary evidence.

Wilson, John Harold. *The Rochester-Savile Letters*. (See under "Editions.")

(D) ARTICLES, NOTES, AND MISCELLANEOUS ITEMS

Allen, Don Cameron. "The Atheist Redeemed: Blount, Oldham, Rochester." In *Doubt's Boundless Sea: Skepticism and Faith in the Renaissance* (Baltimore, Johns Hopkins Press, 1964), pp. 186–223.

Places Rochester in a context of intellectual history.

Auffret, Jean. "Rochester's *Farewell*." *Etudes Anglaises*, *12* (1959), 142–50.

Assuming that Rochester had a hand in the poem, Auffret tries to determine which parts he wrote—incidentally clarifying some topical allusions.

Babington, Percy L. "Dryden not the Author of 'MacFlecknoe.'" *Modern Language Review*, *13* (1918), 25–34.

Wrongly attributes to Oldham both *Mac Flecknoe* and "A Satyr against Reason and Mankind." Correctly assigns to him "Upon the Author of the Play Called Sodom."

Babler, O. F., and Editor. "The Second and Later Bottles." *Notes and Queries*, *197* (1952), 389–90.

Comment on a phrase in one of Rochester's letters to Henry Savile.

Baine, Rodney M. "Rochester or Fishbourne: A Question of Authorship." *Review of English Studies*, *22* (1946), 201–06.

Argues that Christopher Fishbourne probably wrote *Sodom*.

Berman, Ronald. "Rochester and the Defeat of the Senses." *Kenyon Review*, *26* (1964), 354–68.

Criticism.

Brooks, Harold F. "Attributions to Rochester." *London Times Literary Supplement*, 9 May 1935, p. 301.

Demonstrates that Rochester did not write "The Commons' Petition" ("In all humility we crave") or "Upon the Author of the Play Called Sodom."

———. "The Date of Rochester's 'Timon.'" *Notes and Queries*, *174* (1938), 384–85.

Establishes the date of composition.

———. "When Did Dryden Write *MacFlecknoe?*—Some Additional Notes." *Review of English Studies*, *11* (1935), 74–78.

Finds an echo of *Mac Flecknoe* in "Rochester's Farewell."

Bruser, Fredelle. "Disproportion: A Study in the Work of John Wilmot, Earl of Rochester." *University of Toronto Quarterly*, *15* (1945–46), 384–96.

Criticism.

Bullough, Geoffrey. "'A Satyr on the Court Ladies.'" *London Times Literary Supplement*, 18 February 1932, p. 112.

Attempts to identify a lost lampoon attributed to Rochester.

Crocker, S. F. "Rochester's *Satire against Mankind:* A Study of Certain Aspects of the Background." *West Virginia University Studies: III. Philological Papers (Volume 2)*, May 1937, pp. 57–73.

Seeks sources for the poem in Montaigne and other French writers in addition to Boileau.

Dale, Donald A. "Antwerp Editions of Rochester." *Notes and Queries*, *172* (1937), 137. Also "Antwerpen Editions of Rochester," *172*, 206–07 and 332.

On the "1680" editions.

———. "The 1680 'Antwerp' Edition of Rochester's Poems." *The Library*, 4th ser., *20* (1939–40), 105–06.

Calls attention to Pepys's copy.

de Beer, E. S. "John Wilmot, Earl of Rochester: A Conversation and a Speech." *Notes and Queries, 170* (1936), 420.

Two spurious items. The conversation is fictitious, whereas the speech was actually delivered by Lawrence Hyde, Earl of Rochester.

Duclos, Paul-Charles. "John Wilmot, 2° Comte de Rochester." *Revue des Langues Vivantes* (Bruxelles), 22 (1956), 241–56.

A brief account of Rochester's career.

Duncan, Ronald. "Rochester." *Townsman, 3,* no. 12 (1940), pp. 14–21.

A variation of the introduction to Duncan's *Selected Lyrics and Satires.*

Ellis, Frank H. "John Freke and *The History of Insipids.*" *Philological Quarterly,* 44 (1965), 472–83.

Documentary evidence that this lampoon was written by Freke rather than Rochester.

Emslie, Macdonald. "A New Song by Rochester." *London Times Literary Supplement,* 26 February 1954, p. 137.

On the lyric "Tell me no more of constancy."

Erskine-Hill, Howard. "Rochester: Augustan or Explorer?" In *Renaissance and Modern Essays Presented to Vivian de Sola Pinto in celebration of his seventieth birthday,* ed. G. R. Hibbard (London, Routledge and Kegan Paul; New York, Barnes and Noble, 1966), pp. 51–64.

Criticism, especially of "A Satyr against Reason and Mankind," "Upon Nothing," the lines translated from Seneca's *Troades,* "A Very Heroical Epistle," and "An Epistolary Essay."

'Espinasse, Paul G. "Rochester on Charles II." *London Times Literary Supplement,* 1 November 1934, p. 755.

On the text of the impromptu "God bless our good and gracious King."

Fujimura, Thomas H. "Rochester's 'Satyr against Mankind': An Analysis." *Studies in Philology,* 55 (1958), 576–90.

Finds the poem Hobbesian in its attitudes, only more pessimistic.

Giddey, Ernest. "Rochester, Poète Baroque (1647–1680)." *Etudes de Lettres,* ser. 2, 7 (1964), 155–64.

General comments on Rochester's life and poetry.

Grabo, Norman S. "The Profligate and the Puritan." *Notes and Queries,* 207 (1962), 392–93.

A text of "Upon Nothing" was copied into his commonplace book by the New England judge, John Saffin.

Graves, Wallace. "The Uses of Rhetoric in the Nadir of English Morals." *Western Speech,* 28 (1964), 97–105.

Rhetorical analysis of *Sodom.*

Gray, Philip. "Rochester's *Poems on Several Occasions:* New Light on the Dated and Undated Editions, 1680." *The Library,* 4th ser., 19 (1938–39), 185–97.

New bibliographical information on the "1680" editions.

Greene, Graham. "Otway and Mrs. Barry." *London Times Literary Supplement,* 16 April 1931, p. 307.

Refers to "A Session of the Poets."

———. "Rochester and Lee." *London Times Literary Supplement,* 2 November 1935, p. 697.

Evidence that Duke Nemours in Lee's *The Princess of Cleve* may represent Rochester.

Ham, Roswell G. "The Authorship of *A Session of the Poets* (1677)." *Review of English Studies,* 9 (1933), 319–22.

Evidence and arguments that Elkanah Settle wrote this lampoon.

[Hanson, Laurence.] "A Rochester Poem." *The Bodleian Library Record,* 4 (1953), 183–84.

Calls attention to the folio leaflet *Artemisa to Cloe,* 1679.

Harris, Brice. "Dorset's Poem, 'On the Young Statesmen.' " *London Times Literary Supplement,* 4 April 1935, pp. 227–28.

On the authorship of the lampoon beginning "Clarendon had law and sense."

———. "Rochester's 'Remains' and an Old Manuscript." *Notes and Queries, 163* (1932), 170–71.

Notes that approximately 20 poems appear both in Rochester's *Remains,* 1718, and in an early manuscript.

———. " 'A Satyr on the Court Ladies.' " *London Times Literary Supplement,* 20 August 1931, p. 633.

Attempts to identify a lost lampoon attributed to Rochester.

Hartmann, Cyril Hughes. "Rochester's Marriage." *History Today, 5* (1955), 840–49.

An interpretive account of Rochester's courtship and married life, attractively written but adding no new documentary evidence.

Hayward, John. "Rochester on Charles II." *London Times Literary Supplement,* 25 October 1934, p. 735.

On the "1680" editions and the impromptu "God bless our good and gracious King."

Hogan, Patrick G. "Rochester: A Metaphysical Restoration Rake." Abstract of a paper read before the South Central Modern Language Association in October 1951. *Seventeenth-Century News, 10* (1952), 22.

Criticism.

Hook, Lucyle. "The Publication Date of Rochester's *Valentinian.*" *Huntington Library Quarterly, 19* (1956), 401–07.

———. "Something More About Rochester." *Modern Language Notes, 75* (1960), 478–85.

Several letters in the Huntington Library, written in the 1670s, provide new information on the Rochester biography and on "The Debauchee" ("I rise at eleven, I dine about two"), "A Ramble in St. James's Park," "On the Women about Town," and "The Dispute" ("Betwixt Father Patrick and His Highness of late").

Huntley, Frank Livingstone. "Dryden, Rochester, and the Eighth Satire of Juvenal." *Philological Quarterly, 18* (1939), 269–84.

An analysis of the Preface to *All for Love* as satire on Rochester.

Isaacs, J. "The Earl of Rochester's Grand Tour." *Review of English Studies, 3* (1927), 75–76.

Documentary evidence places Rochester at Venice on 1 October and at Padua on 26 October 1664.

Jerome, Judson Blair. "Rochester and the Generation of Wit." Unpublished doctoral dissertation, Ohio State University, 1955. *Dissertation Abstracts, 15* (1955), 1233–34.

Lawrence, W. J. "Rochester and Lee." *London Times Library Supplement,* 9 November 1935, p. 722.

Comment on Greene, "Rochester and Lee" (see above).

Legouis, Pierre. "Rochester et Sa Réputation." *Etudes Anglaises, 1* (1937), 53–69.

General comments.

———. "Three Notes on 'Rochester's' Poems." *Modern Language Notes, 69* (1954), 502–06.

Explains details in "Rochester's Farewell," the lampoon beginning "Must I with patience ever silent sit," and "Tunbridge Wells."

Loane, George G. "Rochester on Charles II." *London Times Literary Supplement,* 4 October 1934, p. 675; also 25 October 1934, p. 735.

On the text of the impromptu "God bless our good and gracious King."

Mackie, J. L. "A New Song by Rochester." *London Times Literary Supplement,* 19 February 1954, p. 121.

On the lyric "Tell me no more of constancy."

Main, C. F. "The Right Vein of Rochester's *Satyr.*" In *Essays in Literary History Presented to J. Milton French,* ed. Rudolf Kirk and C. F. Main (New Brunswick, Rutgers University Press, 1960), pp. 93–112.

Interprets "A Satyr against Reason and Mankind" in light of the genre of formal verse satire.

[Mander, Gerald P.] "Rochester and Dr Bendo." *London Times Literary Supplement*, 13 June 1942, p. 300.

Calls attention to the manuscript volume later published by Pinto as *The Famous Pathologist*.

Moncada, Ernest J. "The Source of an Epigram Attributed to Rochester." *Notes and Queries*, *209* (1964), 95–96.

The epigram is "She was so exquisite a whore."

Moore, John F. "The Originality of Rochester's *Satyr against Mankind*." *PMLA*, *58* (1943), 393–401.

Minimizes the poem's indebtedness to Boileau's eighth satire, Montaigne's essays, or any other specific source.

Nicoll, Allardyce. "Dryden, Howard, and Rochester." *London Times Literary Supplement*, 13 January 1921, p. 27.

Describes B. M. Add. MS. 28692, containing Rochester's *Valentinian* and the scene he wrote for a play by Sir Robert Howard.

Paden, W. D. "Rochester's Satyr." *Books and Libraries at the University of Kansas*, *1*, no. 3 (April 1953), pp. 8–11.

Discusses the folio leaflet *A Satyr against Mankind* [1679].

Palmer, Melvin Delmar. "The Identity of 'M. G.' and 'O. B.' in Rochester's 'An Epistolary Essay from M. G. to O. B. Upon Their Mutual Poems.'" *Modern Language Notes*, 75 (1960), 644–47.

Perceives the irony of the poem, but identifies M. G. and O. B. as Martin Clifford and the Duke of Buckingham.

Pinto, Vivian de Sola. "Godfrey Thacker and Sir Charles Sedley." *Notes and Queries*, *209* (1964), 94–95.

Suggests that Sedley's wife rather than Rochester's is the probable subject of some oblique references in the letters printed in Hook, "Something More About Rochester" (see above).

———. "John Wilmot, Earl of Rochester, and the Right Veine of Satire." *Essays and Studies* (The English Association), new ser., *6* (1953), 56–70. Reprinted in *Seventeenth-Century English Poetry: Modern Essays in Criticism,* ed. William R. Keast (New York, Oxford University Press, 1962), pp. 359–74.
Criticism.

———. "Libertines and Puritans: A Note on some lyrics of the late Seventeenth and early Eighteenth Centuries." *Notes and Queries, 205* (1960), 224–26.
Maintains that Isaac Watts's hymn "Our God, our Help in Ages past" echoes Rochester's songs beginning "An age in her embraces passed" and "All my past life is mine no more."

———. "A Poem Attributed to Rochester." *London Times Literary Supplement,* 5 November 1954, p. 705. Also "Rochester and 'A Young Gentleman,'" 7 October 1955, p. 589.
Suggests that Rochester wrote the lampoon beginning "To make myself for this employment fit."

———. "The Poetry of John Wilmot, Earl of Rochester." *Transactions of the Royal Society of Literature, 13* (1934), 109–33.
Criticism.

———"Rochester and Dryden." *Renaissance and Modern Studies, 5* (1961), 29–48.
Traces the personal relations between the two men, and compares them as poets.

———. "Rochester and Salvator Rosa." *English Miscellany, 7* (1956), 19–24.
Suggests Rosa as a source for "A Satyr against Reason and Mankind" and "Upon Nothing."

———. "Rochester, Dryden, and the Duchess of Portsmouth."

Review of English Studies, 16 (1940), 177–78.

Evidence that Portsmouth instigated the beating of Dryden in Rose Alley on 18 December 1679.

———. "The 1680 'Antwerp' Edition of Rochester's Poems." *The Library,* 4th ser., 20 (1939–40), 105.

A previously unnoticed copy of one of the "1680" editions.

———. "An Unpublished Poem Attributed to Rochester." *London Times Literary Supplement,* 22 November 1934, p. 824. Also "A Poem Attributed to Rochester," 6 December 1934, p. 875, and "Rochester and the Deists," 13 December 1934, p. 895.

The verses beginning "Before by death you newer knowledge gain," although ascribed to Rochester in a seventeenth-century source, are by Sir William Davenant. The third communication calls attention to Charles Blount's three letters to Rochester.

Powley, Edward B. "Rochester on Charles II." *London Times Literary Supplement,* 18 October 1934, p. 715.

On the text of the impromptu "God bless our good and gracious King."

Prinz, Johannes, ed. *Rochesteriana: Being Some Anecdotes Concerning John Wilmot, Earl of Rochester.* Leipzig, privately printed, 1926.

Prints miscellaneous biographical materials.

Quaintance, Richard E. "French Sources of the Restoration 'Imperfect Enjoyment' Poem." *Philological Quarterly,* 42 (1963), 190–99.

Includes the poems beginning "Naked she lay, clasped in my longing arms" (by Rochester), "Fruition was the question in debate" (anonymous), and "One day the amorous Lysander" (by Aphra Behn).

Sprague, Arthur Colby. *Beaumont and Fletcher on the Restoration Stage.* Cambridge, Mass., Harvard University Press,

1926; New York, Benjamin Blom, 1965. Pp. 165–78.
On *Valentinian.*

Thorpe, James. "Authenticity of 'The Wish' as a Rochester Poem." *Modern Language Notes, 62* (1947), 267–68.
Evidence that Rochester did not write the lines beginning "Oh, that I could by some chymic art."

———. "The Earliest Edition of Rochester's Poems." *Princeton University Library Chronicle, 8* (1947), 172–76.
Describes a copy of one of the "1680" editions in the Princeton library.

Todd, William B. "The 1680 Editions of Rochester's *Poems* With Notes on Earlier Texts." *Papers of the Bibliographical Society of America, 47* (1953), 43–58.
Claims that the earliest printing of the *Poems* of 1680 is not the Huntington edition, as Thorpe concluded, but the Pforzheimer edition.

Vieth, David M. "Etherege's 'Man of Mode' and Rochester's 'Artemisa to Cloe.'" *Notes and Queries, 203* (1958), 473–74.
Parallels in ideas between Etherege's play and Rochester's poem.

———. "John Oldham, the Wits, and *A Satyr against Vertue.*" *Philological Quarterly, 32* (1953), 90–93.
Evidence of the circumstances under which Rochester became acquainted with Oldham.

———. "A New Song by Rochester." *London Times Literary Supplement,* 6 November 1953, p. 716.
On the lyric "Tell me no more of constancy."

———. "Order of Contents as Evidence of Authorship: Rochester's *Poems* of 1680." *Papers of the Bibliographical Society of America, 53* (1959), 293–308. Reprinted in *Evidence for Authorship: Essays on Problems of Attribution,* ed. David V. Erdman and Ephim G. Fogel (Ithaca, N.Y., Cornell University Press, 1966), pp. 256–72.

The arrangement of the 61 poems in the "1680" editions is an indispensable aid in solving the difficult problems of their authorship.

———. "Poems by 'My Lord R.': Rochester versus Radclyffe." *PMLA*, 72 (1957), 612–19.

A group of seven lyrics, most of which have been attributed to Rochester, was written by Edward Radclyffe, second Earl of Derwentwater.

———. "Pope and Rochester: An Unnoticed Borrowing." *Notes and Queries*, 211 (1966), 457–58.

Pope twice echoes a line in "An Epistolary Essay."

———. "Rochester and 'A Young Gentleman.' " *London Times Literary Supplement*, 23 September 1955, p. 557.

Evidence against Rochester's authorship of the lampoon beginning "To make myself for this employment fit."

———. "Rochester and Cowley." *London Times Literary Supplement*, 12 October 1951, p. 645.

The quatrain beginning "Is there a man, ye gods, whom I do hate" is by Cowley.

———. "Rochester's 'Scepter' Lampoon on Charles II." *Philological Quarterly*, 37 (1958), 424–32.

On the authorship, early texts, and date of the lampoon "I' th' isle of Britain, long since famous grown."

———. "The Text of Rochester and the Editions of 1680." *Papers of the Bibliographical Society of America*, 50 (1956), 243–63.

The earliest printing of the *Poems* of 1680 is not the Pforzheimer edition, as Todd claimed, but the Huntington edition, as Thorpe originally maintained.

———. "A Textual Paradox: Rochester's 'To a Lady in a Letter.' " *Papers of the Bibliographical Society of America*, 54 (1960), 147–62.

Analyzes the early texts of the lyric beginning "How happy, Chloris, were they free," "How perfect, Chloris, and how free," or "Such perfect bliss, fair Chloris, we."

———. "Two Rochester Songs." *Notes and Queries, 201* (1956), 338–39.

On the authorship and early texts of the lyrics "Insulting beauty, you misspend" and "At last you'll force me to confess."

———. "An Unsuspected Cancel in Tonson's 1691 'Rochester.' " *Papers of the Bibliographical Society of America,* 55 (1961), 130–33.

Sequel to "A Textual Paradox" (see above), with evidence that the 1691 text is expurgated.

Walmsley, D. M. " 'A Trial of the Poets.' " *London Times Literary Supplement,* 28 May 1931, p. 427.

On the lampoon beginning "Since the sons of the muses grew numerous and loud."

Whitfield, Francis. *Beast in View: A Study of the Earl of Rochester's Poetry.* Harvard Honors Theses in English No. 9. Cambridge, Mass., Harvard University Press; London, Humphrey Milford, 1936.

Criticism.

Wilkinson, C. H. "Lord Rochester." *London Times Literary Supplement,* 11 July 1935, p. 448.

An important communication, calling attention to some nineteen poems attributed to Rochester which are printed in *The Triumph of Wit,* 1688, and recording Narcissus Luttrell's dates for a number of broadsides.

Williamson, George. *The Proper Wit of Poetry.* University of Chicago Press, 1961. Pp. 125–30.

Criticism.

———. "The Restoration Petronius." *University of California Chronicle,* 29 (1927), 273–80.

Criticism.

Wilson, John Harold. *The Court Wits of the Restoration: An Introduction.* Princeton University Press, 1948.

Includes scattered comments of much value on Rochester.

———. "The Dating of Rochester's 'Scaen.' " *Review of English Studies, 13* (1937), 455–58.

Rochester probably composed his scene for Sir Robert Howard's play in 1678 rather than 1672.

———. "Rochester: An Overlooked Poem." *Notes and Queries, 187* (1944), 79.

The lyric "Fling this useless book away."

———. "Rochester, Dryden, and the Rose-Street Affair." *Review of English Studies, 15* (1939), 294–301.

An important article challenging the traditional assumption that Rochester was responsible for the beating of Dryden in Rose Alley on 18 December 1679.

———. "Rochester's 'A Session of the Poets.' " *Review of English Studies, 22* (1946), 109–16.

Presents important evidence on the date and authorship of the lampoon beginning "Since the sons of the muses grew numerous and loud."

———. "Rochester's 'Buffoon Conceit.' " *Modern Language Notes, 56* (1941), 372–73.

On the date and authorship of "To the Postboy."

———. "Rochester's Marriage." *Review of English Studies, 19* (1943), 399–403.

The definitive account of Rochester's marriage to Elizabeth Malet.

———. "Rochester's *Valentinian* and Heroic Sentiment." *English Literary History, 4* (1937), 265–73.

Rochester adapted Fletcher's play in the direction of Restoration heroic drama.

———. "Satiric Elements in Rochester's *Valentinian.*" *Philological Quarterly, 16* (1937), 41–48.

Rochester altered the characterization of the emperor to make it a satire on Charles II.

———. "Two Poems Ascribed to Rochester." *Modern Language Notes*, 54 (1939), 458–60.

Doubts Rochester's authorship of the poems beginning "Since death on all lays his impartial hand" and "Fruition was the question in debate." Two poems by Thomas Randolph and three by Aphra Behn were erroneously printed as Rochester's by Hayward and Johns.

Prentice Work

1665-1671

*The dates at the head of each poem, in brackets
to left and right immediately below the title,
are the dates of composition and publication
respectively. See p.xlv of the Introduction,
and also the relevant Notes starting at p.171.*

Song

[Uncertain]

[*1934*]

'Twas a dispute 'twixt heaven and earth
Which had produced the nobler birth.
For heaven appeared Cynthia, with all her train,
    Till you came forth,
      More glorious and more worth   ,5
Than she with all those trembling imps of light
    With which this envious queen of night
Had proudly decked her conquered self in vain.

I must have perished in that first surprise,
    Had I beheld your eyes.   10
Love, like Apollo when he would inspire
Some holy breast, laid all his glories by;
Else the god, clothed in his heavenly fire,
    Would have possessed too powerfully,
And making of his priest a sacrifice,   15
Had so returned unhallowed to the skies.

3

A Pastoral Dialogue between Alexis and Strephon

[Possibly 1674]   [*1682*]

ALEXIS.

There sighs not on the plain
   So lost a swain as I;
Scorched up with love, frozen with disdain,
Of killing sweetness I complain.

STREPHON.

   If 'tis Corinna, die.   5

Since first my dazzled eyes were thrown
   On that bewitching face,
Like ruined birds robbed of their young,
Lamenting, frighted, and alone,
   I fly from place to place.   10

Framed by some cruel powers above,
   So nice she is, and fair,
None from undoing can remove
Since all who are not blind must love—
   Who are not vain, despair.   15

ALEXIS.

The gods no sooner give a grace
   But, fond of their own art,
Severely jealous, ever place,
To guard the glories of a face,
   A dragon in the heart.   20

Proud and ill-natured powers they are,
   Who, peevish to mankind,
For their own honor's sake, with care
Make a sweet form divinely fair,
   And add a cruel mind. 25

STREPHON.

Since she's insensible of love,
   By honor taught to hate,
If we, forced by decrees above,
Must sensible to beauty prove,
   How tyrannous is fate! 30

ALEXIS.

I to the nymph have never named
   The cause of all my pain.

STREPHON.

Such bashfulness may well be blamed,
For since to serve we're not ashamed,
   Why should she blush to reign? 35

ALEXIS.

But if her haughty heart despise
   My humble proffered one,
The just compassion she denies
I may obtain from others' eyes:
   Hers are not fair alone. 40

Devouring flames require new food:
   My heart's consumed almost;
New fires must kindle in her blood,
Or mine go out, and that's as good.

STREPHON.

Wouldst live, when love is lost?   45

Be dead before thy passion dies,
　　For if thou shouldst survive,
What anguish would the heart surprise
To see her flames begin to rise,
　　And thine no more alive!   50

ALEXIS.

Rather, what pleasure should I meet,
　　In my triumphant scorn,
To see my tyrant at my feet
Whilst, taught by her, unmoved I sit,
　　A tyrant in my turn.   55

STREPHON.

Ungentle shepherd, cease, for shame!
　　Which way can you pretend
To merit so divine a flame,
Who to dull life make a mean claim
　　When love is at an end?   60

As trees are by their bark embraced,
　　Love to my soul doth cling;
When, torn by the herd's greedy taste,
The injured plants feel they're defaced,
　　They wither in the spring.   65

My rifled love would soon retire,
　　Dissolving into air,
Should I that nymph cease to admire,
Blest in whose arms I will expire,
　　Or at her feet despair.   70

A Dialogue between Strephon and Daphne

[Uncertain]   [*1691*]

STREPHON.

Prithee now, fond fool, give o'er.
Since my heart is gone before,
To what purpose should I stay?
Love commands another way.

DAPHNE.

Perjured swain, I knew the time   5
When dissembling was your crime;
In pity now employ that art
Which first betrayed, to ease my heart.

STREPHON.

Women can with pleasure feign;
Men dissemble still with pain.   10
What advantage will it prove
If I lie, who cannot love?

DAPHNE.

Tell me, then, the reason why
Love from hearts in love does fly;
Why the bird will build a nest   15
Where he ne'er intends to rest?

STREPHON.

Love, like other little boys,
Cries for hearts, as they for toys—
Which, when gained, in childish play
Wantonly are thrown away.   20

DAPHNE.

Still on wing, or on his knees,
Love does nothing by degrees:
Basely flying when most prized,
Meanly fawning when despised,
Flattering or insulting ever,   25
Generous and grateful never.
All his joys are fleeting dreams,
All his woes severe extremes.

STREPHON.

Nymph, unjustly you inveigh:
Love, like us, must fate obey.   30
Since 'tis nature's law to change,
Constancy alone is strange.
See the heavens in lightnings break,
Next in storms of thunder speak,
Till a kind rain from above   35
Makes a calm—so 'tis in love.
Flames begin our first address;
Like meeting thunder we embrace;
Then, you know, the showers that fall
Quench the fire, and quiet all.   40

DAPHNE.

How should I these showers forget?
'Twas so pleasant to be wet!
They killed love, I knew it well:
I died all the while they fell.
Say, at least, what nymph it is   45
Robs my breast of so much bliss!
If she's fair, I shall be eased:
Through my ruin you'll be pleased.

STREPHON.

Daphne never was so fair,
Strephon scarcely so sincere: 50
Gentle, innocent, and free,
Ever pleased with only me.
Many charms my heart enthrall,
But there's one above them all:
With aversion she does fly   55
Tedious, trading constancy.

DAPHNE.

Cruel shepherd, I submit:
Do what love and you think fit.
Change is fate, and not design;
Say you would have still been mine.   60

STREPHON.

Nymph, I cannot; 'tis too true,
Change has greater charms than you.
Be by my example wise:
Faith to pleasure sacrifice.

DAPHNE.

Silly swain, I'll have you know   65
'Twas my practice long ago.
Whilst you vainly thought me true,
I was false in scorn of you.
By my tears, my heart's disguise,
I thy love and thee despise.   70
Womankind more joy discovers
Making fools, than keeping lovers.

Song

[After spring 1665]   [*1677*]

This song is the first of a pair of love lyrics evidently composed by Rochester and his wife. Lady Rochester's answer is preserved in her own handwriting:

> Nothing adds to love's fond fire
>   More than scorn and cold disdain;
> I, to cherish your desire,
>   Kindness used, but 'twas in vain.
> You insulted on your slave;
>   To be mine you soon refused;
> Hope not then the power to have
>   Which ingloriously you used.
>
> Think not, Thyrsis, I will e'er
>   By my love my empire lose.
> You grow constant through despair:
>   Kindness you would soon abuse.
> Though you still possess my heart,
>   Scorn and rigor I must feign;
> There remains no other art
>   Your love, fond fugitive, to gain.

The last eight lines of Rochester's lyric were sung in his adaptation of Fletcher's *Valentinian* (V.v.).

> Give me leave to rail at you
> (I ask nothing but my due):
> To call you false, and then to say
> You shall not keep my heart a day.
> But, alas! against my will,   5
> I must be your captive still.
> Ah! Be kinder, then, for I
> Cannot change, and would not die.
>
> Kindness has resistless charms;
> All besides but weakly move;   10

Fiercest anger it disarms
And clips the wings of flying love.
Beauty does the heart invade,
Kindness only can persuade;
It gilds the lover's servile chain   15
And makes the slave grow pleased and vain.

A Song

[Uncertain]   [*1693*]

Insulting beauty, you misspend
   Those frowns upon your slave:
Your scorn against such rebels bend
Who dare with confidence pretend
That other eyes their hearts defend   5
   From all the charms you have.

Your conquering eyes so partial are,
   Or mankind is so dull,
That while I languish in despair,
Many proud, senseless hearts declare   10
They find you not so killing fair
   To wish you merciful.

They an inglorious freedom boast;
   I triumph in my chain.
Nor am I unrevenged, though lost,   15
Nor you unpunished, though unjust,
When I alone, who love you most,
   Am killed with your disdain.

A Song

[Uncertain]   [*1685*]

My dear mistress has a heart
    Soft as those kind looks she gave me
When, with love's resistless art
    And her eyes, she did enslave me.
But her constancy's so weak—   5
    She's so wild, and apt to wander—
That my jealous heart would break
    Should we live one day asunder.

Melting joys about her move,
    Killing pleasures, wounding blisses.   10
She can dress her eyes in love,
    And her lips can arm with kisses.
Angels listen when she speaks;
    She's my delight, all mankind's wonder;
But my jealous heart would break   15
    Should we live one day asunder.

Song

[Uncertain]   [*Spring 1676*]

While on those lovely looks I gaze
    To see a wretch pursuing,
In raptures of a blest amaze,
    His pleasing, happy ruin,
'Tis not for pity that I move: 5
    His fate is too aspiring

Whose heart, broke with a load of love,
   Dies wishing and admiring.

But if this murder you'd forgo,
   Your slave from death removing,   10
Let me your art of charming know,
   Or learn you mine of loving.
But whether life or death betide,
   In love 'tis equal measure:
The victor lives with empty pride,   15
   The vanquished die with pleasure.

Song

[Uncertain]   [*Spring 1676*]

This lyric, which survives in Rochester's own handwriting, was first
printed in 1676 as an additional stanza to the song beginning "While
on those lovely looks I gaze" (p. 12), although it is evidently a separate
poem.

At last you'll force me to confess
   You need no arts to vanquish:
Such charms from nature you possess,
   'Twere dullness not to languish.
Yet spare a heart you may surprise,   5
   And give my tongue the glory
To scorn, while my unfaithful eyes
   Betray a kinder story.

Woman's Honor

Love bade me hope, and I obeyed;
　　Phyllis continued still unkind.
"Then you may e'en despair," he said;
　　"In vain I strive to change her mind.

"Honor's got in and keeps her heart;   5
　　Durst he but venture once abroad,
In my own right I'd take your part
　　And show myself the mightier god.

"This huffing Honor domineers
　　In breasts alone where he has place,   10
But if true generous Love appears,
　　The hector dares not show his face."

Let me still languish and complain,
　　Be most inhumanly denied.
I have some pleasure in my pain;   15
　　She can have none with all her pride.

I fall a sacrifice to Love,
　　She lives a wretch for Honor's sake;
Whose tyrant does most cruel prove,
　　The difference is not hard to make.   20

Consider real honor, then:
　　You'll find hers cannot be the same.
'Tis noble confidence in men;
　　In women, mean mistrustful shame.

10. *has place:* takes precedence.

The Submission

[Uncertain] [*c. Sept. 1680*]

To this moment a rebel, I throw down my arms,
Great Love! at first sight of Olinda's bright charms.
Made proud and secure by such forces as these,
You may now be a tyrant as soon as you please.

When innocence, beauty, and wit do conspire 5
To betray, and engage, and inflame my desire,
Why should I decline what I cannot avoid,
And let pleasing hope by base fear be destroyed?

Her innocence cannot contrive to undo me;
Her beauty's inclined, or why should it pursue me? 10
And wit has to pleasure been ever a friend;
Then what room for despair, since delight is love's end?

There can be no danger in sweetness and youth
Where love is secured by good nature and truth.
On her beauty I'll gaze, and of pleasure complain, 15
While every kind look adds a link to my chain.

'Tis more to maintain than it was to surprise,
But her wit leads in triumph the slave of her eyes.
I beheld with the loss of my freedom before,
But, hearing, forever must serve and adore. 20

Too bright is my goddess, her temple too weak.
Retire, divine image! I feel my heart break.
Help, Love! I dissolve in a rapture of charms
At the thought of those joys I should meet in her arms.

Written in a Lady's Prayer Book

[Uncertain]   [*1697*]

These verses are "an imitation (with additions) of two short lyrics by
Malherbe: 'Pour Mettre Devant Les Heures de Caliste' and 'Autre sur
le Mesme Sujet,' first printed in *Les Délices de la Poésie Françoise*, 1615"
(J. Harold Wilson, "Rochester: An Overlooked Poem," *Notes and Queries*,
187 [1944], 79).

I.

Fling this useless book away,
And presume no more to pray.
Heaven is just, and can bestow
Mercy on none but those that mercy show.
With a proud heart maliciously inclined   5
Not to increase, but to subdue mankind,
In vain you vex the gods with your petition;
Without repentance and sincere contrition,
    You're in a reprobate condition.

2.

Phyllis, to calm the angry powers   10
And save my soul as well as yours,
Relieve poor mortals from despair,
And justify the gods that made you fair;
    And in those bright and charming eyes
        Let pity first appear, then love,   15
    That we by easy steps may rise
Through all the joys on earth to those above.

The Discovery

[Before winter 1671–72]   [*1672*]

Celia, the faithful servant you disown
Would, in obedience, keep his love unknown,
But bright ideas such as you inspire
We can no more conceal, than not admire.
My heart at home in my own breast did dwell   5
Like humble hermit in a peaceful cell;
Unknown and undisturbed it rested there,
Stranger alike to hope and to despair,
But Love's tumultuous train does now invade
The sacred quiet of this hallowed shade.   10
His fatal flames shine out to every eye
Like blazing comets in a winter's sky.

How can my passion merit your offense
That challenges so little recompense?
For I am one born only to admire;   15
Too humble e'er to hope, scarce to desire;
A thing whose bliss depends upon your will,
Who would be proud you'd deign to use him ill.

Then give me leave to glory in my chain,
My fruitless sighs, and my unpitied pain.   20
Let me but ever love, and ever be
Th' example of your power and cruelty.
Since so much scorn does in your breast reside,
Be more indulgent to its mother, pride;
Kill all you strike, and trample on their graves,   25
But own the fates of your neglected slaves:
When in the crowd yours undistinguished lies,
You give away the triumph of your eyes.

Perhaps, obtaining this, you'll think I find
More mercy than your anger has designed.   30
But Love has carefully contrived for me
The last perfection of misery,
For to my state those hopes of common peace
Which death affords to every wretch, must cease:
My worst of fates attends me in my grave   35
Since, dying, I must be no more your slave.

The Advice

[Before winter 1671–72]   [*1672*]

All things submit themselves to your command,
Fair Celia, when it does not Love withstand;
The power it borrows from your eyes alone
All but the god must yield to, who has none.
Were he not blind, such are the charms you have,   5
He'd quit his godhead to become your slave,
Be proud to act a mortal hero's part,
And throw himself, for fame, on his own dart.
But fate has otherwise disposed of things,
In different bands subjecting slaves and kings: 10
Fettered in forms of royal state are they,
While we enjoy the freedom to obey.
That fate (like you, resistless) does ordain
To Love, that over beauty he shall reign.
By harmony the universe does move,   15
And what is harmony but mutual love?
Who would resist an empire so divine,
Which universal nature does enjoin?

See gentle brooks, how quietly they glide,
Kissing the rugged banks on either side, 20
While in their crystal streams at once they show,
And with them feed, the flowers which they bestow.
Though rudely thronged by a too-near embrace,
In gentle murmurs they keep on their pace
To their loved sea, for ev'n streams have desires: 25
Cool as they are, they feel Love's powerful fires,
And with such passion that if any force
Stop or molest them in their amorous course,
They swell with rage, break down and ravage o'er
The banks they kissed, the flowers they fed before. 30

Submit then, Celia, ere you be reduced,
For rebels, vanquished once, are vilely used,
And such are you whene'er you dare obey
Another passion, and your love betray.
You are Love's citadel; by you he reigns 35
And his proud empire o'er the world maintains.
He trusts you with his stratagems and arms:
His frowns, his smiles, and all his conquering charms.

Beauty's no more but the dead soil which Love
Manures, and does by wise commerce improve. 40
Sailing by sighs, through seas of tears he sends
Courtships from foreign hearts. For your own ends
Cherish the trade, for as with Indians we
Get gold and jewels for our trumpery,
So to each other, for their useless toys, 45
Lovers afford whole magazines of joys.
But if you're fond of baubles, be, and starve;
Your gewgaw reputation still preserve;
Live upon modesty and empty fame,
Forgoing sense for a fantastic name. 50

Under King Charles II's Picture

[Uncertain]   [*1953*]

Evidently John Roberts was one of Rochester's servants, although no other
record of his existence has come to light.

I, John Roberts, writ this same;
I pasted it, and plastered it, and put it in a frame
In honor of my master's master, King Charles the Second by
    name.

Rhyme to Lisbon

[Uncertain]   [*1738*]

According to several early sources, Charles II and some of his courtiers,
drinking healths, were at a loss for a rhyme for "Lisbon." Rochester
entered, raised his glass, and spoke these lines.

A health to Kate!
Our sovereign's mate,
Of the royal house of Lisbon;
But the Devil take Hyde,
And the bishop beside   5
Who made her bone his bone.

1. *Kate:* Catherine of Braganza, Charles II's Queen.
4. *Hyde:* Edward Hyde, Earl of Clarendon, was popularly blamed for
the Portuguese marriage. On 30 August 1667 he was removed from the
office of Lord Chancellor, which he had held since the Restoration.
5. *bishop:* presumably the Bishop of London, who officiated at the
royal wedding ceremony on the afternoon of 21 May 1662.

Impromptu on Louis XIV

[?Late spring 1669]   [*1745*]

According to a mid-eighteenth century account, some of whose details may be fanciful:

> The *French* Tyrant, in a vain-glorious Boast caus'd the following Verses to be inscrib'd on a Marble Pillar at *Versailles*, to tell the Greatness of his Actions to future Ages, *viz.*

> > Una Dies *Lotheros, Burgundos* Hebdomas una,
> > Una domat *Batavos* Luna; Quid Annus aget?

> In *English* thus:

> > *Lorain* a Day, a Week *Burgundy* won,
> > *Flanders* a Month; what wou'd a Year have done?

> Which being seen by the Lord *Wilmot*, the late ingenious Earl of *Rochester*, he presently writ underneath

the English distich given below.

These lines seem to ridicule the relatively pacific policies of expansion, culminating in the Peace of Aix-la-Chapelle on 2 May 1668, which Louis XIV pursued until 1672, when he plunged into a series of aggressive wars lasting into the next century. Rochester could plausibly have written the couplet during his visit to the French Court in spring of 1669.

Lorraine you stole; by fraud you got Burgundy;
Flanders you bought; but, Gad! you'll pay for 't one day.

1. *Lorraine:* part or all of which was repeatedly occupied by the French between 1633 and 1670. *Burgundy:* technically a part of France long before the reign of Louis XIV, although it continued to be disturbed by foreign territorial claims until 1678, when order was imposed by the French conquest of Franche-Comté.

2. *Flanders:* Under the treaty of Aix-la-Chapelle, Louis XIV with little effort acquired several strategically important towns in the Spanish Netherlands.

Rochester Extempore

[? 1670]   [Unpublished]

> And after singing Psalm the Twelfth,
> He laid his book upon the shelf
> And looked much simply like himself;
> With eyes turned up, as white as ghost,
> He cried, "Ah, Lard! ah, Lard of Hosts!   5
> I am a rascal, that thou know'st!"

Spoken Extempore to a Country Clerk after Having Heard Him Sing Psalms

[Uncertain]   [1709]

According to Alfred Beesley (*The History of Banbury*, London, 1841, p. 488), "the village chroniclers of Adderbury relate many traditional tales of the eccentricities and libertinisms" of the Earl of Rochester. "Amongst others, it is stated that it was at Bodicot (a chapelry to Adderbury) that Rochester made his extempore lines addressed to the psalm-singing clerk or sexton."

> Sternhold and Hopkins had great qualms
> When they translated David's psalms
>   To make the heart full glad;
> But had it been poor David's fate
> To hear thee sing, and them translate,   5
>   By God! 'twould have made him mad.

1: Thomas Sternhold and John Hopkins were authors of the sixteenth-century metrical version of the Psalms which was long used in public worship in English churches. By this date it had become a byword for bad poetry.

To My More Than Meritorious Wife

[After 29 January 1666/7]   [*1747*]

According to one account, Rochester wrote these verses "extempore to his Lady, who sent a servant on purpose desiring to hear from him, being very uneasy at his long Silence."

> I am, by fate, slave to your will
> And shall be most obedient still.
> To show my love, I will compose ye,
> For your fair finger's ring, a posy,
> In which shall be expressed my duty,   5
> And how I'll be forever true t' ye.
> With low-made legs and sugared speeches,
> Yielding to your fair bum the breeches,
> I'll show myself, in all I can,
> Your faithful, humble servant,   10
>
>   John.

Letter from Miss Price to Lord Chesterfield

[Before 4 Dec. 1673]   [*1834*]

These verses seem to have formed an enclosure in a letter to the libertine
Philip Stanhope, second Earl of Chesterfield, from Henrietta Maria Price,
Maid of Honor to the Queen and daughter of Sir Herbert Price, Master
of the Household to Charles II. The transcript in Chesterfield's letterbook is headed "From Mʳˢ Prise Maid of honour to her Majesty who
sent mee a pair of Itallian Gloves." Her letter, unfortunately not dated,
explains, "I had a mind that you should see these inclosed papers which
were writ by the Lord Rochester, and that hath occationd you this
trouble from your humble servant." Using Miss Price as persona, the
poem evidently ridicules an affair between her and Chesterfield; her
covering remark may be an indirect appeal for some kind of retaliation
against Rochester for his effrontery.

> My Lord,
>   These are the gloves that I did mention
> Last night, and 'twas with the intention
> That you should give me thanks and wear them,
> For I most willingly can spare them.
>   When you this packet first do see,   5
> "Damn me!" cry you, "she has writ to me.
> I had better be at Bretby still
> Than troubled with love against my will.
> Besides, this is not all my sorrow:
> She writ today, she'll come tomorrow."   10
> Then you consider the adventure
> And think you never shall content her.
>   But when you do the inside see,
> You'll find things are but as they should be,
> And that 'tis neither love nor passion,   15
> But only for your recreation.

7. *Bretby:* Chesterfield's family estate in Derbyshire.

The Platonic Lady

[Uncertain]   [*1926*]

In contrast to its rather inappropriate title, the text of "The Platonic Lady" is an adaptation of the poem by Petronius beginning "Foeda est in coitu et brevis voluptas" (No. 101 of *Poetae Latini Minores*).

I could love thee till I die,
Wouldst thou love me modestly,
And ne'er press, whilst I live,
For more than willingly I would give:
    Which should sufficient be to prove   5
    I'd understand the art of love.

I hate the thing is called enjoyment:
Besides it is a dull employment,
It cuts off all that's life and fire
From that which may be termed desire;   10
    Just like the bee whose sting is gone
    Converts the owner to a drone.

I love a youth will give me leave
His body in my arms to wreathe;
To press him gently, and to kiss;   15
To sigh, and look with eyes that wish
    For what, if I could once obtain,
    I would neglect with flat disdain.

I'd give him liberty to toy
And play with me, and count it joy.   20

7. *enjoyment:* fruition, an orgasm.

Our freedom should be full complete,
And nothing wanting but the feat.
    Let's practice, then, and we shall prove
    These are the only sweets of love.

23–24: possibly alluding to Marlowe's famous lyric:
        Come live with me and be my love,
        And we will all the pleasures prove . . .

Song

[Spring 1676 or earlier]   [?*1676, 1677*]

As Chloris full of harmless thought
    Beneath the willows lay,
Kind love a comely shepherd brought
    To pass the time away.

She blushed to be encountered so   5
    And chid the amorous swain,
But as she strove to rise and go,
    He pulled her back again.

A sudden passion seized her heart
    In spite of her disdain;   10
She found a pulse in every part,
    And love in every vein.

"Ah, youth!" quoth she, "What charms are these
    That conquer and surprise?
Ah, let me—for unless you please,   15
    I have no power to rise."

She faintly spoke, and trembling lay,
   For fear he should comply,
But virgins' eyes their hearts betray
   And give their tongues the lie.   20

Thus she, who princes had denied
   With all their pompous train,
Was in the lucky minute tried
   And yielded to the swain.

Song

[Uncertain]   [*c. Sept. 1680*]

Fair Chloris in a pigsty lay;
   Her tender herd lay by her.
She slept; in murmuring gruntlings they,
Complaining of the scorching day,
   Her slumbers thus inspire.   5

She dreamt whilst she with careful pains
   Her snowy arms employed
In ivory pails to fill out grains,
One of her love-convicted swains
   Thus hasting to her cried: 10

"Fly, nymph! Oh, fly ere 'tis too late
   A dear, loved life to save;
Rescue your bosom pig from fate
Who now expires, hung in the gate
   That leads to Flora's cave.   15

15. *Flora:* Roman goddess of springtime and flowers, later identified
with the Greek Chloris.

"Myself had tried to set him free
    Rather than brought the news,
But I am so abhorred by thee
That ev'n thy darling's life from me
    I know thou wouldst refuse."   20

Struck with the news, as quick she flies
    As blushes to her face;
Not the bright lightning from the skies,
Nor love, shot from her brighter eyes,
    Move half so swift a pace.   25

This plot, it seems, the lustful slave
    Had laid against her honor,
Which not one god took care to save,
For he pursues her to the cave
    And throws himself upon her.   30

Now piercèd is her virgin zone;
    She feels the foe within it.
She hears a broken amorous groan,
The panting lover's fainting moan,
    Just in the happy minute.   35

Frighted she wakes, and waking frigs.
    Nature thus kindly eased
In dreams raised by her murmuring pigs
And her own thumb between her legs,
    She's innocent and pleased.   40

Early Maturity

1672-1673

(The Third Dutch War)

Song

[Uncertain]   [c. Sept. 1680]

What cruel pains Corinna takes
    To force that harmless frown;
When not one charm her face forsakes,
    Love cannot lose his own.

So sweet a face, so soft a heart,   5
    Such eyes, so very kind,
Betray, alas! the silly art
    Virtue had ill designed.

Poor feeble tyrant, who in vain
    Would proudly take upon her,   10
Against kind nature, to maintain
    Affected rules of honor.

The scorn she bears so helpless proves,
    When I plead passion to her,
That much she fears, but more she loves,   15
    Her vassal should undo her.

Song

[Uncertain]   [*c. Sept. 1680*]

Phyllis, be gentler, I advise;
    Make up for time misspent:
When beauty on its deathbed lies,
    'Tis high time to repent.

Such is the malice of your fate: 5
    That makes you old so soon,
Your pleasure ever comes too late,
    How early e'er begun.

Think what a wretched thing is she
    Whose stars contrive, in spite,   10
The morning of her love should be
    Her fading beauty's night.

Then, if to make your ruin more,
    You'll peevishly be coy,
Die with the scandal of a whore   15
    And never know the joy.

Epistle

[Uncertain]   [*1934*]

Could I but make my wishes insolent,
And force some image of a false content!
But they, like me, bashful and humble grown,
Hover at distance about beauty's throne;
There worship and admire, and then they die   5
Daring no more lay hold of her than I.

   Reason to worth bears a submissive spirit,
But fools can be familiar with merit.
Who but that blundering blockhead Phaëthon
Could e'er have thought to drive about the sun?   10
Just such another durst make love to you
Whom not ambition led, but dullness drew.
No amorous thought could his dull heart incline,
But he would have a passion, for 'twas fine!
That, a new suit, and what he next must say   15
Runs in his idle head the livelong day.

   Hard-hearted saint! since 'tis your will to be
So unrelenting pitiless to me,
Regardless of a love so many years
Preserved 'twixt lingering hopes and awful fears   20
(Such fears in lovers' breasts high value claims,
And such expiring martyrs feel in flames;
My hopes yourself contrived, with cruel care,
Through gentle smiles to lead me to despair),
'Tis some relief, in my extreme distress,   25
My rival is below your power to bless.

Sab: Lost

[Uncertain]   [*1935*]

The circumstances surrounding the composition of this fragment, as well
as the meaning of the cryptic heading which appears in Rochester's holograph draft, remain obscure.

> She yields, she yields! Pale Envy said amen:
> The first of women to the last of men.
> Just so those frailer beings, angels, fell;
> There's no midway, it seems, 'twixt heaven and hell.
> Was it your end, in making her, to show   5
> Things must be raised so high to fall so low?
> Since her nor angels their own worth secures,
> Look to it, gods! the next turn must be yours.
> You who in careless scorn laughed at the ways
> Of humble love, and called 'em rude essays,   10
> Could you submit to let this heavy thing,
> Artless and witless, no way meriting . . .

Two Translations from Lucretius

The first passage, a tentative draft surviving in Rochester's own handwriting, is a free translation of *De Rerum Natura*, I.1–5. The second
passage is a much closer rendering of I.44–49.

I.

[Uncertain]   [*1953*]

> Great Mother of Aeneas, and of Love;
> Delight of mankind, and the powers above;
> Who all beneath those sprinkled drops of light
> Which slide upon the face of gloomy night,

Whither vast regions of that liquid world   5
Where groves of ships on watery hills are hurled,
Or fruitful earth, dost bless, since 'tis by thee
That all things live which the bright sun does see . . .

2.

[Uncertain]   [*1691*]

The gods, by right of nature, must possess
An everlasting age of perfect peace;
Far off removed from us and our affairs;
Neither approached by dangers, or by cares;
Rich in themselves, to whom we cannot add;   5
Not pleased by good deeds, nor provoked by bad.

To Love

[Uncertain]   [*c. Sept. 1680*]

These verses are a close, nearly line-for-line rendering of Ovid's *Amores*,
2.9. A division has been introduced after line 26, following the opinion
of Ovid's recent editors that this elegy constitutes two separate poems.

O Love! how cold and slow to take my part,
Thou idle wanderer about my heart.
Why thy old faithful soldier wilt thou see
Oppressed in my own tents? They murder me.
Thy flames consume, thy arrows pierce thy friends;   5
Rather, on foes pursue more noble ends.
    Achilles' sword would generously bestow
A cure as certain as it gave the blow.
Hunters who follow flying game give o'er
When the prey's caught; hope still leads on before.   10

7–8: After being wounded by Achilles, Telephus was cured by an application of rust from the same spear that caused his wound.

We thine own slaves feel thy tyrannic blows,
Whilst thy tame hand's unmoved against thy foes.
On men disarmed how can you gallant prove?
And I was long ago disarmed by love.
Millions of dull men live, and scornful maids: 15
We'll own Love valiant when he these invades.
Rome from each corner of the wide world snatched
A laurel; else 't had been to this day thatched.

    But the old soldier has his resting place,
And the good battered horse is turned to grass.   20
The harassed whore, who lived a wretch to please,
Has leave to be a bawd and take her ease.
For me, then, who have freely spent my blood,
Love, in thy service, and so boldly stood
In Celia's trenches, were 't not wisely done   25
E'en to retire, and live at peace at home?

No! Might I gain a godhead to disclaim
My glorious title to my endless flame,
Divinity with scorn I would forswear,
Such sweet, dear, tempting mischiefs women are.   30
Whene'er those flames grow faint, I quickly find
A fierce black storm pour down upon my mind.
Headlong I'm hurled, like horsemen who in vain
Their fury-foaming coursers would restrain.
As ships, just when the harbor they attain,   35
By sudden blasts are snatched to sea again,
So Love's fantastic storms reduce my heart
Half-rescued, and the god resumes his dart.
    Strike here, this undefended bosom wound,
And for so brave a conquest be renowned.   40

21–22: This couplet, Rochester's own invention, does not translate the corresponding distich in the Latin original.

Shafts fly so fast to me from every part,
You'll scarce discern your quiver from my heart.
What wretch can bear a livelong night's dull rest,
Or think himself in lazy slumbers blessed?
Fool! Is not sleep the image of pale death?   45
There's time for rest when fate has stopped your breath.
Me may my soft deluding dear deceive:
I'm happy in my hopes whilst I believe.
Now let her flatter, then as fondly chide;
Often may I enjoy, oft be denied.   50

   With doubtful steps the god of war does move
By thy example led, ambiguous Love.
Blown to and fro like down from thy own wing,
Who knows when joy or anguish thou wilt bring?
Yet at thy mother's and thy slave's request,   55
Fix an eternal empire in my breast;
   And let th' inconstant charming sex,
   Whose willful scorn does lovers vex,
   Submit their hearts before thy throne:
   The vassal world is then thy own.   60

The Imperfect Enjoyment

[Uncertain]   [c. Sept. 1680]

For the tradition to which this poem belongs, stemming ultimately from
Ovid's *Amores*, 3.7, and chapters 128–40 of the *Satyricon* of Petronius,
see Richard E. Quaintance, "French Sources of the Restoration 'Imperfect
Enjoyment' Poem," *Philological Quarterly*, 42 (1963), 190–99.

Naked she lay, clasped in my longing arms,
I filled with love, and she all over charms;
Both equally inspired with eager fire,
Melting through kindness, flaming in desire.

With arms, legs, lips close clinging to embrace,   5
She clips me to her breast, and sucks me to her face.
Her nimble tongue, Love's lesser lightning, played
Within my mouth, and to my thoughts conveyed
Swift orders that I should prepare to throw
The all-dissolving thunderbolt below.   10
My fluttering soul, sprung with the pointed kiss,
Hangs hovering o'er her balmy brinks of bliss.
But whilst her busy hand would guide that part
Which should convey my soul up to her heart,
In liquid raptures I dissolve all o'er,   15
Melt into sperm, and spend at every pore.
A touch from any part of her had done 't:
Her hand, her foot, her very look's a cunt.

   Smiling, she chides in a kind murmuring noise,
And from her body wipes the clammy joys,   20
When, with a thousand kisses wandering o'er
My panting bosom, "Is there then no more?"
She cries. "All this to love and rapture's due;
Must we not pay a debt to pleasure too?"

   But I, the most forlorn, lost man alive,   25
To show my wished obedience vainly strive:
I sigh, alas! and kiss, but cannot swive.
Eager desires confound my first intent,
Succeeding shame does more success prevent,
And rage at last confirms me impotent.   30
Ev'n her fair hand, which might bid heat return
To frozen age, and make cold hermits burn,
Applied to my dead cinder, warms no more
Than fire to ashes could past flames restore.
Trembling, confused, despairing, limber, dry,   35
A wishing, weak, unmoving lump I lie.
This dart of love, whose piercing point, oft tried,
With virgin blood ten thousand maids have dyed;

Which nature still directed with such art
That it through every cunt reached every heart— 40
Stiffly resolved, 'twould carelessly invade
Woman or man, nor ought its fury stayed:
Where'er it pierced, a cunt it found or made—
Now languid lies in this unhappy hour,
Shrunk up and sapless like a withered flower. 45

　　Thou treacherous, base deserter of my flame,
False to my passion, fatal to my fame,
Through what mistaken magic dost thou prove
So true to lewdness, so untrue to love?
What oyster-cinder-beggar-common whore 50
Didst thou e'er fail in all thy life before?
When vice, disease, and scandal lead the way,
With what officious haste dost thou obey!
Like a rude, roaring hector in the streets
Who scuffles, cuffs, and justles all he meets, 55
But if his King or country claim his aid,
The rakehell villain shrinks and hides his head;
Ev'n so thy brutal valor is displayed,
Breaks every stew, does each small whore invade,
But when great Love the onset does command, 60
Base recreant to thy prince, thou dar'st not stand.
Worst part of me, and henceforth hated most,
Through all the town a common fucking post,
On whom each whore relieves her tingling cunt
As hogs on gates do rub themselves and grunt, 65
Mayst thou to ravenous chancres be a prey,
Or in consuming weepings waste away;
May strangury and stone thy days attend;

---

59. *stew:* brothel.
67. *weepings:* discharges of moisture from the body.
68. *strangury:* slow and painful urination. *stone:* a concretion, especially in the kidney, urinary bladder, or gall bladder.

May'st thou ne'er piss, who didst refuse to spend
When all my joys did on false thee depend.   70
And may ten thousand abler pricks agree
To do the wronged Corinna right for thee.

A Ramble in St. James's Park

[Before 20 March 1672/3]   [c. Sept. 1680]

Much wine had passed, with grave discourse
Of who fucks who, and who does worse
(Such as you usually do hear
From those that diet at the Bear),
When I, who still take care to see   5
Drunkenness relieved by lechery,
Went out into St. James's Park
To cool my head and fire my heart.
But though St. James has th' honor on 't,
'Tis consecrate to prick and cunt.   10
There, by a most incestuous birth,
Strange woods spring from the teeming earth;
For they relate how heretofore,
When ancient Pict began to whore,
Deluded of his assignation   15
(Jilting, it seems, was then in fashion),
Poor pensive lover, in this place
Would frig upon his mother's face;
Whence rows of mandrakes tall did rise
Whose lewd tops fucked the very skies.   20

4. *the Bear:* a well-known ordinary in Drury Lane. Pepys frequently
dined there.
19. *mandrakes:* The forked root of the mandrake or mandragora, a
plant of medicinal and allegedly magical powers, was traditionally supposed
to represent the legs of a human being.

Each imitative branch does twine
In some loved fold of Aretine,
And nightly now beneath their shade
Are buggeries, rapes, and incests made.
Unto this all-sin-sheltering grove   25
Whores of the bulk and the alcove,
Great ladies, chambermaids, and drudges,
The ragpicker, and heiress trudges.
Carmen, divines, great lords, and tailors,
Prentices, poets, pimps, and jailers,   30
Footmen, fine fops do here arrive,
And here promiscuously they swive.

    Along these hallowed walks it was
That I beheld Corinna pass.
Whoever had been by to see   35
The proud disdain she cast on me
Through charming eyes, he would have swore
She dropped from heaven that very hour,
Forsaking the divine abode
In scorn of some despairing god.   40
But mark what creatures women are:
How infinitely vile, when fair!

    Three knights o' th' elbow and the slur
With wriggling tails made up to her.

    The first was of your Whitehall blades,   45
Near kin t' th' Mother of the Maids;

22. *Aretine:* Pietro Aretino (1492–1556), Italian author, who in 1523 wrote a series of obscene sonnets to accompany an equally obscene set of drawings by the painter Giulio Romano.
26. *bulk:* bench or stall projecting in front of a shop.
29. *Carmen:* carters, carriers.
43. *knights o' th' elbow:* cheating gamblers. *slur:* a method of cheating at dice by sliding a die out of the box so that it does not turn.
46. *Mother of the Maids:* Lady Bridget Sanderson (*c.* 1592–1682), Mother of the Maids of Honor to Queen Catherine from 1669 (possibly from 1662) until her death.

Graced by whose favor he was able
To bring a friend t' th' Waiters' table,
Where he had heard Sir Edward Sutton
Say how the King loved Banstead mutton;   50
Since when he'd ne'er be brought to eat
By 's good will any other meat.
In this, as well as all the rest,
He ventures to do like the best,
But wanting common sense, th' ingredient   55
In choosing well not least expedient,
Converts abortive imitation
To universal affectation.
Thus he not only eats and talks
But feels and smells, sits down and walks,   60
Nay looks, and lives, and loves by rote,
In an old tawdry birthday coat.

    The second was a Grays Inn wit,
A great inhabiter of the pit,
Where critic-like he sits and squints,   65
Steals pocket handkerchiefs, and hints,
From 's neighbor, and the comedy,
To court, and pay, his landlady.

    The third, a lady's eldest son
Within few years of twenty-one,   70
Who hopes from his propitious fate,

    48–49. *Waiters' table . . . Sutton:* Sir Edward Sutton (d. 1695),
baronet, was Gentleman of the Privy Chamber in Ordinary to the King
(Gentleman Usher and Daily Waiter).

    50. *Banstead:* Banstead, in Surrey, was a center of the sheep-raising
industry. Nearby was the Epsom racecourse, much frequented by Charles
II and his courtiers. *mutton:* perhaps, secondarily, "loose woman."

    62. *birthday coat:* gaudy apparel worn for royal birthday celebrations.

    63. *The second:* In some editions of Rochester's works dated 1731 and
later, he is identified as "Captain *Radcliffe*," i.e. Alexander Radcliffe, a
minor poet of the Restoration and member of Grays Inn. *Grays Inn wit:*
Traditionally, law students at the Inns of Court tried to achieve sophisti-
cation by becoming amateur literary critics.

Against he comes to his estate,
By these two worthies to be made
A most accomplished tearing blade.

    One, in a strain 'twixt tune and nonsense,   75
Cries, "Madam, I have loved you long since.
Permit me your fair hand to kiss";
When at her mouth her cunt cries, "Yes!"
In short, without much more ado,
Joyful and pleased, away she flew,   80
And with these three confounded asses
From park to hackney coach she passes.

    So a proud bitch does lead about
Of humble curs the amorous rout,
Who most obsequiously do hunt   85
The savory scent of salt-swoln cunt.

Some power more patient now relate
The sense of this surprising fate.
Gods! that a thing admired by me
Should fall to so much infamy.   90
Had she picked out, to rub her arse on,
Some stiff-pricked clown or well-hung parson,
Each job of whose spermatic sluice
Had filled her cunt with wholesome juice,
I the proceeding should have praised   95
In hope sh' had quenched a fire I raised.
Such natural freedoms are but just:
There's something generous in mere lust.
But to turn damned abandoned jade
When neither head nor tail persuade;   100
To be a whore in understanding,
A passive pot for fools to spend in!

---

92. *well-hung:* furnished with large pendent organs.
93. *job:* an abrupt thrust.

The devil played booty, sure, with thee
To bring a blot on infamy.
　　But why am I, of all mankind,   105
To so severe a fate designed?
Ungrateful! Why this treachery
To humble, fond, believing me,
Who gave you privilege above
The nice allowances of love?   110
Did ever I refuse to bear
The meanest part your lust could spare?
When your lewd cunt came spewing home
Drenched with the seed of half the town,
My dram of sperm was supped up after   115
For the digestive surfeit water.
Full gorgèd at another time
With a vast meal of nasty slime
Which your devouring cunt had drawn
From porters' backs and footmen's brawn,   120
I was content to serve you up
My ballock-full for your grace cup,
Nor ever thought it an abuse
While you had pleasure for excuse—
You that could make my heart away   125
For noise and color, and betray
The secrets of my tender hours
To such knight-errant paramours,
When, leaning on your faithless breast,
Wrapped in security and rest,   130

103. *played booty:* To "play booty" is to join with confederates in
order to victimize another player.
116. *surfeit water:* medicinal beverage to alleviate the aftereffects of
overindulgence in food or drink.
120. *backs:* To "back" is to "cover" or copulate with.
122. *grace cup:* a cup of liquor served after grace at the end of a meal.
125. *make . . . away:* transfer to another's possession.

Soft kindness all my powers did move,
And reason lay dissolved in love!
    May stinking vapors choke your womb
Such as the men you dote upon!
May your depravèd appetite,   135
That could in whiffling fools delight,
Beget such frenzies in your mind
You may go mad for the north wind,
And fixing all your hopes upon 't
To have him bluster in your cunt,   140
Turn up your longing arse t' th' air
And perish in a wild despair!
But cowards shall forget to rant,
Schoolboys to frig, old whores to paint;
The Jesuits' fraternity   145
Shall leave the use of buggery;
Crab-louse, inspired with grace divine,
From earthly cod to heaven shall climb;
Physicians shall believe in Jesus,
And disobedience cease to please us,   150
Ere I desist with all my power
To plague this woman and undo her.
But my revenge will best be timed
When she is married that is limed.
In that most lamentable state   155
I'll make her feel my scorn and hate:
Pelt her with scandals, truth or lies,
And her poor cur with jealousies,
Till I have torn him from her breech,
While she whines like a dog-drawn bitch;   160
Loathed and despised, kicked out o' th' Town
Into some dirty hole alone,

    160. *dog-drawn:* To "dog-draw" is to track venison which has been
illegally killed or wounded by the scent of a dog led with the hand.

To chew the cud of misery
And know she owes it all to me.
  And may no woman better thrive   165
  That dares prophane the cunt I swive!

On the Women about Town

[Shortly before 20 March 1672/3]   [*1704*]

Too long the wise Commons have been in debate
About money and conscience, those trifles of state,
Whilst dangerous grievances daily increase,
And the subject can't riot in safety and peace;
Unless, as against Irish cattle before,   5
You now make an act to forbid Irish whore.

The coots black and white, Clanbrassill and Fox,
Invade us with impudence, beauty, and pox.

1–2: referring to the session of Parliament from 4 February 1672/3 to 29 March 1673. Meeting after an interval of nearly two years, Parliament was exhorted by Charles II to grant the money he needed to carry on the war against the Dutch. Although the Money Bill was finally approved on 29 March, it was delayed while Commons first pressured the King into canceling his Declaration of Indulgence and then passed the Test Act, excluding from civil and military offices all persons who did not take communion in the Anglican Church.

5. *Irish cattle:* In January 1666/7, Parliament passed an act against importing cattle into England from Ireland, thereby depriving the Irish livestock industry of most of its market.

7. *coots:* simpletons. If the word is a proper noun, it may refer to two daughters or other female relatives of Charles Coote, second Earl of Mountrath. *black and white:* brunette and blonde. *Clanbrassill:* Alice, wife of Henry, second Earl of Clanbrassill. At this time she was being "managed" by the Irish interest as a possible mistress for Charles II (*Conway Letters*, ed. Marjorie Hope Nicolson, New Haven, Yale University Press, 1930, p. 339). *Fox:* Although the context implies that she is an Irishwoman, probably the reference is to Elizabeth, elder daughter of Sir Stephen Fox, Clerk of the Green Cloth to Charles II and a man of enormous self-made wealth. On 27 December 1673, in Westminster Abbey, Elizabeth married Charles, third Baron Cornwallis, a notorious gambler.

They carry a fate which no man can oppose:
The loss of his heart and the fall of his nose.   10
Should he dully resist, yet would each take upon her
To beseech him to do 't, and engage him in honor.

O ye merciful powers who of mortals take care,
Make the women more modest, more sound, or less fair!
Is it just that with death cruel love should conspire,   15
And our tarses be burnt by our hearts taking fire?
There's an end of communion if humble believers
Must be damned in the cup like unworthy receivers.

16. *tarses:* penises.

17–18: referring to the belief that one who took the Eucharist while
guilty of sin would be punished by God. For this doctrine the *locus
classicus* is St. Paul. Rochester's words may recall I Corinthians 11:27–29:
"Wherefore whosoever shall eat this bread, and drink this cup of the
Lord, unworthily, . . . eateth and drinketh damnation to himself . . ."
(King James version).

Song

[Probably between Oct. 1671 and April 1676]   [*c. Sept. 1680*]

Quoth the Duchess of Cleveland to counselor Knight,
"I'd fain have a prick, knew I how to come by 't.
I desire you'll be secret and give your advice:
Though cunt be not coy, reputation is nice."

"To some cellar in Sodom Your Grace must retire   5
Where porters with black-pots sit round a coal-fire;
There open your case, and Your Grace cannot fail
Of a dozen of pricks for a dozen of ale."

"Is 't so?" quoth the Duchess. "Aye, by God!" quoth the whore.
"Then give me the key that unlocks the back door,   10
For I'd rather be fucked by porters and carmen
Than thus be abused by Churchill and Jermyn."

1. *Cleveland:* Barbara Palmer, Duchess of Cleveland, who had been
Charles II's mistress *en titre* during the first decade after the Restoration.
Notorious for her nymphomaniac lust, she had a succession of lovers including the two mentioned in line 12. *Knight:* Mary Knight, a celebrated
singer and minor mistress of Charles II.

5. *Sodom:* a London locality known for its brothels and disreputable
inns (Montague Summers, ed., *Dryden: The Dramatic Works*, London,
Nonesuch Press, 1931–32, *1*, 430).

6. *black-pots:* beer-mugs.

7. *case:* clothing or disguise, especially the vizard-masks worn by ladies
of the Restoration Court when in quest of anonymous sexual activity. Cf.
Shakespeare, *1 Henry IV*, II.ii: "Case ye, case ye! on with your vizards!"

10. *back door:* probably the ill-famed "backstairs" of the Privy Closet,
to which only the King and his Keeper, William Chiffinch, were supposed
to have keys.

11. *carmen:* carters, carriers.

12. *Churchill:* John Churchill, the future Duke of Marlborough. He
was almost certainly the father of the daughter born to Cleveland on 16
July 1672. Once, it is said, being surprised by the King in the Duchess's
bedchamber, he tried to escape recognition by leaping out the window.
Jermyn: Henry Jermyn, Master of the Horse to the Duke of York, in
1685 created Baron Dover of Dover. In July 1667, his affair with Cleveland occasioned an angry quarrel between her and the King (Pepys, 30
July).

The Second Prologue at Court to "The Empress of Morocco,"
Spoken by the Lady Elizabeth Howard

[Probably spring 1673]   [*1673*]

Before its public production at the Duke's House on 3 July 1673, Elkanah
Settle's spectacular heroic drama *The Empress of Morocco* was performed
at Court before the King, the parts being taken (as Settle boasted in his
dedication) "by persons of such Birth & Honour, that they borrow'd
no greatness from the charracters they acted." This amateur performance,
whose exact date is uncertain, probably occurred during spring of 1673.
Two prologues were provided, the first contributed by the Earl of Mulgrave. Both were spoken by Lady Elizabeth (Betty) Howard, later Lady
Betty Felton, daughter of James, third Earl of Suffolk.

Wit has of late took up a trick t' appear
Unmannerly, or at the best severe,
And poets share the fate by which we fall
When kindly we attempt to please you all.
'Tis hard your scorn should against such prevail   5
Whose ends are to divert you, though they fail.
You men would think it an ill-natured jest
Should we laugh at you when you did your best.
Then rail not here, though you see reason for 't:
If wit can find itself no better sport,   10
Wit is a very foolish thing at Court.
Wit's business is to please, and not to fright:
'Tis no wit to be always in the right;
You'll find it none, who dare be so tonight.
Few so ill-bred will venture to a play   15
To spy out faults in what we women say.
For us, no matter *what* we speak, but *how:*
How kindly can we say, "I hate you now!"
And for the men, if you'll laugh at 'em, do:
They mind themselves so much, they'll ne'er mind you.   20

But why do I descend to lose a prayer
On those small saints in wit? The god sits *there*.
                    [*To the King*]
To you, great sir, my message hither tends
From youth and beauty, your allies and friends.
See my credentials written in my face: 25
They challenge your protection in this place,
And hither come with such a force of charms
As may give check ev'n to your prosperous arms.
Millions of cupids, hovering in the rear,
Like eagles following fatal troops appear,   30
All waiting for the slaughter which draws nigh
Of those bold gazers who this night must die;
Nor can you 'scape our soft captivity,
From which old age alone must set you free.
Then tremble at the fatal consequence,   35
Since 'tis well known, for your own part, great prince,
'Gainst us you still have made a weak defense.
Be generous and wise, and take our part;
Remember we have eyes, and you a heart.
Else you may find, too late, that we are things   40
Born to kill vassals and to conquer kings.
    But, oh! to what vain conquest I pretend
Whilst Love is our commander, and your friend.
Our victory your empire more assures,
For Love will ever make the triumph yours.   45

28. *your prosperous arms:* with at least a secondary reference to the war
against the Dutch.

Song

Love a woman? You're an ass!
　'Tis a most insipid passion
To choose out for your happiness
　The silliest part of God's creation.

Let the porter and the groom,   5
　Things designed for dirty slaves,
Drudge in fair Aurelia's womb
　To get supplies for age and graves.

Farewell, woman! I intend
　Henceforth every night to sit   10
With my lewd, well-natured friend,
　Drinking to engender wit.

Then give me health, wealth, mirth, and wine,
　And, if busy love entrenches,
There's a sweet, soft page of mine   15
　Does the trick worth forty wenches.

Upon His Drinking a Bowl

[Probably autumn 1673]   [*c. Sept. 1680*]

Curt A. Zimansky observes of this song that "while indirectly from Anacreon, *Odes*, XVII and XVIII, the lines are a translation of Ronsard's poem beginning, 'Vulcan! En faveur de moy . . .'" (*The Critical Works of Thomas Rymer*, New Haven, Yale University Press, 1956, p. 226).

> Vulcan, contrive me such a cup
>   As Nestor used of old.
> Show all thy skill to trim it up;
>   Damask it round with gold.
>
> Make it so large that, filled with sack   5
>   Up to the swelling brim,
> Vast toasts on the delicious lake
>   Like ships at sea may swim.
>
> Engrave no battle on his cheek:
>   With war I've nought to do;   10
> I'm none of those that took Maastricht,
>   Nor Yarmouth leaguer knew.

1–2: As described in the *Iliad*, Nestor's "beautifully wrought cup . . . was set with golden nails, the eared handles upon it were four, and on either side there were fashioned two doves of gold, feeding, and there were double bases beneath it. Another man with great effort could lift it full from the table, but Nestor, aged as he was, lifted it without strain" (trans. Richmond Lattimore, XI, 631–36).

11–12. *took Maastricht . . . Yarmouth leaguer*: two events near the end of the Third Dutch War (1672–1674). In late June 1673, the Dutch fortress of Maastricht surrendered to a French army following a siege; accompanying the French, a small group of English volunteers, led by the Duke of Monmouth, displayed notable courage. "Yarmouth leaguer" (i.e. a military camp) refers to the English expeditionary force which assembled on Blackheath in May 1673 for a projected invasion of Holland, and which was transported in July to Yarmouth. After plans for the invasion had to be abandoned, the force was disbanded on 1 September.

Let it no name of planets tell,
   Fixed stars, or constellations;
For I am no Sir Sidrophel,   15
   Nor none of his relations.

But carve thereon a spreading vine,
   Then add two lovely boys;
Their limbs in amorous folds entwine,
   The type of future joys.   20

Cupid and Bacchus my saints are:
   May drink and love still reign.
With wine I wash away my cares,
   And then to cunt again.

15. *Sir Sidrophel:* the silly astrologer in Butler's *Hudibras*, Part II, Canto 3.

Grecian Kindness

[Uncertain]   [*1691*]

The utmost grace the Greeks could show,
   When to the Trojans they grew kind,
Was with their arms to let 'em go
   And leave their lingering wives behind.
They beat the men, and burnt the town: 5
Then all the baggage was their own.

There the kind deity of wine
   Kissed the soft wanton god of love;
This clapped his wings, that pressed his vine,
   And their best powers united move;   10
While each brave Greek embraced his punk,
Lulled her asleep, and then grew drunk.

Signior Dildo

[*c.* Dec. 1673]   [*1703*]

The occasion of this satirical lyric is the marriage of James, Duke of York,
to Mary of Modena. After a proxy wedding in her native Italy, the new
Duchess and her entourage crossed the Channel on 21 November 1673
to Dover, where the Duke met her and repeated the marriage ceremony.
The ducal party reached London on 26 November.

You ladies all of merry England
Who have been to kiss the Duchess's hand,
Pray, did you lately observe in the show
A noble Italian called Signior Dildo?

This signior was one of Her Highness's train,   5
And helped to conduct her over the main;
But now she cries out, "To the Duke I will go!
I have no more need for Signior Dildo."

At the Sign of the Cross in St. James's Street,
When next you go thither to make yourselves sweet   10
By buying of powder, gloves, essence, or so,
You may chance t' get a sight of Signior Dildo.

You'll take him at first for no person of note
Because he appears in a plain leather coat,
But when you his virtuous abilities know,   15
You'll fall down and worship Signior Dildo.

My Lady Southesk, heavens prosper her for 't!
First clothed him in satin, then brought him to Court;

Heading. *Dildo:* a substitute for the penis.
   9. *St. James's Street:* a fashionable residential and shopping area ad-
jacent to St. James's Palace, where the Duke of York took up residence
with his bride.
   17–20. *Southesk:* Anne, daughter of the Duke of Hamilton and wife

But his head in the circle he scarcely durst show,
So modest a youth was Signior Dildo.   20

The good Lady Suffolk, thinking no harm,
Had got this poor stranger hid under her arm.
Lady Betty by chance came the secret to know,
And from her own mother stole Signior Dildo.

The Countess of Falmouth, of whom people tell   25
Her footmen wear shirts of a guinea an ell,
Might save the expense if she did but know
How lusty a swinger is Signior Dildo.

By the help of this gallant the countess of Ralph
Against the fierce Harrys preserved herself safe.   30

----

of Robert, third Earl of Southesk. One of the most promiscuous noble-women of the Restoration Court, Lady Southesk had already had an affair with the Earl of Chesterfield as early as 1657–58. It was widely rumored that her husband, suspecting a liaison between her and the Duke of York, took revenge by deliberately contracting a case of venereal disease and passing it on to his wife, who then unknowingly infected the Duke.

21–24. *Suffolk:* Barbara, wife of James, third Earl of Suffolk. She was Groom of the Stole to Queen Catherine. *Lady Betty:* the Countess of Suffolk's daughter, Lady Elizabeth Howard. Earlier in the year she had spoken Rochester's prologue for the Court production of Settle's *The Empress of Morocco* (p. 49). In July 1675, much against her parents' wishes, she married Thomas Felton, a Groom of the Bedchamber to the King (*Savile Correspondence*, ed. William Durrant Cooper, Camden Society, 1858, p. 39). Lady Betty Felton and her mother died of fits of apoplexy within days of each other in December 1681 (Narcissus Luttrell, *A Brief Historical Relation of State Affairs*, Oxford, 1857, *1*, 150–51).

25–28. *Countess of Falmouth:* Mary, widow of Charles Berkeley, first Earl of Falmouth, who had been slain in the sea fight against the Dutch on 3 June 1665. By June 1674, when she was secretly married to Charles Sackville, later Earl of Dorset, she had acquired an unsavory reputation. Both she and the Countess-Dowager of Northumberland, the subject of the next stanza, were dazzlingly beautiful women who had been mentioned as possible wives for the Duke of York.

29. *countess of Ralph:* Elizabeth, widow of Joceline Percy, Earl of

She stifled him almost beneath her pillow,
So closely sh' embraced Signior Dildo.

Our dainty fine duchesses have got a trick
To dote on a fool for the sake of his prick:
The fops were undone, did Their Graces but know   35
The discretion and vigor of Signior Dildo.

That pattern of virtue, Her Grace of Cleveland,
Has swallowed more pricks than the ocean has sand;
But by rubbing and scrubbing so large it does grow,
It is fit for just nothing but Signior Dildo.   40

The Duchess of Modena, though she looks high,
With such a gallant is contented to lie,

Northumberland, who had died in 1670. On 24 August 1673 she married
Ralph Montagu, later Earl and Duke of Montagu.

30–32: refers possibly to Henry Harris, the actor, but probably to a
scrape which Rochester's close friend Henry Savile got into with the Countess of Northumberland in September 1671 during a house party at Al-
thorp, the seat of the Sunderland family. Evidently attracted by the
widowed Countess's wealth as much as by her beauty, Savile one night
managed to gain admittance to her bedchamber—having, according to one
account, previously removed the bolt from her door. The lady awoke to
find Savile kneeling at her bedside pouring forth ardent protestations of
love, whereupon in terror she pulled her bellrope, rousing the household.
Hotly pursued by male relatives of the family demanding revenge, Savile
was forced to flee to London and even, rumor had it, to France (*The
Rochester-Savile Letters*, ed. John Harold Wilson, Columbus, Ohio State
University Press, 1941, pp. 7–8).

Rochester's lines imply that he knew a slightly different version of the
story. His plural form "Harrys" may signify that more than one man
named Henry had designs on the Countess, or it may facetiously suggest
how "fierce" Savile appeared to her in her bedchamber.

37–40. *Cleveland:* Barbara Palmer, Duchess of Cleveland, for whom see
the song beginning "Quoth the Duchess of Cleveland to counselor Knight"
(p. 48).

41–44. *Duchess of Modena:* Duchess Laura, Regent of Modena, mother
of the new Duchess of York. She had accompanied her daughter to England.

And for fear the English her secrets should know,
For a Gentleman Usher took Signior Dildo.

The countess o' th' Cockpit (Who knows not her name?   45
She's famous in story for a killing dame),
When all her old lovers forsake her, I trow
She'll then be contented with Signior Dildo.

Red Howard, red Sheldon, and Temple so tall
Complain of his absence so long from Whitehall;   50
Signior Bernard has promised a journey to go
And bring back his countryman Signior Dildo.

Doll Howard no longer with 's Highness must range,
And therefore is proffered this civil exchange:
Her teeth being rotten, she smells best below,   55
And needs must be fitted for Signior Dildo.

St. Albans, with wrinkles and smiles in his face,
Whose kindness to strangers becomes his high place,

45–48. *countess o' th' Cockpit:* identified as Nell Gwyn by John
Harold Wilson (*The Court Wits of the Restoration*, Princeton University
Press, 1948, p. 121). The Cockpit was an area of Whitehall Palace includ-
ing lodgings and a theater where plays were performed during the 1660s.

49: three Maids of Honor to the Queen. *Red . . . red:* The Duke of
York disliked women with red hair. *Howard:* Ann, the younger daughter
of Mrs. Elizabeth Howard, who was the widow of William Howard, son
of the first Earl of Berkshire. In 1677 Ann became the wife of Sir
Gabriel Sylvius. *Sheldon:* Frances Sheldon, whose sister Mary was the wife
of Sir Samuel Tuke. *Temple:* Philippa Temple.

51–52. *Signior Bernard:* probably Don Bernardo de Salinas, a Spanish
diplomat entrusted with the task of persuading England to make a separate
peace with the Dutch. He visited England briefly during the summer of
1673.

53–56. *Doll Howard:* Dorothy, elder sister of Ann Howard (see note
to l. 49, above) and likewise a Maid of Honor to the Queen. Previously
a Maid of Honor to Anne, Duchess of York, until the Duchess's death in
1671, Dorothy became in 1675 the wife of Colonel James Graham, who
held a succession of offices under the Duke of York.

In his coach and six horses is gone to Borgo
To take the fresh air with Signior Dildo.   60

Were this signior but known to the citizen fops,
He'd keep their fine wives from the foremen of shops;
But the rascals deserve their horns should still grow
For burning the Pope and his nephew Dildo.

Tom Killigrew's wife, north Holland's fine flower,   65
At the sight of this signior did fart and belch sour,
And her Dutch breeding farther to show,
Says, "Welcome to England, Mynheer Van Dildo!"

He civilly came to the Cockpit one night,
And proffered his service to fair Madam Knight.   70
Quoth she, "I intrigue with Captain Cazzo;
Your nose in mine arse, good Signior Dildo!"

57–60. *St. Albans:* Henry Jermyn, Earl of St. Albans (d. 1684), Lord Chamberlain and formerly Ambassador to France. Now about 70 years old, he had a half-century's experience as courtier, diplomat, and *bon vivant*. *Borgo:* a town in Italy near Modena.

61–63: The Puritan merchants of London were traditionally ridiculed as cuckolds.

64. *burning the Pope:* The burning of effigies of the Pope was a standard feature of anti-Catholic celebrations among the London citizens. Several Pope-burnings had been part of the Guy Fawkes festivities on 5 November 1673, only a few days before the Catholic Mary of Modena arrived in England. *and his nephew Dildo:* A letter to Rochester from Henry Savile, dated 26 January 1670/1, relates how a box of imported dildoes was confiscated and burned by the customs officers (*The Rochester-Savile Letters*, ed. Wilson, p. 31). A similar incident is the subject of the mock-heroic poem "Dildoides," attributed to Samuel Butler.

65–68. *Tom Killigrew's wife:* Thomas Killigrew, playwright and manager of the King's House, married Charlotte, daughter of John de Hesse, at the Hague on 28 January 1654/5. She was appointed Keeper of the Sweet Coffer for the Queen in May 1662, and First Lady of the Queen's Privy Chamber on 4 June 1662 (*DNB*).

70. *Madam Knight:* Mary Knight, a singer and minor mistress of Charles II. See the song beginning "Quoth the Duchess of Cleveland to counselor Knight" (p. 48).

71. *Cazzo:* in vulgar Italian, "penis."

This signior is sound, safe, ready, and dumb
As ever was candle, carrot, or thumb;
Then away with these nasty devices, and show 75
How you rate the just merits of Signior Dildo.

Count Cazzo, who carries his nose very high,
In passion he swore his rival should die;
Then shut up himself to let the world know
Flesh and blood could not bear it from Signior Dildo. 80

A rabble of pricks who were welcome before,
Now finding the Porter denied 'em the door,
Maliciously waited his coming below
And inhumanly fell on Signior Dildo.

Nigh wearied out, the poor stranger did fly, 85
And along the Pall Mall they followed full cry;
The women, concerned, from every window
Cried, "Oh! for heavens' sake, save Signior Dildo!"

The good Lady Sandys burst into a laughter
To see how the ballocks came wobbling after, 90
And had not their weight retarded the foe,
Indeed 't had gone hard with Signior Dildo.

89. *Lady Sandys:* probably Lady Lucy Sandys, a friend of Nell Gwyn
and frequent visitor at Court.

A Satyr on Charles II

[Shortly before 20 Jan. 1673/4]   [*1697*]

According to a letter dated 20 January 1673/4, whose testimony is cor-
roborated by the headings in several early texts of the following poem,
"my Lord Rochester fled from Court some time since for delivering (by
mistake) into the King's hands a terrible lampoon of his own making
against the King, instead of another the King asked him for" (K. H. D.
Haley, *William of Orange and the English Opposition 1672–4*, Oxford,
Clarendon Press, 1953, pp. 60–61, 172). The opening lines of the poem,
contrasting the peaceful interests of Charles II with the belligerent ambi-
tions of Louis XIV, apparently refer to the approaching end of the Third
Dutch War. By the Treaty of Westminster, signed on 9 February 1673/4,
Charles withdrew from this conflict which the English and French had
waged jointly against the Dutch since early 1672, leaving Louis to pursue
his military conquests on the continent for another four years.

> I' th' isle of Britain, long since famous grown
> For breeding the best cunts in Christendom,
> There reigns, and oh! long may he reign and thrive,
> The easiest King and best-bred man alive.
> Him no ambition moves to get renown   5
> Like the French fool, that wanders up and down
> Starving his people, hazarding his crown.
> Peace is his aim, his gentleness is such,
> And love he loves, for he loves fucking much.
>
>   Nor are his high desires above his strength: 10
> His scepter and his prick are of a length;
> And she may sway the one who plays with th' other,
> And make him little wiser than his brother.
> Poor prince! thy prick, like thy buffoons at Court,
> Will govern thee because it makes thee sport.   15

9. *love he loves:* The meaning may be suggested by Shakespeare, *Antony
and Cleopatra*, I.i.44: "Now for the love of Love and her soft hours."
13. *his brother:* James, Duke of York.

'Tis sure the sauciest prick that e'er did swive,
The proudest, peremptoriest prick alive.
Though safety, law, religion, life lay on 't,
'Twould break through all to make its way to cunt.
Restless he rolls about from whore to whore, 20
A merry monarch, scandalous and poor.

 To Carwell, the most dear of all his dears,
The best relief of his declining years,
Oft he bewails his fortune, and her fate:
To love so well, and be beloved so late. 25
For though in her he settles well his tarse,
Yet his dull, graceless ballocks hang an arse.
This you'd believe, had I but time to tell ye
The pains it costs to poor, laborious Nelly,
Whilst she employs hands, fingers, mouth, and thighs, 30
Ere she can raise the member she enjoys.

 All monarchs I hate, and the thrones they sit on,
From the hector of France to the cully of Britain.

22. *Carwell:* Louise de Keroualle, Duchess of Portsmouth, who had been the King's mistress since October 1671. She was at the height of her ascendancy in Charles's affections.

23. *his declining years:* Charles at this time was 43 years old, Rochester 26.

29–31. *Nelly:* Rochester's advice to Nell Gwyn on how to please the King was to "Cherish his Love where-ever it inclines, and be assur'd you can't commit greater Folly than pretending to be jealous; but, on the contrary, with Hand, Body, Head, Heart and all the Faculties you have, contribute to his Pleasure all you can, and comply with his Desires throughout" (*The Rochester-Savile Letters,* ed. John Harold Wilson, Columbus, Ohio State University Press, 1941, p. 57).

Tragic Maturity

1674-1675

Timon

[April, May, or early June 1674]   [c. Sept. 1680]

This poem is an adaptation or "imitation," in the seventeenth-century sense, of Boileau's third satire. Its principal speaker, who resembles Rochester in his character, activities, and social position, may be named "Timon" in allusion to Timon of Athens, the misanthrope, or to Timon of Phlius, a Greek Skeptic philosopher and satirical poet.

A. What, Timon! does old age begin t' approach,
That thus thou droop'st under a night's debauch?
Hast thou lost deep to needy rogues on tick,
Who ne'er could pay, and must be paid next week?
   Timon. Neither, alas; but a dull dining sot   5
Seized me i' th' Mall, who just my name had got.
He runs upon me, cries, "Dear rogue, I'm thine!
With me some wits of thy acquaintance dine."
I tell him I'm engaged, but as a whore
With modesty enslaves her spark the more,   10
The longer I denied, the more he pressed.
At last I e'en consent to be his guest.

   He takes me in his coach, and as we go,
Pulls out a libel of a sheet or two,
Insipid as the praise of pious queens   15
Or Shadwell's unassisted former scenes,
Which he admired, and praised at every line;

3. *on tick:* on credit.

6. *Mall:* probably not Pall Mall, but the Mall in St. James's Park.

15. *the praise of pious queens:* No work with this exact title is known. The phrase may refer generically to panegyrics on Queen Catherine— who usually bore the King's flagrant sexual infidelity with virtuous patience.

16: Although he repeatedly denied the charge, Thomas Shadwell was accused of having received assistance in writing his comedy *Epsom-Wells,* produced on 2 December 1672. Cf. Dryden, *Mac Flecknoe,* lines 163–64:

> But let no alien Sedley interpose
> To lard with wit thy hungry Epsom prose.

At last it was so sharp it must be mine.
I vowed I was no more a wit than he:
Unpracticed and unblessed in poetry.   20
A song to Phyllis I perhaps might make,
But never rhymed but for my pintle's sake.
I envied no man's fortune nor his fame,
Nor ever thought of a revenge so tame.
He knew my style, he swore, and 'twas in vain   25
Thus to deny the issue of my brain.
Choked with his flattery, I no answer make,
But silent, leave him to his dear mistake,
Which he by this had spread o'er the whole town,
And me with an officious lie undone.   30
Of a well-meaning fool I'm most afraid,
Who sillily repeats what was well said.
    But this was not the worst. When he came home,
He asked, "Are Sedley, Buckhurst, Savile come?"
No, but there were above Halfwit and Huff,   35
Kickum and Dingboy. "Oh, 'tis well enough!
They're all brave fellows," cries mine host. "Let's dine!
I long to have my belly full of wine.
They'll write and fight, I dare assure you:
They're men *tam Marte quam Mercurio*."   40
I saw my error, but 'twas now too late:
No means nor hopes appear of a retreat.
Well, we salute, and each man takes his seat.
"Boy!" says my sot. "Is my wife ready yet?"
A wife, good gods! a fop, and bullies too!   45
For one poor meal what must I undergo?

22. *pintle:* penis.
34. *Sedley:* Sir Charles Sedley. *Buckhurst:* Charles Sackville, Lord
Buckhurst, later Earl of Dorset. *Savile:* Henry Savile, like Sedley and
Buckhurst a fashionable Court wit and friend of Rochester.
40. *tam Marte quam Mercurio:* roughly translated in the preceding
line.

In comes my lady straight. She had been fair,
Fit to give love and to prevent despair,
But age, beauty's incurable disease,
Had left her more desire than power to please.   50
As cocks will strike although their spurs be gone,
She with her old blear eyes to smite begun.
Though nothing else, she in despite of time
Preserved the affectation of her prime:
However you begun, she brought in love,   55
And hardly from that subject would remove.
We chanced to speak of the French king's success;
My lady wondered much how heaven could bless
A man that loved two women at one time,
But more how he to them excused his crime.   60
She asked Huff if love's flame he never felt;
He answered bluntly, "Do you think I'm gelt?"
She at his plainness smiled, then turned to me:
"Love in young minds precedes ev'n poetry:
You to that passion can no stranger be,   65
But wits are given to inconstancy."
      She had run on, I think, till now, but meat
Came up, and suddenly she took her seat.
I thought the dinner would make some amends,
When my good host cries out, "Y' are all my friends!   70
Our own plain fare, and the best terse the Bull
Affords, I'll give you and your bellies full.

---

57. *French king's success:* i.e. in the war on the continent from which
Charles II, Louis XIV's former ally, had just withdrawn by concluding the
separate Treaty of Westminster with the Dutch on 9 February 1673/4.
See lines 151–75, below.

59: Louis XIV's two acknowledged mistresses were Louise de La Vallière
and Madame de Montespan.

71. *terse:* claret. *the Bull:* perhaps the Bull Head tavern in Westminster,
where Pepys enjoyed dining.

As for French kickshaws, sillery and champagne,
Ragouts and fricassees, in troth w' have none."
Here's a good dinner towards, thought I, when straight   75
Up comes a piece of beef, full horseman's weight,
Hard as the arse of Mosely, under which
The coachman sweats as ridden by a witch;
A dish of carrots, each of them as long
As tool that to fair countess did belong,   80
Which her small pillow could not so well hide
But visitors his flaming head espied.
Pig, goose, and capon followed in the rear,
With all that country bumpkins call good cheer,
Served up with sauces, all of eighty-eight,   85
When our tough youth wrestled and threw the weight.
And now the bottle briskly flies about,
Instead of ice, wrapped up in a wet clout.
A brimmer follows the third bit we eat:
Small beer becomes our drink, and wine our meat.   90
The table was so large that in less space
A man might, safe, six old Italians place;
Each man had as much room as Porter, Blount,
Or Harris had in Cullen's bushel cunt.

73. *sillery:* a high-class wine produced near the town of Sillery in Champagne.

77. *Mosely:* "Mother" Mosely, whose name is sometimes linked with Shaftesbury's, operated a house of prostitution in London.

80–82: Evidently this is the same anecdote, involving Henry Savile's invasion of the Countess of Northumberland's bedchamber, which is glanced at in "Signior Dildo," lines 29–32 (pp. 55–56).

85. *eighty-eight:* i.e. 1588, a jingoistic reference to the English defeat of the Spanish armada.

92. *six old Italians:* perhaps an allusion to the banquet of Trimalchio in the *Satyricon* of Petronius.

93–94. *Porter:* probably George Porter, Rochester's raffish crony, who is mentioned more fully in "Dialogue" ("When to the King I bid good morrow"), lines 11–12 (p. 129). *Blount:* unidentified. *Harris:* probably the actor Henry Harris. *Cullen:* Elizabeth, wife of Brien, second Viscount Cullen. She was noteworthy for her beauty and her extravagance.

And now the wine began to work, mine host 95
Had been a colonel; we must hear him boast,
Not of towns won, but an estate he lost
For the King's service, which indeed he spent
Whoring and drinking, but with good intent.
He talked much of a plot and money lent 100
In Cromwell's time. My lady, she
Complained our love was coarse, our poetry
Unfit for modest ears; small whores and players
Were of our harebrained youth the only cares,
Who were too wild for any virtuous league, 105
Too rotten to consummate the intrigue.
Falkland she praised, and Suckling's easy pen,
And seemed to taste their former parts again.
Mine host drinks to the best in Christendom,
And decently my lady quits the room. 110

Left to ourselves, of several things we prate:
Some regulate the stage, and some the state.
Halfwit cries up my lord of Orrery:
Ah, how well Mustapha and Zanger die!
His sense so little forced that by one line 115
You may the other easily divine:
"And which is worse, if any worse can be,
He never said one word of it to me."

107. *Falkland:* During the 1630s, Lucius Carey, second Viscount of Falkland (1610–1643), sponsored a high-minded intellectual coterie at his house at Great Tew near Oxford. *Suckling's easy pen:* Falkland and Sir John Suckling were among the most-admired Cavalier poets.

113. *Orrery:* Roger Boyle, first Earl of Orrery, one of the earliest writers of heroic plays after the Restoration.

114. *Mustapha and Zanger:* sons of the Turkish emperor Solyman in Orrery's *The Tragedy of Mustapha,* produced on 3 April 1665. Both die very honorably in Act V.

117–18: quoted from Orrery's *The Black Prince,* produced on 19 October 1667. The couplet is lines 269–70 of Act II:

> And which is worse, if worse than this can be,
> She for it ne're excus'd her self to me.

There's fine poetry! You'd swear 'twere prose,
So little on the sense the rhymes impose.   120
"Damn me!" says Dingboy. "In my mind, God's wounds,
Etherege writes airy songs and soft lampoons
The best of any man; as for your nouns,
Grammar, and rules of art, he knows 'em not,
Yet writ two talking plays without one plot."   125
Huff was for Settle, and *Morocco* praised;
Said rumbling words, like drums, his courage raised:
"Whose broad-built bulks the boist'rous billows bear;
Safi and Salé, Mogador, Oran,
The famed Arzile, Alcazar, Tetuan."   130
Was ever braver language writ by man?
Kickum for Crowne declared; said in romance
He had outdone the very wits of France:
Witness *Pandion* and his *Charles the Eighth*,
Where a young monarch, careless of his fate,   135
Though foreign troops and rebels shock his state,
Complains another sight afflicts him more,
Viz. "the queen's galleys rowing from the shore,

125. *two talking plays:* The first two of George Etherege's three comedies were *The Comical Revenge; or, Love in a Tub*, produced in March
1664, and *She wou'd if she cou'd*, produced on 6 February 1667/8. His
last and best-known play, *The Man of Mode*, was still two years in the
future.
126: Elkanah Settle's popular heroic drama *The Empress of Morocco*
was first produced privately at Court, probably in spring of 1673, and
publicly on 3 July 1673. Rochester contributed the second prologue for
the Court production; see p. 49.
128–30: quoted from Act II, lines 10, 61–62:

> Their lofty Bulks the foaming Billows bear. . . .
> *Saphee* and *Salli, Mugadore, Oran,*
> The fam'd *Arzille, Alcazer, Tituan,* . . .

134. *Pandion:* John Crowne's romance *Pandion and Amphigenia*, published in 1665. *Charles the Eighth:* Crowne's heroic drama *The History of
Charles the Eighth of France*, produced in late November 1671. It was
published in 1672 and dedicated to Rochester.

Fitting their oars and tackling to be gone,
Whilst sporting waves smiled on the rising sun."   140
Waves smiling on the sun? I'm sure *that's* new,
And 'twas well thought on, give the Devil his due.
Mine host, who had said nothing in an hour,
Rose up and praised the *Indian Emperor:*
"As if our old world modestly withdrew,   145
And here in private had brought forth a new."
There are two lines! Who but *he* durst presume
To make th' old world a new withdrawing room,
Where of another world she's brought to bed?
What a brave midwife is a Laureate's head!   150

   "But pox of all these scribblers! What d' ye think:
Will Souches this year any champagne drink?
Will Turenne fight him? Without doubt," says Huff,
When they two meet, their meeting will be rough."
"Damn me!" says Dingboy. "The French cowards are.   155
They pay, but th' English, Scots, and Swiss make war.
In gaudy troops at a review they shine,
But dare not with the Germans battle join.
What now appears like courage is not so:
'Tis a short pride which from success does grow.   160
On their first blow they'll shrink into those fears

138–40: In Crowne's play, these lines are spoken by Ferdinand, Prince
of Naples, at II.i.85–87.
145–46: The couplet occurs at I.i.3–4 of Dryden's *The Indian Em-
perour*, produced *c.* April 1665.
152–54: This passage refers to the military situation on the Rhine
during spring of 1674. Ludwig de Souches, the general of the Imperial
forces opposing the French, took command in March, news of his appointment reaching England at the end of that month. In April and May it
appeared that he might join battle with the famous Marshal Turenne, Louis
XIV's general on the Rhine. By early June, however, it was known in
England that Souches was moving his army to Flanders, where there was
little chance that he and Turenne would clash. In October he was dismissed from his command in disgrace.

They showed at Cressy, Agincourt, Poitiers.
Their loss was infamous; honor so stained
Is by a nation not to be regained."
"What they were then, I know not; now th' are brave.   165
He that denies it—lies and is a slave,"
Says Huff and frowned. Says Dingboy, "That do I!"
And at that word at t' other's head let fly
A greasy plate, when suddenly they all
Together by the ears in parties fall: 170
Halfwit with Dingboy joins, Kickum with Huff.
Their swords were safe, and so we let them cuff
Till they, mine host, and I had all enough.
Their rage once over, they begin to treat,
And six fresh bottles must the peace complete.   175
    I ran downstairs, with a vow nevermore
To drink beer-glass and hear the hectors roar.

177. *beer-glass:* a glass holding half a pint.

Tunbridge Wells

[Spring 1674]   [*1697*]

At five this morn, when Phoebus raised his head
From Thetis' lap, I raised myself from bed,
And mounting steed, I trotted to the waters,
The rendezvous of fools, buffoons, and praters,
Cuckolds, whores, citizens, their wives and daughters.   5
  My squeamish stomach I with wine had bribed
To undertake the dose that was prescribed;
But turning head, a sudden cursèd view
That innocent provision overthrew,
And without drinking, made me purge and spew.   10
From coach and six a thing unwieldy rolled,
Whose lumber, cart more decently would hold.
As wise as calf it looked, as big as bully,
But handled, proves a mere Sir Nicholas Cully;
A bawling fop, a natural Nokes, and yet   15
He dares to censure as if he had wit.
To make him more ridiculous, in spite
Nature contrived the fool should be a knight.

Heading: Tunbridge Wells developed into a fashionable watering place
during the seventeenth century.
  1. *At five this morn:* Because the healing power of the waters was believed to evaporate with the heat of the sun, they were supposed to be
drunk as soon as possible after sunrise.
  2. *Thetis:* a Nereid, mother of Achilles. Evidently Rochester alludes
to her as goddess of the sea, out of which the sun (Phoebus) would rise
at dawn.
  3: Before the late seventeenth century, the nearest good lodgings were
at Rusthall and Southborough, a mile or two distant from the wells.
  14. *Sir Nicholas Cully:* a dupe in Etherege's first comedy, *The Comical
Revenge; or, Love in a Tub*, produced in March 1664.
  15. *Nokes:* James Nokes, a comic actor of the Duke's Company who was
celebrated for his portrayal of solemn fools. He created the role of Sir
Nicholas Cully.

Though he alone were dismal sight enough,
His train contributed to set him off,   20
All of his shape, all of the selfsame stuff.
No spleen or malice need on them be thrown:
Nature has done the business of lampoon,
And in their looks their characters has shown.

    Endeavoring this irksome sight to balk,   25
And a more irksome noise, their silly talk,
I silently slunk down t' th' Lower Walk.
But often when one would Charybdis shun,
Down upon Scylla 'tis one's fate to run,
For here it was my cursèd luck to find   30
As great a fop, though of another kind,
A tall stiff fool that walked in Spanish guise:
The buckram puppet never stirred its eyes,
But grave as owl it looked, as woodcock wise.
He scorns the empty talking of this mad age,   35
And speaks all proverbs, sentences, and adage;
Can with as much solemnity buy eggs
As a cabal can talk of their intrigues;
Master o' th' Ceremonies, yet can dispense
With the formality of talking sense.   40

27. *Lower Walk:* "Leading from the wells in a south-westerly direction
to nowhere in particular was a level grass walk, 175 yards long, bordered
on both sides by elm trees. This path went by the name of the Upper
Walk, to distinguish it from another known as the Lower Walk running
parallel to it on a lower level a few yards to the east. Between the two,
under the shade of the trees, sat the market women with their baskets of
farm produce. . . . Along the western side of the avenue were ranged
a number of wooden booths, in many of which knick-knacks of every
imaginable variety were sold or raffled for; others served as coffee houses
or taverns" (Margaret Barton, *Tunbridge Wells*, London, Faber and Faber,
1937, p. 117).
    31–32. *As great a fop . . . tall stiff fool:* identified in several early
manuscripts of the poem as Sir Francis Dorrell, knight.
    39. *Master o' th' Ceremonies:* an office later assumed at both Bath and
Tunbridge by Beau Nash.

From hence unto the upper end I ran,
Where a new scene of foppery began.
A tribe of curates, priests, canonical elves,
Fit company for none besides themselves,
Were got together. Each his distemper told,   45
Scurvy, stone, strangury; some were so bold
To charge the spleen to be their misery,
And on that wise disease brought infamy.
But none had modesty enough t' complain
Their want of learning, honesty, and brain,   50
The general diseases of that train.
These call themselves ambassadors of heaven,
And saucily pretend commissions given;
But should an Indian king, whose small command
Seldom extends beyond ten miles of land,   55
Send forth such wretched tools in an ambassage,
He'd find but small effects of such a message.
Listening, I found the cob of all this rabble
Pert Bays, with his importance comfortable.
He, being raised to an archdeaconry   60
By trampling on religion, liberty,

41. *unto the upper end:* to the wells, apparently.

46. *stone, strangury:* See "The Imperfect Enjoyment," line 68 and note (p. 39).

58–69: This passage is a tissue of allusions to the Marvell-Parker controversy. Between 1670 and 1672, Samuel Parker, Archdeacon of Canterbury and later Bishop of Oxford, published several books advocating an extreme Erastian control of religious affairs by the state. About autumn of 1672, the poet Andrew Marvell came to the defense of religious liberty in Part I of *The Rehearsal Transpros'd*, where he whimsically satirized Parker as "Mr. Bayes"—referring, of course, to Buckingham's famous burlesque. When Parker and others angrily replied, Marvell again ridiculed the Archdeacon and his theories in Part II of *The Rehearsal Transpros'd*, published early in 1674.

58. *cob:* leading man.

59. *importance comfortable:* In one of his earlier publications, Parker obliquely mentioned his approaching marriage by remarking that he had

Was grown too great, and looked too fat and jolly,
To be disturbed with care and melancholy,
Though Marvell has enough exposed his folly.
He drank to carry off some old remains   65
His lazy dull distemper left in 's veins.
Let him drink on, but 'tis not a whole flood
Can give sufficient sweetness to his blood
To make his nature or his manners good.

    Next after these, a fulsome Irish crew   70
Of silly Macs were offered to my view.
The things did talk, but th' hearing what they said
I did myself the kindness to evade.
Nature has placed these wretches beneath scorn:
They can't be called so vile as they are born.   75

    Amidst the crowd next I myself conveyed,
For now were come, whitewash and paint being laid,
Mother and daughter, mistress and the maid,
And squire with wig and pantaloon displayed.
But ne'er could conventicle, play, or fair   80
For a true medley, with this herd compare.
Here lords, knights, squires, ladies and countesses,
Chandlers, mum-bacon women, sempstresses

---

been "much concerned . . . in matters of a closer and more comfortable importance to himself and his own affairs." In Part I of *The Rehearsal Transpros'd*, after pretending to be mystified, Marvell facetiously concludes that "comfortable importance" must refer to Parker's mistress. The phrase became a commonplace in Restoration satire.

64: This is Rochester's sole reference to Marvell, who said that "the earle of Rochester was the only man in England that had the true veine of satyre" (John Aubrey, *Brief Lives*, ed. Andrew Clark, Oxford, Clarendon Press, 1898, *2*, 54).

66. *lazy dull distemper:* In his rejoinder to Marvell, Parker explained that he planned to reply sooner but was "prevented by a dull and lazy distemper." In Part II of *The Rehearsal Transpros'd*, Marvell plays with the idea that the phrase may refer to a case of venereal disease.

83. *mum-bacon women:* This phrase seems to be otherwise unrecorded. It may be Rochester's coinage intended to suggest hawkers of heterogeneous items of food, from mum (a kind of beer imported from Brunswick) to bacon.

Were mixed together, nor did they agree
More in their humors than their quality.   85
    Here waiting for gallant, young damsel stood,
Leaning on cane, and muffled up in hood.
The would-be wit, whose business was to woo,
With hat removed and solemn scrape of shoe
Advanceth bowing, then genteelly shrugs,   90
And ruffled foretop into order tugs,
And thus accosts her: "Madam, methinks the weather
Is grown much more serene since you came hither.
You influence the heavens; but should the sun
Withdraw himself to see his rays outdone   95
By your bright eyes, they would supply the morn,
And make a day before the day be born."
With mouth screwed up, conceited winking eyes,
And breasts thrust forward, "Lord, sir!" she replies.
"It is your goodness, and not my deserts,   100
Which makes you show this learning, wit, and parts."
He, puzzled, bites his nail, both to display
The sparkling ring, and think what next to say,
And thus breaks forth afresh: "Madam, egad!
Your luck at cards last night was very bad: 105
At cribbage fifty-nine, and the next show
To make the game, and yet to want those two.
God damn me, madam, I'm the son of a whore
If in my life I saw the like before!"
To peddler's stall he drags her, and her breast   110
With hearts and such-like foolish toys he dressed;

100: Cf. Swift's *Polite Conversation:* "*Miss.* My Lord, that was more their Goodness, than my Desert" (*The Prose Works of Jonathan Swift,* ed. Herbert Davis, Oxford, Basil Blackwell, 1939–, *4,* 155).

106–07: Having moved her scoring pegs through 59 of the 60 holes in the two parallel rows on the cribbage board, she was then unable to advance to the sixtieth hole and the final "game hole."

111. *hearts:* evidently jewelry or ornaments in the shape of a heart.

And then, more smartly to expound the riddle
Of all his prattle, gives her a Scotch fiddle.
    Tired with this dismal stuff, away I ran
Where were two wives, with girl just fit for man—   115
Short-breathed, with pallid lips and visage wan.
Some curtsies past, and the old compliment
Of being glad to see each other, spent,
With hand in hand they lovingly did walk,
And one began thus to renew the talk: 120
"I pray, good madam, if it may be thought
No rudeness, what cause was it hither brought
Your ladyship?" She soon replying, smiled,
"We have a good estate, but have no child,
And I'm informed these wells will make a barren   125
Woman as fruitful as a cony warren."
The first returned, "For this cause I am come,
For I can have no quietness at home.
My husband grumbles though we have got one,
This poor young girl, and mutters for a son.   130
And this is grieved with headache, pangs, and throes;
Is full sixteen, and never yet had *those*."
She soon replied, "Get her a husband, madam:
I married at that age, and ne'er had had 'em;
Was just like her. Steel waters let alone: 135
A back of steel will bring 'em better down."

113. *Scotch fiddle:* slang term for the itch.
125–26: "And here it would be an unpardonable neglect not to mention one virtue in this water, . . . I mean its prolific qualities, of which
every season furnishes renewed and often surprizing proofs. It has indeed
an amazing efficacy in strengthening, and cleansing the generative organs,
and removing the complaint of unfruitfulness . . . besides this, it is in
the highest degree serviceable in all other female complaints . . ." (Thomas
Benge Burr, *The History of Tunbridge-Wells,* London, 1766, pp. 84–
86).
135. *Steel waters:* the chalybeate springs at Tunbridge Wells.
136. *back:* To "back" is to "cover" or copulate with.

And ten to one but they themselves will try
The same means to increase their family.
Poor foolish fribble, who by subtlety
Of midwife, truest friend to lechery,   140
Persuaded art to be at pains and charge
To give thy wife occasion to enlarge
Thy silly head! For here walk Cuff and Kick,
With brawny back and legs and potent prick,
Who more substantially will cure thy wife,   145
And on her half-dead womb bestow new life.
From these the waters got the reputation
Of good assistants unto generation.

   Some warlike men were now got into th' throng,
With hair tied back, singing a bawdy song.   150
Not much afraid, I got a nearer view,
And 'twas my chance to know the dreadful crew.
They were cadets, that seldom can appear:
Damned to the stint of thirty pounds a year.
With hawk on fist, or greyhound led in hand,   155
The dogs and footboys sometimes they command.
But now, having trimmed a cast-off spavined horse,
With three hard-pinched-for guineas in their purse,
Two rusty pistols, scarf about the arse,
Coat lined with red, they here presume to swell: 160
This goes for captain, that for colonel.
So the Bear Garden ape, on his steed mounted,

143. *Cuff and Kick:* the names of "two cheating, sharking, cowardly
Bullies" in Shadwell's comedy *Epsom-Wells*, produced on 2 December
1672.

153. *cadets:* younger sons, who by the law of primogeniture could inherit little or nothing.

162–65. *Bear Garden:* situated in London at the south end of the street
now called Bear Gardens. At a performance on 16 June 1670, Evelyn
relates, "One of the Bulls tossd a Dog full into a Ladys lap, as she sate in
one of the boxes at a Considerable height from the *Arena:* There were
two poore dogs killed; & so all ended with the Ape on horse-back, & I
most heartily weary, of the rude & dirty passetime."

No longer is a jackanapes accounted,
But is, by virtue of his trumpery, then
Called by the name of "the young gentleman."   165
   Bless me! thought I, what thing is man, that thus
In all his shapes, he is ridiculous?
Ourselves with noise of reason we do please
In vain: humanity's our worst disease.
Thrice happy beasts are, who, because they be   170
Of reason void, are so of foppery.
Faith, I was so ashamed that with remorse
I used the insolence to mount my horse;
For he, doing only things fit for his nature,
Did seem to me by much the wiser creature.   175

Upon His Leaving His Mistress

[Uncertain]   [*c. Sept. 1680*]

'Tis not that I am weary grown
Of being yours, and yours alone;
But with what face can I incline
To damn you to be only mine?
 You, whom some kinder power did fashion, 5
 By merit and by inclination,
 The joy at least of one whole nation.

Let meaner spirits of your sex
With humbler aims their thoughts perplex,
And boast if by their arts they can 10
Contrive to make *one* happy man;
 Whilst, moved by an impartial sense,
 Favors like nature you dispense
 With universal influence.

See, the kind seed-receiving earth 15
To every grain affords a birth.
On her no showers unwelcome fall;
Her willing womb retains 'em all.
 And shall my Celia be confined?
 No! Live up to thy mighty mind, 20
 And be the mistress of mankind.

Against Constancy

[Uncertain]   [*Spring 1676*]

Tell me no more of constancy,
    The frivolous pretense
Of cold age, narrow jealousy,
    Disease, and want of sense.

Let duller fools, on whom kind chance   5
    Some easy heart has thrown,
Despairing higher to advance,
    Be kind to one alone.

Old men and weak, whose idle flame
    Their own defects discovers,   10
Since changing can but spread their shame,
    Ought to be constant lovers.

But we, whose hearts do justly swell
    With no vainglorious pride,
Who know how we in love excel,   15
    Long to be often tried.

Then bring my bath, and strew my bed,
    As each kind night returns;
I'll change a mistress till I'm dead—
    And fate change me to worms.   20

Song
(early version)

[Before spring 1676]   [c. Sept. 1680]

How happy, Chloris, were they free,
    Might our enjoyments prove,
But you with formal jealousy
    Are still tormenting love.

Let us, since wit instructs us how,   5
    Raise pleasure to the top:
If rival bottle you'll allow,
    I'll suffer rival fop.

There's not a brisk, insipid spark
    That flutters in the town,   10
But with your wanton eyes you mark
    The coxcomb for your own.

You never think it worth your care
    How empty nor how dull
The heads of your admirers are,   15
    So that their cods be full.

All this you freely may confess,
    Yet we'll not disagree,
For did you love your pleasure less,
    You were not fit for me.   20

19–20: possibly alluding to Lovelace's famous song:

I could not love thee, dear, so much,
Loved I not honor more.

While I, my passion to pursue,
    Am whole nights taking in
The lusty juice of grapes, take you
    The lusty juice of men.

To a Lady in a Letter
(final version)

[Uncertain]   [*Spring 1676*]

Such perfect bliss, fair Chloris, we
    In our enjoyments prove,
'Tis pity restless jealousy
    Should mingle with our love.

Let us, since wit has taught us how,   5
    Raise pleasure to the top:
You rival bottle must allow,
    I'll suffer rival fop.

Think not in this that I design
    A treason 'gainst love's charms,   10
When, following the god of wine,
    I leave my Chloris' arms,

Since you have that, for all your haste
    (At which I'll ne'er repine),
Will take its liquor off as fast   15
    As I can take off mine.

There's not a brisk, insipid spark
    That flutters in the town,

But with your wanton eyes you mark
  Him out to be your own;   20

Nor do you think it worth your care
  How empty and how dull
The heads of your admirers are,
  So that their cods be full.

All this you freely may confess,   25
  Yet we ne'er disagree,
For did you love your pleasure less,
  You were no match for me.

Whilst I, my pleasure to pursue,
  Whole nights am taking in   30
The lusty juice of grapes, take you
  The juice of lusty men.

Song

[Uncertain]   [1935]

It is tempting to imagine that this lyric, which survives in Rochester's
own handwriting, was addressed to some actress who was his mistress, perhaps Elizabeth Barry.

Leave this gaudy gilded stage,
  From custom more than use frequented,
Where fools of either sex and age
  Crowd to see themselves presented.

To love's theater, the bed,   5
  Youth and beauty fly together,

And act so well it may be said
   The laurel there was due to either.

'Twixt strifes of love and war, the difference lies in this:
When neither overcomes, love's triumph greater is.   10

The Fall

[Uncertain]   [*c. Sept. 1680*]

How blest was the created state
   Of man and woman, ere they fell,
Compared to our unhappy fate:
   We need not fear another hell.

Naked beneath cool shades they lay;   5
   Enjoyment waited on desire;
Each member did their wills obey,
   Nor could a wish set pleasure higher.

But we, poor slaves to hope and fear,
   Are never of our joys secure;   10
They lessen still as they draw near,
   And none but dull delights endure.

Then, Chloris, while I duly pay
   The nobler tribute of my heart,
Be not you so severe to say   15
   You love me for the frailer part.

The Mistress

[Uncertain]   [*1691*]

An age in her embraces passed
    Would seem a winter's day,
Where life and light with envious haste
    Are torn and snatched away.

But oh, how slowly minutes roll   5
    When absent from her eyes,
That feed my love, which is my soul:
    It languishes and dies.

For then no more a soul, but shade,
    It mournfully does move   10
And haunts my breast, by absence made
    The living tomb of love.

You wiser men, despise me not
    Whose lovesick fancy raves
On shades of souls, and heaven knows what: 15
    Short ages live in graves.

Whene'er those wounding eyes, so full
    Of sweetness, you did see,
Had you not been profoundly dull,
    You had gone mad like me.   20

Nor censure us, you who perceive
    My best beloved and me
Sigh and lament, complain and grieve:
    You think we disagree.

Alas! 'tis sacred jealousy,   25
    Love raised to an extreme:
The only proof 'twixt her and me
    We love, and do not dream.

Fantastic fancies fondly move
    And in frail joys believe,   30
Taking false pleasure for true love;
    But pain can ne'er deceive.

Kind jealous doubts, tormenting fears,
    And anxious cares, when past,
Prove our hearts' treasure fixed and dear,   35
    And make us blest at last.

A Song

[Uncertain]   [*1691*]

Absent from thee, I languish still;
    Then ask me not, when I return?
The straying fool 'twill plainly kill
    To wish all day, all night to mourn.

Dear! from thine arms then let me fly,   5
    That my fantastic mind may prove
The torments it deserves to try
    That tears my fixed heart from my love.

When, wearied with a world of woe,
    To thy safe bosom I retire   10
Where love and peace and truth does flow,
    May I contented there expire,

Lest, once more wandering from that heaven,
    I fall on some base heart unblest,
Faithless to thee, false, unforgiven,   15
    And lose my everlasting rest.

A Song of a Young Lady to Her Ancient Lover

[Uncertain]   [*1691*]

    Ancient person, for whom I
    All the flattering youth defy,
    Long be it ere thou grow old,
    Aching, shaking, crazy, cold;
        But still continue as thou art,   5
        Ancient person of my heart.

    On thy withered lips and dry,
    Which like barren furrows lie,
    Brooding kisses I will pour
    Shall thy youthful [heat] restore   10
    (Such kind showers in autumn fall,
    And a second spring recall);
        Nor from thee will ever part,
        Ancient person of my heart.

    Thy nobler part, which but to name   15
    In our sex would be counted shame,

By age's frozen grasp possessed,
From [his] ice shall be released,
And soothed by my reviving hand,
In former warmth and vigor stand.   20
All a lover's wish can reach
For thy joy my love shall teach,
And for thy pleasure shall improve
All that art can add to love.
    Yet still I love thee without art,   25
    Ancient person of my heart.

Love and Life

[Uncertain]   [*1677*]

All my past life is mine no more;
    The flying hours are gone,
Like transitory dreams given o'er
Whose images are kept in store
    By memory alone.   5

Whatever is to come is not:
    How can it then be mine?
The present moment's all my lot,
And that, as fast as it is got,
    Phyllis, is wholly thine.   10

Then talk not of inconstancy,
    False hearts, and broken vows;
If I, by miracle, can be
This livelong minute true to thee,
    'Tis all that heaven allows.   15

Epilogue to "Love in the Dark,"
As It Was Spoke by Mr. Haines

[Shortly before 10 May 1675]   [*1675*]

This epilogue was composed for the comedy *Love in the Dark*, produced
at the King's House on 10 May 1675 and written by Sir Francis Fane,
Junior, who afterward dedicated the play to his friend Rochester in
adulatory terms. Rochester's epilogue concerns itself with the "war" between the two London playhouses, then at its height. The rival Duke's
House kept the upper hand by mounting more lavish spectacles than the
impecunious King's House could afford—employing dances, songs, instrumental music, elaborate scenery, and stage machinery. Rochester con-
centrates his ridicule upon two such spectacular works by Thomas Shadwell, the operatic version of *The Tempest*, acted 30 April 1674, and
especially the dramatic opera *Psyche*, first performed on 27 February
1674/5. Both were also burlesqued in farces by Thomas Duffet, a playwright retained by the King's House for this special purpose, and both
receive derogatory notice in Dryden's *Mac Flecknoe*.

> As charms are nonsense, nonsense seems a charm
> Which hearers of all judgment does disarm,
> For songs and scenes a double audience bring,
> And doggerel takes which smiths in satin sing.
> Now to machines and a dull masque you run,   5
> We find that wit's the monster you would shun,

Heading. *Mr. Haines:* Joseph Haines, among the most popular comic
actors of the Restoration. In *Love in the Dark* he played Visconti, one
of three "Gentlemen of *Milan*."

    1. *charms:* in the strict sense, spells couched in formulas of words or
verse. Both *The Tempest* and *Psyche* abound in magical occurrences.

    4. *smiths in satin:* the Cyclops who, as Act III of *Psyche* opens, are seen
in the palace of Cupid "at work at a Forge, forging great Vases of Silver."
They dance, "hammering the Vases upon Anvils," and then present a
song (*The Complete Works of Thomas Shadwell*, ed. Montague Summers,
London, Fortune Press, 1927, 2, 306).

    6. *the monster you would shun:* In Act II, an oracle seemingly con-
signs Psyche to death from a serpent which has terrorized the city by
devouring the inhabitants. In Act III, having killed the serpent, Prince
Nicander and Polynices enter in triumph with its severed head (Summers,
2, 297, 312–13).

And by my troth, 'tis most discreetly done:
For since with vice and folly wit is fed,
Through mercy 'tis most of you are not dead.
Players turn puppets now at your desire: 10
In their mouths nonsense, in their tails a wire,
They fly through clouds of clouts and showers of fire.
A kind of losing loadum is their game,
Where the worst writer has the greatest fame.

    To get vile plays like theirs shall be our care,   15
But of such awkward actors we despair.
False taught at first,
Like bowls ill-biased, still the more they run,
They're further off than when they first begun.
In comedy their unweighed action mark: 20
There's one is such a dear familiar spark
He yawns as if he were but half awake,
And fribbling for free speaking does mistake.
False accent and neglectful action too
They have both so nigh good, yet neither true,   25
That both together, like an ape's mock face,
By near resembling man do man disgrace.

    Through-paced ill actors may perhaps be cured;
Half-players, like half-wits, can't be endured.
Yet these are they who durst expose the age   30
Of the great wonder of our English stage,
Whom nature seemed to form for your delight,
And bid him speak as she bid Shakespeare write.

11–12: In Act III of *Psyche*, "Furies descend and strike the Altar, and break it, and every one flies away with a fire-brand in's hand." The "clouds of clouts" are prominent in the scene of heaven, with the palace of Jupiter, with which the play concludes (Summers, 2, 314, 336).

13. *losing loadum:* form of an old English card game in which the loser wins.

31. *great wonder of our English stage:* Michael Mohun, a chief actor of the King's House. In *Love in the Dark* he played the libertine wit Trivultio, one of the three "Gentlemen of *Milan.*"

Those blades indeed are cripples in their art—
Mimic his foot, but not his speaking part.   35
Let them the Traitor or Volpone try;
Could they
Rage like Cethegus, or like Cassius die,
They ne'er had sent to Paris for such fancies
As monsters' heads and merry-andrews' dances.   40

    Withered perhaps, not perished we appear,
But they were blighted, and ne'er came to bear.
Th' old poets dressed your mistress wit before;
These draw you on with an old painted whore,
And sell, like bawds, patched plays for maids twice o'er.   45
Yet they may scorn our House and actors too,
Since they have swelled so high to hector you.
They cry, "Pox o' these Covent Garden men!
Damn 'em, not one of them but keeps out ten.
Were they once gone, we for those thundering blades   50
Should have an audience of substantial trades,

36–38: Four of Mohun's best-known parts were the title roles in James
Shirley's tragedy *The Traitor* and Jonson's *Volpone*, Cethegus in Jonson's
Catiline His Conspiracy, and Cassius in Shakespeare's *Julius Caesar* (*The
London Stage 1660–1800. Part I: 1660–1700*, ed. William Van Lennep,
Carbondale, Southern Illinois University Press, 1965, pp. 21, 86, 149,
191).

40. *monsters' heads:* perhaps alluding to masks worn by the devils and
Furies in the scene of hell which begins Act V of *Psyche* (Summers, *2*,
327). There may also be a reference to Caliban in *The Tempest. merry-
andrews' dances:* The dances for *Psyche* were created by the famous French
master St. André. Cf. Dryden, *Mac Flecknoe*, lines 53–54:

> St. André's feet ne'er kept more equal time,
> Not ev'n the feet of thy own *Psyche's* rhyme.

44–45: Shadwell's *The Tempest* is an operatic adaptation of the Dryden-
Davenant version of the work, which in turn derives from Shakespeare's
play. Shadwell's *Psyche* is based upon the highly successful French tragedy-
ballet *Psyché*, later transformed into an opera by Fontenelle.

48. *Covent Garden:* in the fashionable West End, as opposed to the
mercantile district of London.

Who love our muzzled boys and tearing fellows,
My lord, great Neptune, and *Great nephew, Aeolus.*
Oh, how the merry citizen's in love
With   55
Psyche, the goddess of each field and grove!
He cries, 'I' faith, methinks 'tis well enough,'
But you roar out and cry, ' 'Tis all damned stuff!' "
    So to their House the graver fops repair,
While men of wit find one another here.   60

52–53. *muzzled boys . . . Aeolus:* The masque at the end of Shadwell's *The Tempest* includes the lines "My Lord: Great *Neptune,* for my
sake . . ." and "Great Nephew *Aeolus* make no noise, / Muzzle your
roaring Boys" (Summers, *2,* 265, 266).
56: In Act I of *Psyche,* Pan's recitative begins, "Great *Psyche,* Goddess
of each Field and Grove" (Summers, *2,* 285).

A Satyr against Reason and Mankind

[Before 23 March 1675/6]   [*June 1679*]

Based to some extent on Boileau's eighth satire, this famous poem is also
indebted to Hobbes, Montaigne, and the tradition of *le libertinage*
generally.

    Were I (who to my cost already am
One of those strange, prodigious creatures, man)
A spirit free to choose, for my own share,
What case of flesh and blood I pleased to wear,
I'd be a dog, a monkey, or a bear,   5
Or anything but that vain animal
Who is so proud of being rational.
    The senses are too gross, and he'll contrive
A sixth, to contradict the other five,
And before certain instinct, will prefer   10
Reason, which fifty times for one does err;

Reason, an *ignis fatuus* in the mind,
Which, leaving light of nature, sense, behind,
Pathless and dangerous wandering ways it takes
Through error's fenny bogs and thorny brakes;   15
Whilst the misguided follower climbs with pain
Mountains of whimseys, heaped in his own brain;
Stumbling from thought to thought, falls headlong down
Into doubt's boundless sea, where, like to drown,
Books bear him up awhile, and make him try   20
To swim with bladders of philosophy;
In hopes still to o'ertake th' escaping light,
The vapor dances in his dazzling sight
Till, spent, it leaves him to eternal night.
Then old age and experience, hand in hand,   25
Lead him to death, and make him understand,
After a search so painful and so long,
That all his life he has been in the wrong.
Huddled in dirt the reasoning engine lies,
Who was so proud, so witty, and so wise.   30
    Pride drew him in, as cheats their bubbles catch,
And made him venture to be made a wretch.
His wisdom did his happiness destroy,
Aiming to know that world he should enjoy.
And wit was his vain, frivolous pretense   35
Of pleasing others at his own expense,
For wits are treated just like common whores:
First they're enjoyed, and then kicked out of doors.
The pleasure past, a threatening doubt remains
That frights th' enjoyer with succeeding pains.   40
Women and men of wit are dangerous tools,
And ever fatal to admiring fools:

23. *dazzling:* dazzled.
31. *bubbles:* dupes.

Pleasure allures, and when the fops escape,
'Tis not that they're belov'd, but fortunate,
And therefore what they fear at heart, they hate.   45

   But now, methinks, some formal band and beard
Takes me to task. Come on, sir; I'm prepared.

   "Then, by your favor, anything that's writ
Against this gibing, jingling knack called wit
Likes me abundantly; but you take care   50
Upon this point, not to be too severe.
Perhaps my muse were fitter for this part,
For I profess I can be very smart
On wit, which I abhor with all my heart.
I long to lash it in some sharp essay,   55
But your grand indiscretion bids me stay
And turns my tide of ink another way.

   "What rage ferments in your degenerate mind
To make you rail at reason and mankind?
Blest, glorious man! to whom alone kind heaven   60
An everlasting soul has freely given,
Whom his great Maker took such care to make
That from himself he did the image take
And this fair frame in shining reason dressed
To dignify his nature above beast;   65
Reason, by whose aspiring influence
We take a flight beyond material sense,
Dive into mysteries, then soaring pierce
The flaming limits of the universe,
Search heaven and hell, find out what's acted there,   70
And give the world true grounds of hope and fear."

   Hold, mighty man, I cry, all this we know

46. *formal band and beard:* Many Restoration clergymen wore Geneva
bands.

69: an echo of Lucretius, *De Rerum Natura*, I.73, "flammantia moenia
mundi."

From the pathetic pen of Ingelo,
From Patrick's *Pilgrim*, Sibbes' soliloquies,
And 'tis this very reason I despise: 75
This supernatural gift, that makes a mite
Think he's the image of the infinite,
Comparing his short life, void of all rest,
To the eternal and the ever blest;
This busy, puzzling stirrer-up of doubt   80
That frames deep mysteries, then finds 'em out,
Filling with frantic crowds of thinking fools
Those reverend bedlams, colleges and schools;
Borne on whose wings, each heavy sot can pierce
The limits of the boundless universe;   85
So charming ointments make an old witch fly
And bear a crippled carcass through the sky.
'Tis this exalted power, whose business lies
In nonsense and impossibilities,
This made a whimsical philosopher   90
Before the spacious world, his tub prefer,
And we have modern cloistered coxcombs who
Retire to think, 'cause they have nought to do.
    But thoughts are given for action's government;
Where action ceases, thought's impertinent.   95

73. *Ingelo:* the Reverend Nathaniel Ingelo (? 1621–1683). His long
religious-allegorical romance, *Bentivolio and Urania* (1660), was reprinted
several times during the Restoration period.
  74. *Patrick's "Pilgrim": The Parable of the Pilgrim* (1664), by Simon
Patrick (1626–1707), later Bishop of Ely. It resembles Bunyan's *Pilgrim's
Progress. Sibbes' soliloquies:* Richard Sibbes (1577–1635), a Puritan
divine, wrote numerous religious works of an inspirational nature.
  85: The idea of an infinite universe was still a novelty in the seventeenth
century; compare line 69, above.
  86–87: According to popular superstition, witches anointed themselves
in order to fly through the air.
  90–91: Diogenes the Cynic, well known for dwelling in a tub, taught
that virtue consists in the avoidance of all physical pleasure and that pain
and hunger are positively helpful in the pursuit of goodness.

Our sphere of action is life's happiness,
And he who thinks beyond, thinks like an ass.
Thus, whilst against false reasoning I inveigh,
I own right reason, which I would obey:
That reason which distinguishes by sense   100
And gives us rules of good and ill from thence,
That bounds desires with a reforming will
To keep 'em more in vigor, not to kill.
Your reason hinders, mine helps to enjoy,
Renewing appetites yours would destroy.   105
My reason is my friend, yours is a cheat;
Hunger calls out, my reason bids me eat;
Perversely, yours your appetite does mock:
This asks for food, that answers, "What's o'clock?"
This plain distinction, sir, your doubt secures: 110
'Tis not true reason I despise, but yours.
      Thus I think reason righted, but for man,
I'll ne'er recant; defend him if you can.
For all his pride and his philosophy,
'Tis evident beasts are, in their degree,   115
As wise at least, and better far than he.
Those creatures are the wisest who attain,
By surest means, the ends at which they aim.
If therefore Jowler finds and kills his hares
Better than Meres supplies committee chairs,   120
Though one's a statesman, th' other but a hound,
Jowler, in justice, would be wiser found.
      You see how far man's wisdom here extends;

120. *Meres:* Sir Thomas Meres (1635–1715), a prominent member of the Country (later Whig) party, M. P. for Lincoln, and a Commissioner of the Admiralty from 1679 to 1684. *supplies committee chairs:* On several occasions when the House of Commons resolved into a committee of the whole house, Meres occupied the chair.

Look next if human nature makes amends:
Whose principles most generous are, and just, 125
And to whose morals you would sooner trust.
Be judge yourself, I'll bring it to the test:
Which is the basest creature, man or beast?
Birds feed on birds, beasts on each other prey,
But savage man alone does man betray. 130
Pressed by necessity, they kill for food;
Man undoes man to do himself no good.
With teeth and claws by nature armed, they hunt
Nature's allowance, to supply their want.
But man, with smiles, embraces, friendship, praise, 135
Inhumanly his fellow's life betrays;
With voluntary pains works his distress,
Not through necessity, but wantonness.

For hunger or for love they fight and tear,
Whilst wretched man is still in arms for fear. 140
For fear he arms, and is of arms afraid,
By fear to fear successively betrayed;
Base fear, the source whence his best passions came:
His boasted honor, and his dear-bought fame;
That lust of power, to which he's such a slave, 145
And for the which alone he dares be brave;
To which his various projects are designed;
Which makes him generous, affable, and kind;
For which he takes such pains to be thought wise,
And screws his actions in a forced disguise, 150
Leading a tedious life in misery
Under laborious, mean hypocrisy.
Look to the bottom of his vast design,
Wherein man's wisdom, power, and glory join:
The good he acts, the ill he does endure, 155
'Tis all from fear, to make himself secure.

Merely for safety, after fame we thirst,
For all men would be cowards if they durst.

    And honesty's against all common sense:
Men must be knaves, 'tis in their own defence.   160
Mankind's dishonest; if you think it fair
Amongst known cheats to play upon the square,
You'll be undone.
Nor can weak truth your reputation save:
The knaves will all agree to call you knave.   165
Wronged shall he live, insulted o'er, oppressed,
Who dares be less a villain than the rest.

    Thus, sir, you see what human nature craves:
Most men are cowards, all men should be knaves.
The difference lies, as far as I can see,   170
Not in the thing itself, but the degree,
And all the subject matter of debate
Is only: Who's a knave of the first rate?

    All this with indignation have I hurled
At the pretending part of the proud world,   175
Who, swollen with selfish vanity, devise
False freedoms, holy cheats, and formal lies
Over their fellow slaves to tyrannize.
    But if in Court so just a man there be
(In Court a just man, yet unknown to me)   180
Who does his needful flattery direct,
Not to oppress and ruin, but protect
(Since flattery, which way soever laid,
Is still a tax on that unhappy trade);
If so upright a statesman you can find,   185
Whose passions bend to his unbiased mind,
Who does his arts and policies apply
To raise his country, not his family,

Nor, whilst his pride owned avarice withstands,
Receives close bribes through friends' corrupted hands— 190
   Is there a churchman who on God relies;
Whose life, his faith and doctrine justifies?
Not one blown up with vain prelatic pride,
Who, for reproof of sins, does man deride;
Whose envious heart makes preaching a pretense, 195
With his obstreperous, saucy eloquence,
To chide at kings, and rail at men of sense;
None of that sensual tribe whose talents lie
In avarice, pride, sloth, and gluttony;
Who hunt good livings, but abhor good lives; 200
Whose lust exalted to that height arrives
They act adultery with their own wives,
And ere a score of years completed be,
Can from the lofty pulpit proudly see
Half a large parish their own progeny; 205
Nor doting bishop who would be adored
For domineering at the council board,
A greater fop in business at fourscore,
Fonder of serious toys, affected more,
Than the gay, glittering fool at twenty proves 210
With all his noise, his tawdry clothes, and loves;
   But a meek, humble man of honest sense,
Who, preaching peace, does practice continence;
Whose pious life's a proof he does believe
Mysterious truths, which no man can conceive. 215
If upon earth there dwell such God-like men,
I'll here recant my paradox to them,
Adore those shrines of virtue, homage pay,
And, with the rabble world, their laws obey.
   If such there be, yet grant me this at least: 220
Man differs more from man, than man from beast.

Fragment

[Uncertain]   [*1935, 1953*]

What vain, unnecessary things are men!
How well we do without 'em! Tell me, then,
Whence comes that mean submissiveness we find
This ill-bred age has wrought on womankind?
Fall'n from the rights their sex and beauties gave   5
To make men wish, despair, and humbly crave,
Now 'twill suffice if they vouchsafe to *have*.

    T' th' Pall Mall, playhouse, and the drawing room,
Their women-fairs, these women-coursers come
To chaffer, choose, and ride their bargains home.   10
At the appearance of an unknown face,
Up steps the arrogant, pretending ass,
Pulling by th' elbow his companion Huff,
Cries, "Look! de God, that wench is well enough:
Fair and well-shaped, good lips and teeth, 'twill do;   15
She shall be tawdry for a month or two
At my expense, be rude and take upon her,
Show her contempt of quality and honor,
And, with the general fate of errant woman,
Be very proud awhile, then very common."   20

    Ere bear this scorn, I'd be shut up at home,
Content with humoring myself alone;
Force back the humble love of former days
In pensive madrigals and ends of plays,
When, if my lady frowned, th' unhappy knight   25

Was fain to fast and lie alone that night.
But whilst th' insulting wife the breeches wore,
The husband took her clothes to g[i]ve his ——,
Who now maintains it with a gentler art:
Thus tyrannies to commonwealths convert.   30

    Then, after all, you find, whate'er we say,
Things must go on in their lewd natural way.
Besides, the beastly men, we daily see,
Can please themselves alone as well as we.
Therefore, kind ladies of the town, to you   35
For our stol'n ravished men we hereb[y] sue.
By this time you have found out, we suppos[e],
That they're as arrant tinsel as their cloth[es]:
Poor broken properties, that cannot serve
To treat such persons so as they deserv[e].   40
Mistake us not, we do not here pretend
That, like the young sparks, you can condescend
To love a beastly playhouse creature. Foh!
We dare not think so meanly of you. No,
'Tis not the player pleases, but the part: 45
She may like Rollo who despises Hart.

    To theaters, as temples, you are brought,
Where Love is worshipped, and his precepts taught.
You must go home and practice, for 'tis here
Just as in other preaching places, where   50
Great eloquence is shown 'gainst sin a[n]d papists
By men who live idolaters and atheist[s].
These two were dainty trades indeed, could each
Live up to half the miracles they teach;
Both are a . . .   55

46. *Rollo:* Beaumont and Fletcher's melodrama *The Bloody Brother*, usually known during the Restoration period as *Rollo Duke of Normandy* or simply *Rollo*. *Hart:* Charles Hart, one of the principal actors of the King's Company, who excelled in kingly and heroic roles such as Rollo.

A Letter from Artemisia in the Town to Chloe in the Country

[?1675]   [1679]

Chloe,
              In verse by your command I write.
Shortly you'll bid me ride astride, and fight:
These talents better with our sex agree
Than lofty flights of dangerous poetry.
Amongst the men, I mean the men of wit   5
(At least they passed for such before they writ),
How many bold adventurers for the bays,
Proudly designing large returns of praise,
Who durst that stormy, pathless world explore,
Were soon dashed back, and wrecked on the dull shore,   10
Broke of that little stock they had before!
How would a woman's tottering bark be tossed
Where stoutest ships, the men of wit, are lost?
When I reflect on this, I straight grow wise,
And my own self thus gravely I advise: 15
     Dear Artemisia, poetry's a snare;
Bedlam has many mansions; have a care.
Your muse diverts you, makes the reader sad:
You fancy you're inspired; he thinks you mad.
Consider, too, 'twill be discreetly done   20
To make yourself the fiddle of the town,
To find th' ill-humored pleasure at their need,
Cursed if you fail, and scorned though you succeed!
Thus, like an arrant woman as I am,

21. *fiddle:* mirth-maker, jester.

No sooner well convinced writing's a shame,   25
That whore is scarce a more reproachful name
Than poetess—
Like men that marry, or like maids that woo,
'Cause 'tis the very worst thing they can do,
Pleased with the contradiction and the sin,   30
Methinks I stand on thorns till I begin.

    Y' expect at least to hear what loves have passed
In this lewd town, since you and I met last;
What change has happened of intrigues, and whether
The old ones last, and who and who's together.   35
But how, my dearest Chloe, shall I set
My pen to write what I would fain forget?
Or name that lost thing, love, without a tear,
Since so debauched by ill-bred customs here?
Love, the most generous passion of the mind,   40
The softest refuge innocence can find,
The safe director of unguided youth,
Fraught with kind wishes, and secured by truth;
That cordial drop heaven in our cup has thrown
To make the nauseous draught of life go down;   45
On which one only blessing, God might raise
In lands of atheists, subsidies of praise,
For none did e'er so dull and stupid prove
But felt a god, and blessed his power in love—
This only joy for which poor we were made   50
Is grown, like play, to be an arrant trade.
The rooks creep in, and it has got of late
As many little cheats and tricks as that.

    But what yet more a woman's heart would vex,
'Tis chiefly carried on by our own sex;   55
Our silly sex! who, born like monarchs free,

52. *rooks:* swindlers, sharpers, especially in gaming.

Turn gypsies for a meaner liberty,
. And hate restraint, though but from infamy.
They call whatever is not common, nice,
And deaf to nature's rule, or love's advice,   60
Forsake the pleasure to pursue the vice.
To an exact perfection they have wrought
The action, love; the passion is forgot.
'Tis below wit, they tell you, to admire,
And ev'n without approving, they desire.   65
Their private wish obeys the public voice;
'Twixt good and bad, whimsey decides, not choice.
Fashions grow up for taste; at forms they strike;
They know what they would have, not what they like.
Bovey's a beauty, if some few agree   70
To call him so; the rest to that degree
Affected are, that with their ears they see.

     Where I was visiting the other night
Comes a fine lady, with her humble knight,
Who had prevailed on her, through her own skill,   75
At his request, though much against his will,
To come to London.
As the coach stopped, we heard her voice, more loud
Than a great-bellied woman's in a crowd,
Telling the knight that her affairs require   80
He, for some hours, obsequiously retire.
I think she was ashamed to have him seen:
Hard fate of husbands! The gallant had been,
Though a diseased, ill-favored fool, brought in.

   70. *Bovey:* identified by marginal glosses in several early texts as Sir
Ralph Bovey, baronet (d. 1679).
   74. *fine lady:* Her character resembles that of Melantha in Dryden's
comedy *Marriage À-la-Mode,* which was produced about April 1672 and
published in 1673 with a dedication to Rochester. Both women are hyper-
conscious of social norms, loquacious, and fond of affected French terms
as well as the expression "Let me die."

"Dispatch," says she, "that business you pretend,   85
Your beastly visit to your drunken friend!
A bottle ever makes you look so fine;
Methinks I long to smell you stink of wine!
Your country drinking breath's enough to kill:
Sour ale corrected with a lemon peel.   90
Prithee, farewell! We'll meet again anon."
The necessary thing bows, and is gone.
  She flies upstairs, and all the haste does show
That fifty antic postures will allow,
And then bursts out: "Dear madam, am not I   95
The altered'st creature breathing? Let me die,
I find myself ridiculously grown,
Embarrassée with being out of town,
Rude and untaught like any Indian queen:
My country nakedness is strangely seen.   100
  "How is love governed, love that rules the state,
And pray, who are the men most worn of late?
When I was married, fools were *à la mode*.
The men of wit were then held *incommode*,
Slow of belief, and fickle in desire,   105
Who, ere they'll be persuaded, must inquire
As if they came to spy, not to admire.
With searching wisdom, fatal to their ease,
They still find out why what may, should not please;
Nay, take themselves for injured when we dare   110
Make 'em think better of us than we are,
And if we hide our frailties from their sights,
Call us deceitful jilts and hypocrites.
They little guess, who at our arts are grieved,
The perfect joy of being well deceived;   115
Inquisitive as jealous cuckolds grow:
Rather than not be knowing, they will know

What, being known, creates their certain woe.
Women should these, of all mankind, avoid,
For wonder by clear knowledge is destroyed.   120
Woman, who is an arrant bird of night,
Bold in the dusk before a fool's dull sight,
Should fly when reason brings the glaring light.
    "But the kind, easy fool, apt to admire
Himself, trusts us; his follies all conspire   125
To flatter his, and favor our desire.
Vain of his proper merit, he with ease
Believes we love him best who best can please.
On him our gross, dull, common flatteries pass,
Ever most joyful when most made an ass.   130
Heavy to apprehend, though all mankind
Perceive us false, the fop concerned is blind,
Who, doting on himself,
Thinks everyone that sees him of his mind.
These are true women's men."   135
                              Here forced to cease
Through want of breath, not will to hold her peace,
She to the window runs, where she had spied
Her much esteemed dear friend, the monkey, tied.
With forty smiles, as many antic bows,
As if 't had been the lady of the house,   140
The dirty, chattering monster she embraced,
And made it this fine, tender speech at last:
"Kiss me, thou curious miniature of man!
How odd thou art! how pretty! how japan!
Oh, I could live and die with thee!" Then on   145
For half an hour in compliment she run.
    I took this time to think what nature meant
When this mixed thing into the world she sent,
So very wise, yet so impertinent:

One who knew everything; who, God thought fit,   150
Should be an ass through choice, not want of wit;
Whose foppery, without the help of sense,
Could ne'er have rose to such an excellence.
Nature's as lame in making a true fop
As a philosopher; the very top   155
And dignity of folly we attain
By studious search, and labor of the brain,
By observation, counsel, and deep thought:
God never made a coxcomb worth a groat.
We owe that name to industry and arts: 160
An eminent fool must be a fool of parts.
And such a one was she, who had turned o'er
As many books as men; loved much, read more;
Had a discerning wit; to her was known
Everyone's fault and merit, but her own.   165
All the good qualities that ever blessed
A woman so distinguished from the rest,
Except discretion only, she possessed.
    But now, "*Mon cher* dear Pug," she cries, "*adieu!*"
And the discourse broke off does thus renew: 170
    "You smile to see me, whom the world perchance
Mistakes to have some wit, so far advance
The interest of fools, that I approve
Their merit, more than men's of wit, in love.
But, in our sex, too many proofs there are   175
Of such whom wits undo, and fools repair.
This, in my time, was so observed a rule
Hardly a wench in town but had her fool.
The meanest common slut, who long was grown
The jest and scorn of every pit buffoon,   180
Had yet left charms enough to have subdued
Some fop or other, fond to be thought lewd.

Foster could make an Irish lord a Nokes,
And Betty Morris had her City cokes.
A woman's ne'er so ruined but she can   185
Be still revenged on her undoer, man;
How lost soe'er, she'll find some lover, more
A lewd, abandoned fool than she a whore.

   "That wretched thing Corinna, who had run
Through all the several ways of being undone,   190
Cozened at first by love, and living then
By turning the too dear-bought trick on men—
Gay were the hours, and winged with joys they flew,
When first the town her early beauties knew;
Courted, admired, and loved, with presents fed;   195
Youth in her looks, and pleasure in her bed;
Till fate, or her ill angel, thought it fit
To make her dote upon a man of wit,
Who found 'twas dull to love above a day;
Made his ill-natured jest, and went away.   200
Now scorned by all, forsaken, and oppressed,
She's a *memento mori* to the rest;
Diseased, decayed, to take up half a crown
Must mortgage her long scarf and manteau gown.

   183. *Foster:* evidently the girl who figures mysteriously in a letter of
September 1671 from John Muddyman to Rochester: "Now my Lord
as to a concerne of your owne. Fate has taken care to vindicate your proceeding with Foster, whoe is discovered to bee a damsell of low degre,
and very fit for the latter part of your treatment, noe northerne lass but a
mere dresser at Hazard's scoole, her uncle a wyght that wields the puisant
spiggot at Kensington, debaucht by Mr. Buttler a gentleman of the cloak
and gallow-shoe, an order of knighthood very fatall to maydenhead" (Historical Manuscripts Commission Reports, *Bath MSS.*, 2, 153). *Irish lord:*
unidentified. *Nokes:* James Nokes, a comic actor of the Duke's Company
who was celebrated for his portrayal of solemn fools.
   184. *Betty Morris:* the prostitute whom in 1671 Dorset characterized
as "bonny black Bess" in his well-known burlesque lyric "Methinks the
poor town has been troubled too long." She is mentioned again in "An
Allusion to Horace," lines 111–14 (pp. 125–26). *City:* the mercantile
district of London, in contrast to the fashionable "Town." *cokes:* simple-
ton, dupe.

Poor creature! who, unheard of as a fly,   205
In some dark hole must all the winter lie,
And want and dirt endure a whole half year
That for one month she tawdry may appear.

   "In Easter Term she gets her a new gown,
When my young master's worship comes to town,   210
From pedagogue and mother just set free,
The heir and hopes of a great family;
Which, with strong ale and beef, the country rules,
And ever since the Conquest have been fools.
And now, with careful prospect to maintain   215
This character, lest crossing of the strain
Should mend the booby breed, his friends provide
A cousin of his own to be his bride.
And thus set out
With an estate, no wit, and a young wife   220
(The solid comforts of a coxcomb's life),
Dunghill and pease forsook, he comes to town,
Turns spark, learns to be lewd, and is undone.
Nothing suits worse with vice than want of sense:
Fools are still wicked at their own expense.   225

   "This o'ergrown schoolboy lost Corinna wins,
And at first dash to make an ass begins:
Pretends to like a man who has not known
The vanities nor vices of the town;
Fresh in his youth, and faithful in his love;   230
Eager of joys which he does seldom prove;
Healthful and strong, he does no pains endure
But what the fair one he adores can cure;
Grateful for favors, does the sex esteem,
And libels none for being kind to him;   235
Then of the lewdness of the times complains:
Rails at the wits and atheists, and maintains

'Tis better than good sense, than power or wealth,
To have a love untainted, youth, and health.

  "The unbred puppy, who had never seen   240
A creature look so gay, or talk so fine,
Believes, then falls in love, and then in debt;
Mortgages all, ev'n to the ancient seat,
To buy this mistress a new house for life;
To give her plate and jewels, robs his wife.   245
And when t' th' height of fondness he is grown,
'Tis time to poison him, and all's her own.
Thus meeting in her common arms his fate,
He leaves her bastard heir to his estate,
And, as the race of such an owl deserves,   250
His own dull lawful progeny he starves.

  "Nature, who never made a thing in vain,
But does each insect to some end ordain,
Wisely contrived kind keeping fools, no doubt,
To patch up vices men of wit wear out."   255
Thus she ran on two hours, some grains of sense
Still mixed with volleys of impertinence.

  But now 'tis time I should some pity show
To Chloe, since I cannot choose but know
Readers must reap the dullness writers sow.   260
By the next post such stories I will tell
As, joined with these, shall to a volume swell,
As true as heaven, more infamous than hell.
But you are tired, and so am I.
                                        Farewell.

A Very Heroical Epistle in Answer to Ephelia

[Shortly after 4 July 1675]   [*1679*]

This fictitious verse letter satirizes Rochester's enemy John Sheffield, Earl of Mulgrave, whose conceit concerning his accomplishments as lover, soldier, and poet became legendary at the Restoration Court. The dramatic speaker of the poem, representing Mulgrave, is made to appear ridiculous because his self-centered attitudes implicitly violate traditional standards of conduct and morality.

"A Very Heroical Epistle" is the second of a pair of verse letters in the fashion originating in Ovid's *Heroides*. In the first letter, usually called "Ephelia to Bajazet" and probably composed by George Etherege, "Ephelia" reproaches "Bajazet" for his infidelity, while Rochester's poem is "Bajazet's" arrogant rejoinder. The name "Bajazet," alluding to the haughty Turkish emperor in Marlowe's *Tamburlaine*, continued to be applied to Mulgrave for years afterward.

Madam,
    If you're deceived, it is not by my cheat,
For all disguises are below the great.
What man or woman upon earth can say
I ever used 'em well above a day?
How is it, then, that I inconstant am?   5
He changes not who always is the same.

    In my dear self I center everything:
My servants, friends, my mistress, and my King;
Nay, heaven and earth to that one point I bring.
Well mannered, honest, generous, and stout   10
(Names by dull fools to plague mankind found out)
Should I regard, I must myself constrain,
And 'tis my maxim to avoid all pain.

    You fondly look for what none e'er could find,
Deceive yourself, and then call me unkind,   15
And by false reasons would my falsehood prove:
For 'tis as natural to change, as love.

You may as justly at the sun repine
Because alike it does not always shine.
No glorious thing was ever made to stay: 20
My blazing star but visits, and away.
As fatal, too, it shines as those i' th' skies:
'Tis never seen but some great lady dies.

The boasted favor you so precious hold
To me's no more than changing of my gold: 25
Whate'er you gave, I paid you back in bliss;
Then where's the obligation, pray, of this?
If heretofore you found grace in my eyes,
Be thankful for it, and let that suffice.
But women, beggar-like, still haunt the door   30
Where they've received a charity before.

O happy sultan, whom we barbarous call,
How much refined art thou above us all!
Who envies not the joys of thy serail?
Thee like some god the trembling crowd adore;   35
Each man's thy slave, and womankind thy whore.
Methinks I see thee, underneath the shade
Of golden canopies supinely laid,
Thy crouching slaves all silent as the night,
But, at thy nod, all active as the light!   40
Secure in solid sloth thou there dost reign,
And feel'st the joys of love without the pain.
Each female courts thee with a wishing eye,
Whilst thou with awful pride walk'st careless by,
Till thy kind pledge at last marks out the dame   45

21. *blazing star:* Mulgrave's star of the Order of the Garter, which he
received on 23 April 1674.
22–23: A comet was believed to portend some major disaster, especially
the death of an important person. The word "dies" carries a sexual *double-
entendre.*
25. *changing of my gold:* making change.

Thou fanciest most to quench thy present flame.
Then from thy bed submissive she retires,
And thankful for the grace, no more requires.

No loud reproach nor fond unwelcome sound
Of women's tongues thy sacred ear dares wound.   50
If any do, a nimble mute straight ties
The true love knot, and stops her foolish cries.

Thou fear'st no injured kinsman's threatening blade,
Nor midnight ambushes by rivals laid;
While here with aching hearts our joys we taste,   55
Disturbed by swords, like Damocles his feast.

53–54: These lines refer to the Earl of Mulgrave's widely publicized and rather ridiculous affair with Mall Kirke, one of the Duchess of York's Maids of Honor. The "midnight ambush" took place in September 1674, when the Duke of Monmouth, one of Mulgrave's rivals in Mall's affections, had the Earl apprehended by the guard as he emerged from her lodgings in Whitehall and kept him locked up for the rest of the night. Approximately nine months later, Mall gave birth to a boy. Although it was far from certain that Mulgrave was the father, Mall's brother, Captain Percy Kirke (who in 1685 became infamous as the commander of "Kirke's Lambs"), assumed the "injured kinsman's" part by challenging Mulgrave. In the duel, fought on 4 July 1675, Mulgrave was severely but not critically wounded.

The Disabled Debauchee

[?1675]   [c. Sept. 1680]

The verse form of this poem is the so-called "heroic stanza," which was
widely used in the seventeenth century for works of an epic character
such as Davenant's *Gondibert* and Dryden's *Annus Mirabilis.*

As some brave admiral, in former war
    Deprived of force, but pressed with courage still,
Two rival fleets appearing from afar,
    Crawls to the top of an adjacent hill;

From whence, with thoughts full of concern, he views   5
    The wise and daring conduct of the fight,
Whilst each bold action to his mind renews
    His present glory and his past delight;

From his fierce eyes flashes of fire he throws,
    As from black clouds when lightning breaks away;   10
Transported, thinks himself amidst the foes,
    And absent, yet enjoys the bloody day;

So, when my days of impotence approach,
    And I'm by pox and wine's unlucky chance
Forced from the pleasing billows of debauch   15
    On the dull shore of lazy temperance,

My pains at least some respite shall afford
    While I behold the battles you maintain
When fleets of glasses sail about the board,
    From whose broadsides volleys of wit shall rain.   20

Nor let the sight of honorable scars,
    Which my too forward valor did procure,

Frighten new-listed soldiers from the wars:
  Past joys have more than paid what I endure.

Should any youth (worth being drunk) prove nice, 25
  And from his fair inviter meanly shrink,
'Twill please the ghost of my departed vice
  If, at my counsel, he repent and drink.

Or should some cold-complexioned sot forbid,
  With his dull morals, our bold night-alarms, 30
I'll fire his blood by telling what I did
  When I was strong and able to bear arms.

I'll tell of whores attacked, their lords at home;
  Bawds' quarters beaten up, and fortress won;
Windows demolished, watches overcome; 35
  And handsome ills by my contrivance done.

Nor shall our love-fits, Chloris, be forgot,
  When each the well-looked linkboy strove t' enjoy,
And the best kiss was the deciding lot
  Whether the boy fucked you, or I the boy. 40

With tales like these I will such thoughts inspire
  As to important mischief shall incline:
I'll make him long some ancient church to fire,
  And fear no lewdness he's called to by wine.

Thus, statesmanlike, I'll saucily impose, 45
  And safe from action, valiantly advise;
Sheltered in impotence, urge you to blows,
  And being good for nothing else, be wise.

Upon Nothing

[Before 14 May 1678]   [1679]

Orthodox Christian theology holds that God created the universe out
of nothing (the usual version) or chaos (the variation adopted by Milton
in *Paradise Lost*). Hence, according to a paradoxical tradition which
developed as a corollary, this nonexistent nothing is the source or un-
formed raw material of all things in the Creation, without which they
could not exist.

Nothing! thou elder brother even to Shade:
Thou hadst a being ere the world was made,
And well fixed, art alone of ending not afraid.

Ere Time and Place were, Time and Place were not,
When primitive Nothing Something straight begot;   5
Then all proceeded from the great united What.

Something, the general attribute of all,
Severed from thee, its sole original,
Into thy boundless self must undistinguished fall;

Yet Something did thy mighty power command,   10
And from thy fruitful Emptiness's hand
Snatched men, beasts, birds, fire, water, air, and land.

Matter, the wicked'st offspring of thy race,
By Form assisted, flew from thy embrace,
And rebel Light obscured thy reverend dusky face.   15

With Form and Matter, Time and Place did join;
Body, thy foe, with these did leagues combine
To spoil thy peaceful realm, and ruin all thy line;

But turncoat Time assists the foe in vain,
And bribed by thee, destroys their short-lived reign,   20
And to thy hungry womb drives back thy slaves again.

Though mysteries are barred from laic eyes,
And the divine alone with warrant pries
Into thy bosom, where the truth in private lies,

Yet this of thee the wise may truly say: 25
Thou from the virtuous nothing dost delay,
And to be part of thee the wicked wisely pray.

Great Negative, how vainly would the wise
Inquire, define, distinguish, teach, devise,
Didst thou not stand to point their blind philosophies!   30

Is or Is Not, the two great ends of Fate,
And True or False, the subject of debate,
That perfect or destroy the vast designs of state—

When they have racked the politician's breast,
Within thy bosom most securely rest,   35
And when reduced to thee, are least unsafe and best.

But Nothing, why does Something still permit
That sacred monarchs should in council sit
With persons highly thought at best for nothing fit,

While weighty Something modestly abstains   40
From princes' coffers, and from statesmen's brains,
And Nothing there like stately Nothing reigns?

Nothing! who dwellst with fools in grave disguise,
For whom they reverend shapes and forms devise,
Lawn sleeves and furs and gowns, when they like thee look
     wise: 45

French truth, Dutch prowess, British policy,
Hibernian learning, Scotch civility,
Spaniards' dispatch, Danes' wit are mainly seen in thee;

The great man's gratitude to his best friend,
Kings' promises, whores' vows—towards thee they bend,   50
Flow swiftly into thee, and in thee ever end.

   45. *Lawn sleeves:* part of a bishop's regalia.

An Allusion to Horace, the Tenth Satyr
of the First Book

[Winter of 1675–76]   [*c. Sept. 1680*]

This poem is an "imitation" in the same sense as Pope's "Imitations of
Horace" and is apparently the first such work in the English language.
Based on Horace, *Satires*, 1.10, it requires a close knowledge of the Latin
original so that the reader will be aware, not only of clever adaptations of
Roman circumstances to English ones, but of ironic discrepancies between
the two.

   "An Allusion to Horace" is the earliest overt sign of the enmity between Rochester and Dryden which affected the attitudes of both men
for the rest of their lives. Dryden delayed any direct answer until his
Preface to *All for Love*, published in March 1678.

    Well, sir, 'tis granted I said Dryden's rhymes
    Were stol'n, unequal, nay dull many times.

What foolish patron is there found of his
So blindly partial to deny me this?
But that his plays, embroidered up and down 5
With wit and learning, justly pleased the town
In the same paper I as freely own.

    Yet having this allowed, the heavy mass
That stuffs up his loose volumes must not pass;
For by that rule I might as well admit 10
Crowne's tedious scenes for poetry and wit.
'Tis therefore not enough when your false sense
Hits the false judgment of an audience
Of clapping fools, assembling a vast crowd
Till the thronged playhouse crack with the dull load; 15
Though ev'n that talent merits in some sort
That can divert the rabble and the Court,
Which blundering Settle never could attain,
And puzzling Otway labors at in vain.
But within due proportions circumscribe 20
Whate'er you write, that with a flowing tide

3. *foolish patron:* John Sheffield, Earl of Mulgrave, to whom Dryden dedicated his heroic drama *Aureng-Zebe,* published in February 1675/6. In his dedication, Dryden thanks Mulgrave for recommending the play to the King's perusal before its production on 17 November 1675, and for providing Dryden an opportunity to discuss his proposed epic with the King and the Duke of York.

11. *Crowne:* According to a possibly apocryphal story, Rochester contrived to have John Crowne commissioned in Dryden's place to write the masque *Calisto,* which was given a sumptuous production at Court on 15 February 1674/5. For a more favorable reference to Crowne, see "Timon," lines 132–42 (pp. 70–71).

18. *blundering Settle:* Elkanah Settle's *Love and Revenge* (produced 9 November 1674) and *The Conquest of China* (produced 28 May 1675) failed to repeat his earlier popular success in *The Empress of Morocco.*

19. *puzzling Otway:* Thomas Otway's clumsy first play, *Alcibiades,* had been produced in late September 1675. His highly successful second effort, *Don Carlos,* was recommended by Rochester to the King and the Duke of York before its first performance on 8 June 1676, and his third play, *Titus and Berenice* with the *Cheats of Scapin* (1677), was dedicated to Rochester.

The style may rise, yet in its rise forbear
With useless words t' oppress the wearied ear.
Here be your language lofty, there more light:
Your rhetoric with your poetry unite.   25
For elegance' sake, sometimes allay the force
Of epithets: 'twill soften the discourse.
A jest in scorn points out and hits the thing
More home than the morosest satyr's sting.

Shakespeare and Jonson did herein excel,   30
And might in this be imitated well;
Whom refined Etherege copies not at all,
But is himself a sheer original;
Nor that slow drudge in swift Pindaric strains,
Flatman, who Cowley imitates with pains,   35
And rides a jaded muse, whipped with loose reins.

When Lee makes temperate Scipio fret and rave,
And Hannibal a whining amorous slave,
I laugh, and wish the hot-brained fustian fool
In Busby's hands, to be well lashed at school.   40

Of all our modern wits, none seems to me
Once to have touched upon true comedy

32–33. *refined Etherege:* George Etherege's third and last comedy,
The Man of Mode, was produced on 11 March 1675/6.
34–36. *Flatman:* Thomas Flatman (1637–88), a miniature-painter and
poetaster who specialized in bad Pindaric odes. He wrote an elegy for
Rochester's death in 1680.
37–38: Scipio and Hannibal are characters in Nathaniel Lee's second
play, the ranting heroic tragedy *Sophonisba,* which was produced on 30
April 1675. Lee's first play, *Nero* (1675), had been dedicated to Rochester.
40. *Busby:* Richard Busby (1606–95), the famous headmaster of Westminster School—which Lee did not, however, attend.
41–53. *hasty Shadwell:* Thomas Shadwell's ninth and most recent play,
The Libertine, was produced on 15 June 1675. He often boasted of his
speed in composition—claiming, for example, that *The Libertine* was
completed in approximately three weeks. Rochester's praise of Shadwell
here and in line 121 represents a drastic change from his earlier comments
in "Timon," line 16 (p. 65), and the epilogue to *Love in the Dark* (p.
91). *slow Wycherley:* At this time William Wycherley had completed

But hasty Shadwell and slow Wycherley.

Shadwell's unfinished works do yet impart

Great proofs of force of nature, none of art: 45

With just, bold strokes he dashes here and there,

Showing great mastery, with little care,

And scorns to varnish his good touches o'er

To make the fools and women praise 'em more.

But Wycherley earns hard whate'er he gains: 50

He wants no judgment, nor he spares no pains.

He frequently excels, and at the least

Makes fewer faults than any of the best.

    Waller, by nature for the bays designed,

With force and fire and fancy unconfined,   55

In panegyrics does excel mankind.

He best can turn, enforce, and soften things

To praise great conqu'rors, or to flatter Kings.

For pointed satyrs, I would Buckhurst choose:

The best good man with the worst-natured muse.   60

    For songs and verses mannerly obscene,

That can stir nature up by springs unseen,

And without forcing blushes, warm the Queen—

Sedley has that prevailing gentle art,

That can with a resistless charm impart   65

---

three of his four comedies, notably *The Country-Wife*, which was produced on 12 January 1674/5. His other masterpiece, *The Plain-Dealer*,
was not produced until 11 December 1676. In his Preface to *All for
Love*, Dryden takes Rochester to task for calling "a slow man hasty, or
a hasty writer a slow drudge."

54–58. *Waller:* These lines well describe Edmund Waller's forte, the
writing of commendatory verses. *great conqu'rors . . . Kings:* Waller had
contributed panegyrics on both Cromwell and Charles II.

59–60. *Buckhurst:* Charles Sackville, Lord Buckhurst, later Earl of
Dorset. His best-known satire is his ironical encomium of Edward Howard
beginning "Come on, ye critics! find one fault who dare," which he wrote
in 1669.

61–70. *Sedley:* Sir Charles Sedley is remembered chiefly as a writer of
songs.

The loosest wishes to the chastest heart;
Raise such a conflict, kindle such a fire,
Betwixt declining virtue and desire,
Till the poor vanquished maid dissolves away
In dreams all night, in sighs and tears all day.   70

    Dryden in vain tried this nice way of wit,
For he to be a tearing blade thought fit.
But when he would be sharp, he still was blunt:
To frisk his frolic fancy, he'd cry, "Cunt!"
Would give the ladies a dry bawdy bob,   75
And thus he got the name of Poet Squab.
But, to be just, 'twill to his praise be found
His excellencies more than faults abound;
Nor dare I from his sacred temples tear
That laurel which he best deserves to wear.   80

    But does not Dryden find ev'n Jonson dull;
Fletcher and Beaumont uncorrect, and full
Of lewd lines, as he calls 'em; Shakespeare's style

---

75. *dry bawdy bob:* A "dry-bob" is coition without emission.

76. *Poet Squab:* a popular nickname for Dryden which was apparently first applied to him in this passage.

80. *laurel:* Dryden had been Poet Laureate since 1668.

81–84: These lines are a very loose summary of opinions expressed by Dryden in his controversy with Shadwell during the years 1668–73, especially in his "Defence of the Epilogue: or An Essay on the Dramatic Poetry of the Last Age" which he appended to *The Conquest of Granada* (1672). In this essay, which includes several references to Horace, *Satires*, 1.10—the same work Rochester imitates in "An Allusion to Horace"—Dryden analyzes what he regards as faults in the language of Jonson, Fletcher (and Beaumont), and Shakespeare.

81. *Jonson:* In his controversy with Shadwell, Dryden maintained that Jonson excelled in judgment but was not noteworthy for wit, which Dryden was inclined to restrict to "sharpness of conceit." Shadwell, insisting upon a broader definition of wit, argued that it was essential for writing Jonsonian comedy of humors.

82–83. *Fletcher and Beaumont:* Although he nowhere uses the exact phrase "lewd lines," Dryden in the "Defence of the Epilogue" criticizes the unrefined language of Fletcher, as well as that of Jonson and Shakespeare.

Stiff and affected; to his own the while
Allowing all the justness that his pride   85
So arrogantly had to these denied?
And may not I have leave impartially
To search and censure Dryden's works, and try
If those gross faults his choice pen does commit
Proceed from want of judgment, or of wit;   90
Or if his lumpish fancy does refuse
Spirit and grace to his loose, slattern muse?
Five hundred verses every morning writ
Proves you no more a poet than a wit.
Such scribbling authors have been seen before;   95
Mustapha, The English Princess, forty more
Were things perhaps composed in half an hour.
To write what may securely stand the test
Of being well read over, thrice at least
Compare each phrase, examine every line,   100
Weigh every word, and every thought refine.

   Scorn all applause the vile rout can bestow,
And be content to please those few who know.
Canst thou be such a vain, mistaken thing
To wish thy works might make a playhouse ring   105
With the unthinking laughter and poor praise
Of fops and ladies, factious for thy plays?
Then send a cunning friend to learn thy doom
From the shrewd judges in the drawing room.
I've no ambition on that idle score,   110
But say with Betty Morris heretofore,

83–84. *Shakespeare . . . Stiff and affected:* an inaccurate account of
Dryden's actual words in the "Defence of the Epilogue."
   96. *Mustapha:* Orrery's *The Tragedy of Mustapha,* produced on 3
April 1665. Cf. "Timon," lines 113–14 (p. 69). *The English Princess:*
John Caryll's tragedy *The English Princess, or, The Death of Richard the
III,* produced on 7 March 1666/7.
   111. *Betty Morris:* the prostitute whom Rochester had mentioned previ-
ously in line 184 of "Artemisia to Chloe" (p. 110).

When a Court lady called her Buckley's whore,
"I please one man of wit, am proud on 't too:
Let all the coxcombs dance to bed to you!"
Should I be troubled when the purblind knight,   115
Who squints more in his judgment than his sight,
Picks silly faults, and censures what I write;
Or when the poor-fed poets of the town,
For scraps and coach room, cry my verses down?
I loathe the rabble; 'tis enough for me   120
If Sedley, Shadwell, Shepherd, Wycherley,
Godolphin, Butler, Buckhurst, Buckingham,
And some few more, whom I omit to name,
Approve my sense: I count their censure fame.

112. *Buckley:* Henry Bulkeley, Master of the Household to Charles II
and James II.

115–17. *purblind knight:* Sir Carr Scroope, baronet (1649–80), a
minor poet and wit. His poor eyesight is often ridiculed in contemporary
lampoons. These three lines are the earliest trace of the literary quarrel
between Rochester and Scroope; see the headnote to "On the Supposed
Author of a Late Poem in Defence of Satyr" (p. 132).

121. *Shepherd:* Sir Fleetwood Shepherd (1634–98), the courtier, wit,
and versifier whose most convincing display of literary judgment was his
discovery of the poet Matthew Prior.

122. *Godolphin:* Sidney Godolphin, first Earl of Godolphin. In 1679,
he joined with Hyde and Sunderland to form the governing junto known
as the "Chits." *Butler:* probably Samuel Butler, author of *Hudibras,* though
just possibly Lord John Butler, a son of the Duke of Ormonde, who in
1666 had been among the unsuccessful suitors for the hand of Elizabeth
Malet, Rochester's wife. *Buckingham:* George Villiers, second Duke of
Buckingham.

Disillusionment and Death

1676-1680

Dialogue

[*c.* Jan. 1675/6]   [Unpublished]

Nell.   When to the King I bid good morrow
         With tongue in mouth, and hand on tarse,
   Portsmouth may rend her cunt for sorrow,
   And Mazarin may kiss mine arse.

Portsmouth.   When England's monarch's on my belly,   5
         With prick in cunt, though double crammed,
   Fart of mine arse for small whore Nelly,
   And great whore Mazarin be damned.

King.   When on Portsmouth's lap I lay my head,
         And Knight does sing her bawdy song,   10
   I envy not George Porter's bed,
         Nor the delights of Madam Long.

1. *Nell:* Nell Gwyn.
2. *tarse:* penis.
3. *Portsmouth:* Louise de Keroualle, Duchess of Portsmouth, Charles II's reigning mistress before the advent of Mazarin.
4. *Mazarin:* Hortense Mancini, Duchess Mazarin, the newest of the King's mistresses, arrived in England in December 1675.
7–8. *small whore Nelly . . . great whore Mazarin:* Nell Gwyn was "small and slender but well rounded" whereas Mazarin was the "tallest of all the mistresses" (John Harold Wilson, *Nell Gwyn: Royal Mistress*, New York, Pellegrini and Cudahy, 1952, pp. 43, 188).
10. *Knight:* Mary Knight, singer and one of Charles II's minor mistresses. She figures in the song beginning "Quoth the Duchess of Cleveland to counselor Knight" (p. 48) and is mentioned in "Signior Dildo," lines 69–72 (p. 58).
11. *George Porter:* One of Rochester's more disreputable cronies, George Porter (? 1622–1683) was the eldest son of Endymion Porter and Groom of the Bedchamber to Charles II. He married Diana, daughter of George Goring, first Earl of Norwich, by whom he had eight children. During the Civil War he had held a high rank under his brother-in-law, Lord Goring, who described him as "the best company, but the worst officer that ever served the king" (*DNB*).
12. *Madam Long:* Jane Long, one of the original actresses of the Duke's

People.   Now heavens preserve our faith's defender
            From Paris plots and Roman cunt;
            From Mazarin, that new pretender,   15
            And from that *politique*, Grammont.

Company. She created the role of the Widow in Etherege's *The Comical Revenge; or, Love in a Tub*, 1664. Sometime in 1673 she left the stage to become George Porter's mistress. On 17 December 1677, Henry Savile wrote to Rochester that Porter "is grown soe ravenous that now hee surfeits of every thing hee sees but Mrs. Long and his sonn Nobbs which hee can never have enough on" (*The Rochester-Savile Letters*, ed. John Harold Wilson, Columbus, Ohio State University Press, 1941, p. 52).

16. *Grammont:* Philibert, Comte de Grammont, author of the famous *Memoirs* of the Court of Charles II. He acted as Mazarin's social pilot during her first few weeks at Court, leaving England by April 1676 as escort for the Duchess of Cleveland, who was going to Paris (*Memoirs of Count Grammont*, ed. Gordon Goodwin, Edinburgh, John Grant, 1908, *1*, xxi).

To the Postboy

[Shortly after 27 June 1676]   [*1926, 1941, 1963*]

These strange half-boastful, half-penitential verses were seemingly prompted by Rochester's part in the notorious melee at Epsom on Saturday night, 17 June 1676, to which lines 9–12 refer. See Introduction, pp. xxviii–xxix.

Rochester.   Son of a whore, God damn you! can you tell
               A peerless peer the readiest way to Hell?
               I've outswilled Bacchus, sworn of my own make
               Oaths would fright Furies, and make Pluto
                   quake;
               I've swived more whores more ways than
                   Sodom's walls   5
               E'er knew, or the College of Rome's Cardinals.
               Witness heroic scars—Look here, ne'er go!—

Cerecloths and ulcers from the top to toe!
Frighted at my own mischiefs, I have fled
And bravely left my life's defender dead;   10
Broke houses to break chastity, and dyed
That floor with murder which my lust denied.
Pox on 't, why do I speak of these poor things?
I have blasphemed my God, and libeled Kings!
The readiest way to Hell—Come, quick!   15

Boy.   Ne'er stir:
The readiest way, my Lord, 's by Rochester.

8. *Cerecloths:* cloth impregnated with wax, commonly used as a plaster in surgery.

9–12: At the start of the Epsom incident, Rochester, Etherege, a certain Captain Downs, and several other gentlemen-rakes were administering a blanket-tossing to some fiddlers who refused to play for them. When a barber who came to investigate was threatened with the same treatment, he shrewdly guided them to the constable's house by pretending it was the house of the handsomest woman in town. Rochester and his crew broke down the doors in search of a whore and beat the constable—evidently the action described in lines 11–12.

The constable escaped and returned with the watch, however, whereupon order was restored. The watch had begun to disperse when Rochester inexplicably drew his sword upon the constable. Downs seized hold of Rochester to stop him while the constable resummoned the watch, one of whom, misunderstanding the situation, gave Downs a crashing blow on the head. The other rioters fled as Downs fought vainly on without a sword. He died of his wounds ten days later.

14. *blasphemed my God:* perhaps in "A Satyr against Reason and Mankind" (p. 94), which evoked several verse replies from clergymen. *libeled Kings:* probably in "A Satyr on Charles II" (p. 60).

On the Supposed Author of a Late Poem
in Defence of Satyr

[*c.* autumn 1676]   [*c. Sept. 1680*]

"On the Supposed Author" is a central document in Rochester's quarrel with Sir Carr Scroope. Rochester's initial attack on Scroope in "An Allusion to Horace," lines 115–17 (p. 126), was answered by the baronet in his "In Defence of Satyr," which is based on Horace, *Satires*, 1.4, with some hints probably from 2.1. Scroope's passage on Rochester refers to the Epsom brawl of 17 June 1676 and may also, in the phrase "buffoon conceit," suggest that by writing his verses "To the Postboy" (p. 130) Rochester was trying to shrug off responsibility for the death of Captain Downs ten days later:

> But why am I this bugbear to ye all?
> My pen is dipped in no such bitter gall.
> He that can rail at one he calls his friend,
> Or hear him absent wronged, and not defend;
> Who, for the sake of some ill-natured jest,
> Tells what he should conceal, invents the rest;
> To fatal midnight frolics can betray
> His brave companion, and then run away,
> Leaving him to be murdered in the street,
> Then put it off with some buffoon conceit—
> This, this is he you should beware of all,
> Yet him a pleasant, witty man you call.
> To whet your dull debauches up and down,
> You seek him as top fiddler of the town.

To this passage, probably composed during summer of 1676, Rochester is retorting in "On the Supposed Author," which Scroope in turn countered with an epigram:

> Rail on, poor feeble scribbler, speak of me
> In as bad terms as the world speaks of thee.
> Sit swelling in thy hole like a vexed toad,
> And full of pox and malice, spit abroad.
> Thou canst blast no man's fame with thy ill word:
> Thy pen is full as harmless as thy sword.

With this cool riposte Scroope withdrew from the quarrel, although it was continued by Rochester in "The Mock Song" (p. 136) and "On Poet Ninny" (p. 141) and by other satirists following Rochester's lead.

To rack and torture thy unmeaning brain
In satyr's praise, to a low untuned strain,
In thee was most impertinent and vain,
When in thy person we more clearly see
That satyr's of divine authority,   5
For God made one on man when he made thee:
To show there are some men, as there are apes,
Framed for mere sport, who differ but in shapes.

In thee are all those contradictions joined
That make an ass prodigious and refined.   10
A lump deformed and shapeless wert thou born,
Begot in love's despite and nature's scorn,
And art grown up the most ungraceful wight,
Harsh to the ear, and hideous to the sight;
Yet love's thy business, beauty thy delight.   15
Curse on that silly hour that first inspired
Thy madness to pretend to be admired:
To paint thy grisly face, to dance, to dress,
And all those awkward follies that express
Thy loathsome love and filthy daintiness;   20
Who needs will be an ugly *beau garçon*,
Spit at and shunned by every girl in town,
Where, dreadfully, love's scarecrow thou art placed
To fright the tender flock that long to taste,
While every coming maid, when you appear,   25
Starts back for shame, and straight turns chaste for fear.
For none so poor or prostitute have proved,
Where you made love, t' endure to be beloved.

'Twere labor lost, or else I would advise,
But thy half wit will ne'er let thee be wise.   30
Half witty, and half mad, and scarce half brave;
Half honest, which is very much a knave—
Made up of all these halves, thou canst not pass
For anything entirely but an ass.

Impromptu on Charles II

[Uncertain]   [*1707*]

According to one source, these famous verses were "posted on Whitehall gate." The antiquary Thomas Hearne describes them as "the lord Rochester's verses upon the king, on occasion of his majestie's saying, he would leave every one to his liberty in talking, when himself was in company, and would not take what was said at all amiss." Still another account relates that "the King praising the translation of the Psalms, says my Lord Rochester, 'An't please your majesty, I'll show you presently how they run,' and thus begun."

> God bless our good and gracious King,
>   Whose promise none relies on;
> Who never said a foolish thing,
>   Nor ever did a wise one.

Impromptu on the English Court

[?1676]   [*1745*]

Several early sources agree that (as Thomas Hearne wrote) Charles II
and some of his courtiers "being in company, my lord Rochester, upon
the king's request, made the following verses."

> Here's Monmouth the witty,
> And Lauderdale the pretty,
> And Frazier, that learned physician;
> But above all the rest,
> Here's the Duke for a jest,   5
> And the King for a grand politician.

1. *Monmouth:* James, Duke of Monmouth, illegitimate son of Charles
II. Though courageous, handsome, and graceful in manner, he lacked in-
telligence.

2. *Lauderdale:* John Maitland, first Duke of Lauderdale, at this time
virtual dictator of Scotland. "He made a very ill appearance: he was very
big: his hair red, hanging oddly about him: his tongue was too big for
his mouth, which made him bedew all that he talked to" (Burnet, *History
of His Own Time*).

3. *Frazier:* Sir Alexander Frazier, the King's principal physician.

5. *the Duke:* James, Duke of York, whose lack of a sense of humor is
amply illustrated in the way he governed England when he became King
James II.

The Mock Song

[Probably winter 1676–77]   [*c. Sept. 1680*]

This poem is a burlesque of a song probably composed by Rochester's
enemy Sir Carr Scroope:

> I cannot change as others do,
>   Though you unjustly scorn,
> Since that poor swain that sighs for you
>   For you alone was born.
> No, Phyllis, no, your heart to move,
>   A surer way I'll try,
> And to revenge my slighted love,
>   Will still love on, will still love on, and die.
>
> When killed with grief Amyntas lies,
>   And you to mind shall call
> The sighs that now unpitied rise,
>   The tears that vainly fall,
> That welcome hour that ends his smart
>   Will then begin your pain,
> For such a faithful, tender heart
>   Can never break, can never break in vain.

Scroope's lines may have been addressed to Cary Frazier (see next poem)
while he was courting her during late 1676 and early 1677. If so, "The
Mock Song" may satirize her as well as Scroope and his delicate lyric.

"I swive as well as others do;
    I'm young, not yet deformed;
My tender heart, sincere and true,
    Deserves not to be scorned.
Why, Phyllis, then, why will you swive   5
    With forty lovers more?"
"Can I," said she, "with nature strive?
    Alas I am, alas I am a whore!

"Were all my body larded o'er
    With darts of love, so thick   10

That you might find in every pore
    A well-stuck standing prick,
Whilst yet my eyes alone were free,
    My heart would never doubt,
In amorous rage and ecstasy,   15
    To wish those eyes, to wish those eyes fucked out."

On Cary Frazier

[?1677]   [*1963*]

Cary Frazier, Maid of Honor to Queen Catherine and a celebrated
beauty of the Court of Charles II, was the daughter of Sir Alexander
Frazier, the King's principal physician. Her mother was one of the
Queen's Dressers.

    Her father gave her dildoes six;
        Her mother made 'em up a score;
    But she loves nought but living pricks,
        And swears by God she'll frig no more.

On Mrs. Willis

[Uncertain]   [*c. Sept. 1680*]

    Against the charms our ballocks have
        How weak all human skill is,
    Since they can make a man a slave
        To such a bitch as Willis!

Heading. *Mrs. Willis:* Sue Willis, a prostitute who operated on the
fringes of the Court circle. On 24 June 1677, Rochester's friend Henry
Savile wrote to his brother, Viscount Halifax, "My Ld Culpepper is also
returned from Paris with Mrs. Willis, whom he carry'd thither to buy
whatsoever pleased her there and this nation could not afford" (*Savile
Correspondence*, ed. William Durrant Cooper, Camden Society, 1858,
p. 62).

Whom that I may describe throughout,   5
    Assist me, bawdy powers;
I'll write upon a double clout,
    And dip my pen in flowers.

Her look's demurely impudent,
    Ungainly beautiful;   10
Her modesty is insolent,
    Her wit both pert and dull.

A prostitute to all the town,
    And yet with no man friends,
She rails and scolds when she lies down,   15
    And curses when she spends.

Bawdy in thoughts, precise in words,
    Ill-natured though a whore,
Her belly is a bag of turds,
    And her cunt a common shore.   20

8. *flowers:* menstrual discharge.
20. *shore:* sewer.

Song

[Uncertain]   [*c. Sept. 1680*]

By all love's soft, yet mighty powers,
  It is a thing unfit
That men should fuck in time of flowers,
  Or when the smock's beshit.

Fair nasty nymph, be clean and kind,   5
  And all my joys restore
By using paper still behind
  And spunges for before.

My spotless flames can ne'er decay
  If after every close,   10
My smoking prick escape the fray
  Without a bloody nose.

If thou wouldst have me true, be wise
  And take to cleanly sinning;
None but fresh lovers' pricks can rise   15
  At Phyllis in foul linen.

Epilogue to "Circe"

[Shortly before 12 May 1677]   [*1677*]

Circe, a Tragedy, by Charles Davenant, the twenty-one-year-old son of Sir William Davenant, was produced at the Duke's House on 12 May 1677. The prologue to this highly successful mythological opera was contributed by Dryden.

Some few, from wit, have this true maxim got,
That *'tis still better to be pleased than not*,
And therefore never their own torment plot;
While the malicious critics still agree
To loathe each play they come, and pay, to see.   5
The first know 'tis a meaner part of sense
To find a fault than taste an excellence;
Therefore they praise and strive to like, while these
Are dully vain of being hard to please.
Poets and women have an equal right   10
To hate the dull, who, dead to all delight,
Feel pain alone, and have no joy but spite.
'Twas impotence did first this vice begin:
Fools censure wit as old men rail of sin,
Who envy pleasure which they cannot taste,   15
And, good for nothing, would be wise at last.
Since therefore to the women it appears
That all these enemies of wit are theirs,
Our poet the dull herd no longer fears.
Whate'er his fate may prove, 'twill be his pride   20
To stand or fall with beauty on his side.

16: Cf. "The Disabled Debauchee," line 48: "And being good for nothing else, be wise" (p. 117).

On Poet Ninny

[?April 1678]   [c. Sept. 1680]

"On Poet Ninny" is apparently the last of Rochester's surviving satires on Sir Carr Scroope. Poet Ninny is the character who represents Edward Howard in Thomas Shadwell's first play, *The Sullen Lovers*, produced on 2 May 1668.

Crushed by that just contempt his follies bring
On his crazed head, the vermin fain would sting;
But never satyr did so softly bite,
Or Gentle George himself more gently write.
Born to no other but thy own disgrace,   5
Thou art a thing so wretched and so base
Thou canst not ev'n offend, but with thy face;
And dost at once a sad example prove
Of harmless malice, and of hopeless love,
All pride and ugliness! Oh, how we loathe   10
A nauseous creature so composed of both!
How oft have we thy capering person seen,
With dismal look, and melancholy mien,
The just reverse of Nokes, when he would be
Some mighty hero, and makes love like thee.   15

1–2: evidently alluding to lampoons on Scroope and to his attempt to answer them, perhaps in such verses as the epigram beginning "Rail on, poor feeble scribbler, speak of me." See the headnote to "On the Supposed Author of a Late Poem in Defence of Satyr" (p. 132).

3: an allusion to the concluding couplet of Dorset's famous satire on Edward Howard:

> Thou sett'st thy name to what thyself dost write:
> Did ever libel yet so sharply bite?

4. *Gentle George:* George Etherege.

14–15. *Nokes:* James Nokes, a comic actor of the Duke's Company who was celebrated for his portrayal of solemn fools. He created the role of Ninny in *The Sullen Lovers*.

Thou art below being laughed at; out of spite,
Men gaze upon thee as a hideous sight,
And cry, "There goes the melancholy knight!"
There are some modish fools we daily see,
Modest and dull: why, they are wits to thee!   20
For, of all folly, sure the very top
Is a conceited ninny and a fop;
With face of farce, joined to a head romancy,
There's no such coxcomb as your fool of fancy.
But 'tis too much on so despised a theme: 25
No man would dabble in a dirty stream.
The worst that I could write would be no more
Than what thy very friends have said before.

My Lord All-Pride

[Late 1670s]   [*1679*]

This attack on John Sheffield, Earl of Mulgrave, answers some unidentified
verses of his—probably not, as scholars assumed formerly, his much-
publicized "An Essay upon Satyr," which seems to belong to a slightly
later date. Like the terms "Bajazet" and "King John," "Lord All-Pride"
became a popular sobriquet for Mulgrave, whose boasted accomplishments
as poet, soldier, and lover are all ridiculed in Rochester's lampoon.

Bursting with pride, the loathed impostume swells;
Prick him, he sheds his venom straight, and smells.
But 'tis so lewd a scribbler, that he writes
With as much force to nature as he fights;
Hardened in shame, 'tis such a baffled fop   5
That every schoolboy whips him like a top.
And, with his arm and head, his brain's so weak

1–2: Evidently Mulgrave has written a lampoon in reply to lampoons
on him—as in "An Essay upon Satyr," circulated in November 1679, he
retaliated against satirists like Rochester who had been sniping at him for
at least four years. *impostume:* purulent swelling, abscess.
7–12: Charges that poems which Mulgrave passed off as his own were

That his starved fancy is compelled to rake
Among the excrements of others' wit
To make a stinking meal of what they shit;   10
So swine, for nasty meat, to dunghill run,
And toss their gruntling snouts up when they've done.

    Against his stars the coxcomb ever strives,
And to be something they forbid, contrives.
With a red nose, splay foot, and goggle eye,   15
A plowman's looby mien, face all awry,
With stinking breath, and every loathsome mark,
The Punchinello sets up for a spark.
With equal self-conceit, too, he bears arms,
But with that vile success his part performs   20
That he burlesques his trade, and what is best
In others, turns like Harlequin to jest.
So have I seen, at Smithfield's wondrous fair,
When all his brother monsters flourish there,
A lubbard elephant divert the town   25
With making legs, and shooting off a gun.

    Go where he will, he never finds a friend;
Shame and derision all his steps attend.
Alike abroad, at home, i' th' camp and Court,
This Knight o' th' Burning Pestle makes us sport.   30

------

really written partly by Dryden and others tended to center on "An Essay
upon Satyr."

    16. *looby:* lubber, lout.

    18. *Punchinello:* Punchinello or Polichinello was a seventeenth-century
Italian puppet character, the ancestor of Punch, which was introduced into
London about 1660.

    23. *Smithfield:* where Bartholomew Fair was held.

    25. *lubbard:* lubberly. *elephant:* On 1 September 1679, Robert Hooke
noted that at Bartholomew Fair he "Saw Elephant wave colours, shoot a
gun, bend and kneel, carry a castle and a man, etc." (*The Diary of Robert
Hooke*, ed. Henry W. Robinson and Walter Adams, London, Taylor and
Francis, 1935, p. 423).

    30. *Knight o' th' Burning Pestle:* in allusion to Francis Beaumont's
famous burlesque, but possibly referring to Mulgrave's "red nose" and
probably containing a sexual *double-entendre*.

An Epistolary Essay from M. G. to O. B. upon
Their Mutual Poems

[Shortly after 21 Nov. 1679]   [*c. Sept. 1680*]

Apparently attempting to repeat the technique he had used earlier in
"A Very Heroical Epistle in Answer to Ephelia" (p. 113), Rochester in
"An Epistolary Essay" satirizes John Sheffield, Earl of Mulgrave, by de-
picting him as persona. In the later poem, the self-centered speaker
renders himself ridiculous by unconsciously violating traditional concep-
tions of good writing. The initials "M. G." are the first letters of the two
syllables of Mulgrave's name; "O. B.," whatever the initials may stand
for, represents John Dryden.

The "Epistolary Essay" seems to be Rochester's principal retort to
the attack on him in Mulgrave's "An Essay upon Satyr," which he men-
tions in a letter of 21 November 1679. Most contemporaries, including
Rochester in his letter, believed that Dryden was at least part-author of
"An Essay upon Satyr." The lampoon aroused considerable resentment,
which expressed itself most forcibly in the beating of Dryden in Rose
Alley on the night of 18 December 1679.

Dear friend,
                    I hear this town does so abound
With saucy censurers, that faults are found
With what of late we, in poetic rage
Bestowing, threw away on the dull age.
But howsoe'er envy their spleen may raise   5
To rob my brow of the deservèd bays,
Their thanks at least I merit, since through me
They are partakers of your poetry.
And this is all I'll say in my defence:
T' obtain one line of your well-worded sense,   10
I'd be content t' have writ the *British Prince*.

11. *British Prince:* Edward Howard's epic *The Brittish Princes*, published about May 1669, became a byword in the Restoration for bad
poetry. Howard was Dryden's brother-in-law.

I'm none of those who think themselves inspired,
Nor write with the vain hopes to be admired,
But from a rule I have upon long trial:
T' avoid with care all sort of self-denial.   15
Which way soe'er desire and fancy lead,
Contemning fame, that path I boldly tread.
And if, exposing what I take for wit,
To my dear self a pleasure I beget,
No matter though the censuring critic fret.   20
Those whom my muse displeases are at strife
With equal spleen against my course of life,
The least delight of which I'd not forgo
For all the flattering praise man can bestow.
If I designed to please, the way were then   25
To mend my manners rather than my pen.
The first's unnatural, therefore unfit,
And for the second, I despair of it,
Since grace is not so hard to get as wit.

Perhaps ill verses ought to be confined   30
In mere good breeding, like unsavory wind.
Were reading forced, I should be apt to think
Men might no more write scurvily than stink.
But 'tis your choice whether you'll read or no;
If likewise of your smelling it were so,   35
I'd fart, just as I write, for my own ease,
Nor should you be concerned unless you please.
I'll own that you write better than I do,
But I have as much need to write as you.
What though the excrement of my dull brain   40
Runs in a costive and insipid strain,
Whilst your rich head eases itself of wit:
Must none but civet cats have leave to shit?

In all I write, should sense and wit and rhyme

Fail me at once, yet something so sublime   45
Shall stamp my poem, that the world may see
It could have been produced by none but me.
And that's my end, for man can wish no more
Than so to write, as none e'er writ before.

    But why am I no poet of the times?   50
I have allusions, similes, and rhymes,
And wit—or else 'tis hard that I alone
Of the whole race of mankind should have none.
Unequally the partial hand of heaven
Has all but this one only blessing given.   55
The world appears like a large family
Whose lord, oppressed with pride and poverty,
That to a few great plenty he may show,
Is fain to starve the numerous train below:
Just so seems Providence, as poor and vain,   60
Keeping more creatures than it can maintain;
Here 'tis profuse, and there it meanly saves,
And for one prince it makes ten thousand slaves.
In wit alone 't has been munificent,
Of which so just a share to each is sent   65
That the most avaricious is content:
Who ever thought—the due division's such—
His own too little, or his friend's too much?
Yet most men show, or find great want of wit,
Writing themselves, or judging what is writ.   70

---

45. *sublime:* a surprisingly early allusion to Longinus, whose *Peri Hupsous* was first made generally available to Englishmen in Boileau's French translation published in 1674.

64–68: Cf. Descartes, *Discourse on Method*, the opening sentence of Part I: "Good sense is, of all things among men, the most equally distributed; for every one thinks himself so abundantly provided with it, that those even who are the most difficult to satisfy in everything else, do not usually desire a larger measure of this quality than they already possess."

But I, who am of sprightly vigor full,
Look on mankind as envious and dull.
Born to myself, myself I like alone
And must conclude my judgment good, or none.
For should my sense be nought, how could I know   75
Whether another man's be good or no?
Thus I resolve of my own poetry
That 'tis the best, and that's a fame for me.
If then I'm happy, what does it advance
Whether to merit due, or arrogance?   80
"Oh! but the world will take offense thereby."
Why then, the world will suffer for 't, not I.
Did e'er this saucy world and I agree
To let it have its beastly will of me?
Why should my prostituted sense be drawn   85
To every rule their musty customs spawn?
"But men will censure you." 'Tis ten to one
Whene'er they censure, they'll be in the wrong.
There's not a thing on earth that I can name
So foolish and so false as common fame.   90
It calls the courtier knave, the plain man rude,
Haughty the grave, and the delightful lewd,
Impertinent the brisk, morose the sad,
Mean the familiar, the reserved one mad.
Poor helpless woman is not favored more: 95
She's a sly hypocrite, or public whore.
Then who the devil would give *this* to be free
From th' innocent reproach of infamy?
    These things considered make me, in despite
Of idle rumor, keep at home and write.   100

97. *this:* probably implying a gesture such as snapping the fingers.

Epigram on Thomas Otway

[*c.* Jan. 1679/80]   [*1953*]

This epigram preserves the sole hint of ill will toward Otway during the last four years of Rochester's life. After a dig at Otway's first play in "An Allusion to Horace," written in winter of 1675–76 (p. 121), Rochester had helped assure the success of the dramatist's second effort, *Don Carlos* (produced 8 June 1676). Otway's third play, *Titus and Berenice* with the *Cheats of Scapin* (pub. *c.* February 1676/7), was dedicated to the Earl. Possibly Rochester thought he was attacked as "*Lord Lampoon* and *Monsieur Song*" in Otway's poem *The Poet's Complaint of his Muse*, which was published on or about 22 January 1679/80.

> To form a plot,
> The blustering bard whose rough, unruly rhyme
> Gives Plutarch's *Lives* the lie in every line,
> Who rapture before nature does prefer
> (And now himself turned his own imager),   5
> Defaceth God's in every character.

2–3: Apparently these lines refer to Otway's potboiler *The History and Fall of Caius Marius*, even though most of the play is technically in blank verse rather than rhyme. Produced about September 1679, it is an attempt to combine Shakespeare's *Romeo and Juliet* with Roman material drawn from Plutarch and also from Lucan.

5. *his own imager:* Otway's *Poet's Complaint* includes extensive auto-biographical passages.

Answer to a Paper of Verses
Sent Him by Lady Betty Felton
and Taken out of the Translation of Ovid's "Epistles," *1680*

[*c.* Feb. 1679/80]   [*1693*]

The rough syntax of this poem suggests an extemporaneous composition.
Perhaps, enjoying a "jovial night" at a London tavern, Rochester dashed
it off upon being interrupted by some reproachful verses sent by Lady
Betty, who had copied them out of the epistles from forsaken women to
their lovers in the recently published translations of Ovid's *Heroides*.
Grammont relates a somewhat similar story concerning Frances Jennings
and Henry Jermyn (*Memoirs of Count Grammont*, ed. Gordon Goodwin, Edinburgh, John Grant, 1908, *2*, 163–64).

> What strange surprise to meet such words as these
> (Such terms of horror were ne'er chose to please)—
> To meet, midst pleasures of a jovial night,
> Words that can only give amaze and fright:
> No gentle thought that does to love invite!   5
> Were it not better for your arms t' employ
> Grasping a lover in pursuit of joy,
> Than handling sword and pen, weapons unfit?
> Your sex gains conquest by their charms and wit.
> Of writers slain I could with pleasure hear,   10
> Approve of fights, o'erjoyed to cause a tear—
> So slain, I mean, that she should soon revive,
> Pleased in my arms to find herself alive.

Heading. *Lady Betty Felton:* wife of Thomas Felton and daughter of
the Earl of Suffolk. In 1673, as Lady Elizabeth Howard, she spoke
Rochester's prologue for the Court production of Settle's *The Empress of
Morocco* (p. 49), and she and her mother are mentioned in lines 21–24
of *Signior Dildo* (p. 55). By 1680, her allegedly licentious behavior made
her increasingly a subject of lampoons. *Translation of Ovid's "Epistles,"*
1680: a volume of translations of 23 epistles from Ovid's *Heroides*, contributed by Dryden and others. A highly successful collection which passed
through many editions, it was first published about February 1679/80.

A Translation from Seneca's "Troades," Act II, Chorus

[Shortly before 7 Feb. 1679/80]   [*c. Sept. 1680*]

Rochester's verses are adapted from lines 397–408 of the *Troades*. He sent a copy to the deist Charles Blount, who in his reply, dated 7 February 1679/80, observed eloquently,

> I Had the Honour Yesterday to receive from the Hands of an Humble Servant of your Lordship's, your most incomperable Version of that Passage of *Seneca's*, where he begins with,—*Post mortem nihil est, ipsaque mors nihil*, &c.—and must confess, with your Lordship's Pardon, that I cannot but esteem the Translation to be, in some measure, a confutation of the Original; since what less than a divine and immortal Mind could have produced what you have there written? Indeed, the Hand that wrote it may become *Lumber*, but sure, the Spirit that dictated it, can never be so: No, my Lord, your mighty Genius is a most sufficient Argument of its own Immortality; and more prevalent with me, than all the Harangues of the Parsons, or Sophistry of the Schoolmen. (*The Miscellaneous Works of Charles Blount, Esq.*, London, 1695, p. [1]117.)

After death nothing is, and nothing, death:
The utmost limit of a gasp of breath.
Let the ambitious zealot lay aside
His hopes of heaven, whose faith is but his pride;
    Let slavish souls lay by their fear,   5
    Nor be concerned which way nor where
    After this life they shall be hurled.
Dead, we become the lumber of the world,
And to that mass of matter shall be swept
Where things destroyed with things unborn are kept.   10
    Devouring time swallows us whole;
Impartial death confounds body and soul.

For Hell and the foul fiend that rules
God's everlasting fiery jails
(Devised by rogues, dreaded by fools),
With his grim, grisly dog that keeps the door,
Are senseless stories, idle tales,
Dreams, whimseys, and no more.

Poems Possibly by Rochester

To His Sacred Majesty, on His Restoration in the Year 1660

[Shortly after 29 May 1660]   [*1660*]

Anthony à Wood says of this and the following two poems that "these three copies were made, as 'twas then well known, by Robert Whitehall a physician of Merton college, who pretended to instruct the count (then twelve [actually thirteen] years of age) in the art of poetry, and on whom he absolutely doted" (*Athenae Oxonienses*, ed. Philip Bliss, London, F. C. and J. Rivington, 1813–20, *3*, 1232). Although Wood's statement is probably correct, the poems were unquestionably printed as Rochester's with his knowledge and consent.

"To His Sacred Majesty" originally appeared in a volume of verses published at Oxford to celebrate the Restoration of Charles II on 29 May 1660.

> Virtue's triumphant shrine! who dost engage
> At once three kingdoms in a pilgrimage;
> Which in ecstatic duty strive to come
> Out of themselves, as well as from their home;
> Whilst England grows one camp, and London is   5
> Itself the nation, not metropolis,
> And loyal Kent renews her arts again,
> Fencing her ways with moving groves of men;
> Forgive this distant homage, which doth meet
> Your blest approach on sedentary feet;   10
> And though my youth, not patient yet to bear
> The weight of arms, denies me to appear

3–4: When Charles II arrived at Dover on 23 May 1660, the beaches were dense with spectators who had come to welcome him.

7–8: During Charles's progress from Canterbury to London on 28 and 29 May, the roads were lined with people all the way.

> In steel before you, yet, Great Sir, approve
> My manly wishes, and more vigorous love;
> In whom a cold respect were treason to   15
> A father's ashes, greater than to you;
> Whose one ambition 'tis for to be known,
> By daring loyalty, your Wilmot's son.

16. *A father's ashes:* For the activities of Rochester's father as a royalist general during Charles II's exile, see Introduction, p. xviii.

In Obitum Serenissimae Mariae Principis Arausionensis

[Shortly after 24 Dec. 1660]   [*1660/1*]

Both this and the following poem were printed in a volume of commemorative verses on the death of Mary, Princess Royal of England and Princess of Orange. The sister of Charles II and mother of William III, she died of smallpox at Whitehall on Christmas eve, 1660. (See also the headnote to the preceding poem.)

> Impia blasphemi sileant convitia vulgi;
>   Absolvo medicos, innocuamque manum.
> Curassent alios facili medicamine morbos:
>   Ulcera cum veniunt, ars nihil ipsa valet.
> Vultu femineo quaevis vel pustula vulnus   5
>   Lethale est, pulchras certior ense necat.
> Mollia vel temeret si quando mitior ora,
>   Evadat forsan femina, diva nequat.
> Cui par est animae corpus, quae tota venustas,
>   Formae qui potis est, haec superesse suae?   10

To Her Sacred Majesty, the Queen Mother,
on the Death of Mary, Princess of Orange

[Shortly after 24 Dec. 1660]   [*1660/1*]

This poem is addressed to Henrietta Maria, widow of the martyred
Charles I. Charles II and the deceased Princess Mary were her eldest son
and daughter. (See also the headnotes to the two preceding poems.)

Respite, great Queen, your just and hasty fears:
There's no infection lodges in our tears.
Though our unhappy air be armed with death,
Yet sighs have an untainted, guiltless breath.
  O stay awhile, and teach your equal skill   5
To understand and to support our ill.
You that in mighty wrongs an age have spent,
And seem to have outlived ev'n banishment;
Whom traitorous mischief sought its earliest prey
When unto sacred blood it made its way,   10
And thereby did its black design impart
To take his head, that wounded first his heart;
You that unmoved great Charles his ruin stood,
When that three nations sunk beneath the load;
Then a young daughter lost, yet balsam found   15
To stanch that new and freshly bleeding wound,
And after this, with fixed and steady eyes,
Beheld your noble Gloucester's obsequies,

9–12: possibly alluding to the impeachment of the Queen by the
House of Commons on 23 May 1643. On 14 July 1644 she sailed for
France, never to see her husband again.

13. *great Charles his ruin:* the beheading of Charles I on 30 January
1649.

15. *a young daughter lost:* Elizabeth, Henrietta Maria's second daughter, died of a fever at Carisbrooke Castle on 8 September 1650.

18. *noble Gloucester's obsequies:* Henry, Duke of Gloucester, Henrietta
Maria's youngest son, died of smallpox in London on 13 September 1660.

And then sustained the royal princess' fall:
You only can lament her funeral.   20

   But you will hence remove, and leave behind
Our sad complaints, lost in the empty wind—
Those winds that bid you stay, and loudly roar
Destruction, and drive back unto the shore.
Shipwreck to safety, and the envy fly   25
Of sharing in this scene of tragedy,
Whilst sickness, from whose rage you post away,
Relents, and only now contrives your stay.
The lately fatal and infectious ill
Courts the fair princess, and forgets to kill.   30

   In vain on fevers curses we dispense,
And vent our passions' angry eloquence.
In vain we blast the ministers of fate,
And the forlorn physicians imprecate;
Say they to death new poisons add, and fire;   35
Murder securely for reward and hire;
Art's basilisks, that kill whome'er they see,
And truly write bills of mortality;
Who, lest the bleeding corpse should them betray,
First drain those vital speaking streams away.   40
And will you by your flight take part with these?
Become yourself a third and new disease?
If they have caused our loss, then so have you,
Who take yourself and the fair princess too.
For we, deprived, an equal damage have   45
When France doth ravish hence, as when the grave,
   But that your choice th' unkindness doth improve
   And dereliction adds unto remove.

21–30, 44–46: After arriving in England in October 1660, Henrietta
Maria (despite the plea in these lines) returned to France in January
1660/1, taking with her the "fair princess" Henrietta ("Minette"), her
youngest daughter and the future Duchess of Orleans. Their departure
was delayed by bad weather and by the Princess's ill-health.

A Rodomontade on His Cruel Mistress

[Uncertain] [*1671*]

Trust not that thing called woman: she is worse
Than all ingredients crammed into a curse.
Were she but ugly, peevish, proud, a whore,
Poxed, painted, perjured, so she were no more,
I could forgive her, and connive at this,   5
Alleging still she but a woman is.
But she is worse: in time she will forestall
The Devil, and be the damning of us all.

Against Marriage

[1675 or earlier] [Unpublished]

Out of mere love and arrant devotion,
Of marriage I'll give you this galloping notion.
  It's the bane of all business, the end of all pleasure,
The consumption of wit, youth, virtue, and treasure.
It's the rack of our thoughts, the nightmare of sleep,   5
That sets us to work before the day peep.
It makes us make brick without stubble or straw,
And a cunt has no sense of conscience or law.
  If you needs must have flesh, take the way that is noble:
In a generous wench there is nothing of trouble.   10
You come on, you come off—say, do what you please—
And the worst you can fear is but a disease,
And diseases, you know, will admit of a cure,
But the hell-fire of marriage none can endure.

7: See Exodus 5:6–19.

A Song

[Uncertain]   [*1682*]

NYMPH.

Injurious charmer of my vanquished heart,
 Canst thou feel love, and yet no pity know?
Since of myself from thee I cannot part,
 Invent some gentle way to let me go.
  For what with joy thou didst obtain,   5
   And I with more did give,
  In time will make thee false and vain,
   And me unfit to live.

SHEPHERD.

Frail angel, that wouldst leave a heart forlorn
 With vain pretense falsehood therein might lie, 10
Seek not to cast wild shadows o'er your scorn:
 You cannot sooner change than I can die.
  To tedious life I'll never fall,
   Thrown from thy dear, loved breast;
  He merits not to live at all   15
   Who cares to live unblest.

CHORUS.

Then let our flaming hearts be joined
 While in that sacred fire;
Ere thou prove false, or I unkind,
 Together both expire.   20

Epigram on Samuel Pordage

[1673 or earlier]   [*1723*]

According to an anecdote recorded about 1730 by John Boyle, fifth Earl of Orrery, the playwright Samuel Pordage, having "taken Infinite Pains" composing his tragedy *Herod and Mariamne*, "was very unwilling to lose his Labour, after the Work had not only receiv'd the approbation of Himself, but of several of his poetical Friends also. A Patron was still wanting; & after consulting some of his Acquaintances, who should have the honour of patronizing so accomplish'd a Play, It was resolv'd, nemine contradicente, that Wilmot Earl of Rochester was the most worthy of such a Favour. To This End, the Author, tho not personally, or nominally known to my Lord Rochester, waited upon him & left the Play for his Lordship's Perusal, and liv'd for some Days on the Expectation of his approaching Applause. At the Expiration of about a Week, He went a second Time to my Lord's House, where He found the Manuscript in the Hands of the Porter, with this Distick write upon the Cover of It":

> Poet, whoe'er thou art, God damn thee;
> Go hang thyself, and burn thy *Mariamne*.

On Rome's Pardons

[Uncertain]   [*c. Sept. 1680*]

> If Rome can pardon sins, as Romans hold,
> And if those pardons can be bought and sold,
> It were no sin t' adore and worship gold.
>
> If they can purchase pardons with a sum
> For sins they may commit in time to come,
> And for sins past, 'tis very well for Rome.

At this rate they are happiest that have most:
They'll purchase heaven at their own proper cost.
Alas, the poor! All that are so are lost.

Whence came this knack, or when did it begin?   10
What author have they, or who brought it in?
Did Christ e'er keep a customhouse for sin?

Some subtle devil, without more ado,
Did certainly this sly invention brew
To gull 'em of their souls and money too.   15

Works Cited by Cue Titles in the Notes

SECONDARY SOURCES

ARP
David M. Vieth, *Attribution in Restoration Poetry: A Study of Rochester's "Poems" of 1680*, Yale Studies in English 153, New Haven and London, Yale University Press, 1963.

Case
Arthur E. Case, *A Bibliography of English Poetical Miscellanies 1521–1750*, Oxford, The Bibliographical Society, 1935.

Day and Murrie
Cyrus Lawrence Day and Eleanore Boswell Murrie, *English Song-Books 1651–1702*, Oxford, The Bibliographical Society, 1940.

Gyldenstolpe
Bror Danielsson and David M. Vieth, eds., *The Gyldenstolpe Manuscript Miscellany of Poems by John Wilmot, Earl of Rochester, and other Restoration Authors*, Stockholm Studies in English XVII (Acta Universitatis Stockholmiensis), Stockholm, Almqvist & Wiksell, 1967.

Lord, *POAS, 1*

*Poems on Affairs of State: Augustan Sa-
tirical Verse 1660–1714*, Volume I:
1660–1678, ed. George deF. Lord, New
Haven and London, Yale University
Press, 1963.

Mengel, *POAS, 2*

————, Volume II: 1678–1681, ed.
Elias F. Mengel, Jr., New Haven and
London, Yale University Press, 1965.

EARLY EDITIONS OF ROCHESTER'S WORKS

(For a fuller listing of early Rochester
editions, see *ARP*, pp. 8–15, 500–06, and
also *Gyldenstolpe*, pp. 319–20. The sym-
bols in the lefthand column below are explained in *ARP*, p. 9.)

A-1680-HU

*Poems on Several Occasions By the Right
Honourable, the E. of R ———. Printed
at Antwerp, 1680.*

A-1680-PF

*Poems on Several Occasions By the Right
Honourable the E. of R —————Printed
at Antwerp, 1680.*

A-1685

*Poems on Several Occasions. Written by
a late Person of Honour. London,
Printed for A. Thorncome, and are to be
Sold by most Booksellers. 1685.*

A-1701

*Poems on Several Occasions. By the R.
H. the E. of R. London, Printed for*

A. T. and are to be Sold by most Booksellers. *1701.*

B-1691   Poems, &c. on Several Occasions: with Valentinian, a Tragedy. Written by the Right Honourable John Late Earl of Rochester. London, Printed for Jacob Tonson at the Judge's-Head in Chancery-Lane near Fleet-Street, *1691.*

C-1707-a   The Miscellaneous Works of the Right Honourable the Late Earls of Rochester And Roscommon. . . . London Printed: And sold by B. Bragge, at the Raven in Pater-Noster-Row, against Ivy-Lane. *1707.*

C-1709   The Works of the Right Honourable The Earls of Rochester, and Roscommon. . . . The Third Edition. . . . London: Printed for E. Curll, at the Peacock without Temple-Bar, *1709.*

C-1714-1   The Works Of the Earls of Rochester, Roscommon, Dorset, &c. In Two Volumes. Adorn'd with Cuts. The Fourth Edition. London: Printed for E. Curll, at the Dial and Bible against St. Dunstan's Church in Fleet-street. M.DCC.-XIV. . . .

C-1718-1   The Works Of the Earls of Rochester, Roscomon, Dorset, &c. In Two Vol-

umes. Adorn'd with Cuts. London:
Printed in the Year M.DCC.XVIII. . . .

C-1718-2   *Poems on Several Occasions, By the Earl*
                      of Roscomon, &c. With Some Memoirs
                      of his Life. Volume II. London: Printed
                      in the Year M.DCC.XVIII.

C-1735   *The Works Of the Earls of Rochester,*
                      Roscomon, and Dorset: Also those of the
                      Dukes of Devonshire, and Buckingham-
                      shire; . . . London: Printed by T.
                      Goodourl, 1735. . . .

D-1718   *Remains of the Right Honourable John,*
                      Earl of Rochester. . . . London: Printed
                      for Tho. Dryar; and sold by T. Harbin
                      in the New-Exchange in the Strand; W.
                      Chetwood at Cato's Head in Russel-
                      Court, near the Play-House; and by the
                      Booksellers of London and Westminster.
                      1718. . . .

D-1761   *The Poetical Works Of that Witty Lord*
                      John Earl of Rochester: . . . London:
                      Printed in the Year M DCC LXI.

                      MANUSCRIPTS

Chetham   Chetham's Library, Hunt's Bank, Man-
                      chester, England.

Edinburgh   Library of the University of Edinburgh,
                      Scotland.

Gyldenstolpe	In the Royal Library, Stockholm. MS. Vu. 69 is reproduced in full in *Gyldenstolpe*.
Huntington	Henry E. Huntington Library, San Marino, California.
Illinois	University of Illinois Library.
Lambeth	Lambeth Palace Library.
Ohio	Ohio State University Library.
Osborn	Private collection of Mr. James M. Osborn, New Haven, Connecticut.
Portland	In the library of the University of Nottingham.
Sackville (Knole)	In the County Archives, Maidstone, Kent. Sackville (Knole) MSS. 79 is classified as K. A. O: U269F24.
Taylor	Private collection of Mr. Robert H. Taylor, Princeton, New Jersey. The numbering of the Taylor MSS. is explained in *ARP*, p. 494.
Vienna	Österreichische Nationalbibliothek, Vienna.
Yale	Yale University Library. The "Yale MS." is fully described in *ARP*, Chapter 3, pp. 56–100.

Notes on the Texts, Authorship, and Dates of the Poems

p. 3   SONG (" 'Twas a dispute 'twixt heaven and earth")

TEXT.   Copy-text: Portland MS. PwV 31 in Rochester's own hand, fols. 2ʳ-2ᵛ. The original has no heading. Before l.4, "WTill" is scored out. In l. 13 the
word "powrfull," which originally appeared between
"The" and "god," has been scored out, and "Els"
has been written at the beginning of the line in the
lefthand margin. Later in this same line, a word
which appears to be "that" is partly deleted and
overwritten "his." In l. 16, "Must have" is scored
out and "Had soe" written above it.

For further·information on the text, authorship,
and other aspects of this poem, see *ARP*, Chapter 7,
pp. 204–30.

DATE.   The exact date of composition is unknown, although the old-fashioned style of the poem, reminis-
cent of Ben Jonson's lyrics, suggests an early work.
It was first published in *Welbeck Miscellany No. 2.
A Collection of Poems by Several Hands,* ed. Francis
Needham (Bungay, Suffolk, R. Clay and Sons,
1934), p. 51.

p. 4   A PASTORAL DIALOGUE BETWEEN ALEXIS
AND STREPHON ("There sighs not on the plain")

TEXT.   Copy-text: *A Pastoral Dialogue between Alexis
and Strephon, Written by the Right Honourable,
The Late Earl of Rochester, At the Bath, 1674,* London, 1682.

Departures from copy-text: 25 add] adds. 59
make] makes. These two obvious misprints have
been corrected as in the text in B-1691, p. 10, which
was evidently printed from the broadside of 1682.

AUTHORSHIP. Assigned to Rochester in the broadside of 1682, and reprinted with the same attribution in B-1691.

DATE. Although the copy-text may be correct in claiming that Rochester wrote these verses "at the Bath, 1674," their conventional character points to an earlier date of composition. They were first published in the broadside of 1682.

p. 7   A DIALOGUE BETWEEN STREPHON AND DAPHNE ("Prithee now, fond fool, give o'er")

TEXT. Copy-text: B-1691, p. 3, from which all other known texts apparently descend.

AUTHORSHIP. Attributed to Rochester in B-1691.

DATE. The date of composition is unknown. The poem was first published in B-1691.

p. 10   SONG ("Give me leave to rail at you")

TEXT. Copy-text: Yale MS., p. 136, used without verbal alteration. For other early texts, see *ARP*, pp. 414–16, and *Gyldenstolpe*, p. 336. Lady Rochester's answer is taken, with accidentals modernized, from the holograph manuscript at the University of Nottingham, Portland MS. PwV 31, fol. 12^r.

AUTHORSHIP. See *ARP*, pp. 414–16.

DATE. The poem was probably not written until after Rochester began courting his future wife at the beginning of May 1665. The initial eight lines were published in *Songs for i 2 & 3 Voyces Composed by*

Henry Bowman, [1677] (Day and Murrie 44), p. 31.

p. 11 A SONG ("Insulting beauty, you misspend")

TEXT. Copy-text: *Examen Poeticum,* 1693 (Case 172-3-a), p. ¹381, from which all other known texts apparently descend. For further information on the text and authorship of this poem, see my article, "Two Rochester Songs," *Notes and Queries,* 201 (1956), 338–39.

DATE. The date of composition is unknown. The poem was first published in *Examen Poeticum,* 1693.

p. 12 A SONG ("My dear mistress has a heart")

TEXT. Copy-text: *Miscellany, Being A Collection of Poems By several Hands,* 1685 (Case 177), p. 43.

AUTHORSHIP. Attributed to Rochester in *Miscellany,* 1685, which was edited by Aphra Behn. Reprinted with the same ascription in B-1691, p. 64.

DATE. The date of composition is unknown. The poem was first published in *Miscellany,* 1685.

p. 12 SONG ("While on those lovely looks I gaze")

TEXT. Copy-text: Yale MS., p. 151. Other texts consulted: A-1680-HU, p. 71; *A New Collection of the Choicest Songs,* 1676 (Case 161), sig. A8ʳ; Portland MS. PwV 40, p. 64; Gyldenstolpe MS., p. 177; Harvard MS. Eng. 636F, p. 67. For additional early texts, see *ARP,* pp. 429–31.
  Departures from copy-text: 13 betide] beside.

AUTHORSHIP.   See *ARP*, pp. 429–31.

DATE.   The exact date of composition is unknown. The poem was first published in *A New Collection,* which was licensed 28 April 1676 and advertised in the *Term Catalogues* on 12 June 1676.

p. 13   SONG ("At last you'll force me to confess")

TEXT.   Copy-text: Portland MS. PwV 31 in Rochester's own hand, fol. 3ʳ. In l. 5, between "spare" and "A," the word "the" is scored out.

A variant version of this song, perhaps descended from a separate authorial draft, was first printed in *Examen Poeticum,* 1693 (Case 172-3-a), p. ¹424:

> Too late, alas! I must confess
>   You need no arts to move me:
> Such charms by nature you possess,
>   'Twere madness not to love ye.
>
> Then spare a heart you may surprise,
>   And give my tongue the glory
> To boast, though my unfaithful eyes
>   Betray a kinder story.

The 1693 text is headed "Another Song In Imitation of Sir *John Eaton's* Songs" and is preceded by "A Song by Sir *John Eaton*" ("Tell me not I my time mispend").

For further information on the text and authorship of Rochester's lyric, see *ARP*, Chapter 7, pp. 204–30, and my article, "Two Rochester Songs," *Notes and Queries, 201* (1956), 338–39.

DATE.   The exact date of composition is unknown. The poem was first published in *A New Collection of the Choicest Songs,* 1676 (Case 161), sig. A8ʳ, which was licensed 28 April 1676 and advertised in the *Term Catalogues* on 12 June 1676.

p. 14 WOMAN'S HONOR ("Love bade me hope, and I obeyed")

TEXT. Copy-text: A-1680-HU, p. 66, used without verbal alteration. For other early texts, see *ARP*, pp. 421–22, and *Gyldenstolpe*, p. 335.

AUTHORSHIP. See *ARP*, pp. 421–22.

DATE. The exact date of composition is unknown. The poem was first published in A-1680-HU.

p. 15 THE SUBMISSION ("To this moment a rebel, I throw down my arms")

TEXT. Copy-text: Gyldenstolpe MS., p. 165, used without verbal alteration. Yale MS., p. 144, is verbally identical except for the heading. For other early texts, see *ARP*, pp. 423–24, and *Gyldenstolpe*, pp. 335–36.

AUTHORSHIP. See *ARP*, pp. 423–24.

DATE. The exact date of composition is unknown. The poem was first published in A-1680-HU, p. 67.

p. 16 WRITTEN IN A LADY'S PRAYER BOOK ("Fling this useless book away")

TEXT. Copy-text: *Familiar Letters: Written by the Right Honourable John late Earl of Rochester. And several other Persons of Honour and Quality*, London, 1697, *1*, 173. The division into two poems, corresponding to the two lyrics of the French original, is introduced in the reprinting of the poem in *A Collection of Miscellany Poems, Letters, &c. By Mr. Brown, &c.*, 1699 (Case 216), p. 85. The heading is adapted from the letter written by Tom Brown which presents these verses.

AUTHORSHIP. See the article by Wilson cited in the headnote. The verses are also attributed to Rochester in the text of 1699.

DATE. The date of composition is unknown. These lines were first published in *Familiar Letters*, 1697.

p. 17 THE DISCOVERY ("Celia, the faithful servant you disown")

TEXT. Copy-text: B-1691, p. 19. Other text consulted: *A Collection of Poems, Written upon several Occasions, By several Persons*, 1672 (Case 151), p. ²57. (B-1691 is the basis for the line-order and the readings of ll. 13–28, the text of 1672 for the readings of ll. 1–12 and 29–36).

Departures from copy-text: 1 the] that. 2 unknown] his own. 9] Now Love with a tumultuous train invades. 10 this hallowed shade] those hallowed shades. 12 winter's] winter. 31 contrived] designed. 33 those] the. 34 death affords to every wretch] every wretch enjoys in death. 35 attends] attend.

AUTHORSHIP. Attributed to Rochester in B-1691.

DATE. Composed prior to its first publication in Hobart Kemp's *A Collection of Poems*, 1672, which was entered in the *Stationers' Register* on 28 October 1671 and advertised in the *Term Catalogues* on 7 February 1671/2.

p. 18 THE ADVICE ("All things submit themselves to your command")

TEXT. Copy-text: B-1691, p. 16. Other text consulted: *A Collection of Poems, Written upon several Occasions, By several Persons,* 1672 (Case 151), p. ²60.

Departures from copy-text: 10 subjecting] subjected. 25 their loved sea, for ev'n streams have] the loved sea, for streams have their. 29 with rage, break down] break down with rage. 30 the flowers] and flowers. 33–38] *lacking; supplied from the 1672 text with correction in l. 35 of an apparent misprint,* citadels *for* citadel.

AUTHORSHIP. Attributed to Rochester in B-1691.

DATE. Composed prior to its first publication in Hobart Kemp's *A Collection of Poems,* 1672, which was entered in the *Stationers' Register* on 28 October 1671 and advertised in the *Term Catalogues* on 7 February 1671/2.

p. 20 UNDER KING CHARLES II'S PICTURE ("I, John Roberts, writ this same")

TEXT. Copy-text: B. M. Harl. MS. 7316, fol. 23ᵛ. For further information on the text and authorship of these verses, see *ARP*, Chapter 7, especially pp. 229–30.

DATE. The date of composition is unknown. The poem was first printed by Vivian de Sola Pinto in *Poems by John Wilmot, Earl of Rochester* (London, Routledge and Kegan Paul, 1953), p. xlv.

p. 20   RHYME TO LISBON ("A health to Kate")

TEXT.   Copy-text: B. M. Add. MS. 29921, fol. 3ᵛ, used without verbal alteration. The heading, lacking in the copy-text, is supplied from the version of the poem in *A Choice Collection of Poetry*, 1738 (Case 417-1), p. 61.

The anecdote in the headnote can be found in the copy-text and, more elaborately, accompanying the text in *The Agreeable Companion*, 1745 (Case 447), p. 342.

AUTHORSHIP.   Attributed to Rochester in B. M. Add. MS. 29921, in *A Choice Collection of Poetry*, 1738, and in *The Agreeable Companion*, 1745.

DATE.   The date of composition is unknown. The poem was apparently first published in *A Choice Collection of Poetry*, 1738.

p. 21   IMPROMPTU ON LOUIS XIV ("Lorraine you stole; by fraud you got Burgundy")

TEXT.   Copy-text: *The Agreeable Companion*, 1745 (Case 447), p. 344, from which the anecdote in the headnote is also taken.

AUTHORSHIP.   Attributed to Rochester in the copy-text, in Bodl. MS. Tanner 89, fol. 261ʳ, and in Bodl. MS. Sancroft 53, p. 39. This evidence is reinforced by the congruence of the apparent date of the poem with the date of Rochester's visit to Paris in 1669.

DATE.   See headnote. The couplet was apparently first published in *The Agreeable Companion*, 1745.

p. 22   ROCHESTER EXTEMPORE ("And after singing Psalm the Twelfth")

> TEXT.   Copy-text: Osborn MS. Chest II, Number 14, p. 1200, which is the only text known to have survived.

> AUTHORSHIP.   Attributed to Rochester in the copy-text.

> DATE.   Dated 1670 in the copy-text.

p. 22   SPOKEN EXTEMPORE TO A COUNTRY CLERK . . . ("Sternhold and Hopkins had great qualms")

> TEXT.   Copy-text: C-1709, p. ^{2}75, used without verbal alteration. It seems impossible to determine which of several surviving versions of this impromptu is most nearly authentic.

> AUTHORSHIP.   Attributed to Rochester in C-1709 and sources descended from it; *A Choice Collection of Poetry*, 1738 (Case 417-1), p. 61; B. M. Harl. MS. 7316, fol. 18^r; Bodl. MS. Add. B. 105, fol. 32^r.

> DATE.   The date of composition is unknown. The poem was apparently first published in C-1709.

p. 23   TO MY MORE THAN MERITORIOUS WIFE ("I am, by fate, slave to your will")

> TEXT.   Copy-text: *The Museum: or, The Literary and Historical Register*, Vol. III, No. XXXI (23 May 1747), p. 156, used without verbal alteration. Independently descended versions appear in B. M.

Harl. MS. 7316, fol. 12ʳ, and in *The Literary Magazine: or, Universal Review: From January to August,* London, 1758, p. 24. The quotation in the headnote comes from the text of 1758.

AUTHORSHIP.   The poem is attributed to Rochester in all three surviving versions. In *The Museum,* 1747, it is printed as one of seven authentic letters from Rochester to his wife and son.

DATE.   Probably these verses were written after Rochester's marriage on 29 January 1666/7. They seem not to have reached print until 1747.

p. 24   LETTER FROM MISS PRICE TO LORD CHESTERFIELD ("These are the gloves that I did mention")

TEXT.   Copy-text: B. M. Add. MS. 19253 (Chesterfield's letterbook). The verses are set off from Miss Price's comment by two long horizontal strokes of the pen, apparently signifying that they were an enclosure in the original letter.

AUTHORSHIP.   See Miss Price's statement quoted in the headnote. This poem may be one of the many lampoons on her which Grammont claims Rochester wrote.

DATE.   Composed before 4 December 1673, when Miss Price relinquished her position as Maid of Honor to marry a certain Alexander Stanhope, doubtless a relative of Chesterfield. She died, probably in childbirth, and was buried in Westminster Abbey on 23 October 1674 (*Angliae Notitia, Calen-*

dar of Treasury Books, Calendar of State Papers,
Domestic Series, *passim; Westminster Abbey Regis-*
ters, ed. Joseph Lemuel Chester, London, 1876, p.
11). Rochester's poem was published in *Letters of*
Philip, Second Earl of Chesterfield (London, 1834),
pp. 136–37, and in *Philip Stanhope, Second Earl of*
Chesterfield (London, Fanfrolico, [1930]), n. p.

p. 25   THE PLATONIC LADY ("I could love thee till I
die")

TEXT.   Copy-text: Bodl. MS. Add. A. 301, p. 24,
which is the only text of this lyric known to have
survived. In l. 13, where the word "will" is scored
out and "she'd" written above it, the context requires the deleted reading; evidently the copyist
misunderstood the condensed syntax of the line. The
division into four stanzas is not present in the manuscript but seems clearly called for.

AUTHORSHIP.   According to the Bodleian manuscript,
the poem is "By Lord Rochester."

DATE.   There is no evidence of the date of composition, although the relatively clumsy syntax of this
song suggests an early work. It was first published
by John Hayward in *Collected Works of John*
Wilmot, Earl of Rochester (London, Nonesuch
Press, 1926), p. 142.

p. 26   SONG ("As Chloris full of harmless thought")

TEXT.   Copy-text: *Corydon and Cloris or, The*
Wanton Sheepherdess, [?1676]. This broadside version, evidently the earliest printing of the poem, is

prefaced by ten lines and followed by eight more which do not occur in any other independently descended text. Since they are transparently an attempt to provide the poem with a moralistic conclusion, they can be dismissed as probably spurious. Other texts consulted: *The Wits Academy: or, The Muses Delight*, London, 1677 (not in Case), p. ²115; *The Last and Best Edition of New Songs*, 1677 (Case 163), sig. B3ʳ; *New Ayres and Dialogues*, 1678 (Day and Murrie 46), p. 14; *Choice Ayres & Songs*, 1679 (Day and Murrie 48), p. 8; A-1680-HU, p. 58; A-1680-PF, p. 58; B. M. Sloane MS. 1009, fol. 389ᵛ. For additional early texts, see *ARP*, pp. 407–10.

Departures from copy-text: *Heading* Song] Corydon and Cloris or, The Wanton Sheepherdess.

AUTHORSHIP.   See *ARP*, pp. 407–10.

DATE.   This song seems to have been printed at least three separate times in 1676. Although the undated broadside *Corydon and Cloris* is often assigned to 1677 (*ARP*, p. 497), it refers to "a pleasant Playhouse new Tune: Or, *Amorett* and *Phillis*." The reference is apparently to the song "As Amoret with Phillis sat" in *The Man of Mode*, produced 11 March 1675/6; hence the broadside was probably published during the months immediately following. According to its title page, *The Wits Academy*, 1677, was licensed 10 April 1676. Similarly, *The Last and Best Edition of New Songs*, 1677, was licensed 20 November 1676 and advertised in the *Term Catalogues* on 22 November. Rochester may, of course, have composed this lyric as late as spring of 1676, but its relatively conventional character suggests that it is an early poem.

p. 27 SONG ("Fair Chloris in a pigsty lay")

TEXT. Copy-text: Gyldenstolpe MS., p. 169. Other texts consulted: Portland MS. PwV 40, p. 60; Harvard MS. Eng. 636F, p. 77; Osborn MS. Chest II, Number 32; Yale MS., p. 133; A-1680-HU, p. 61; D-1718, p. 70. For additional early texts, see *ARP*, pp. 413–14.

Departures from copy-text: 26 slave] swain.

AUTHORSHIP. See *ARP*, pp. 413–14.

DATE. The exact date of composition is unknown. The poem was first published in A-1680-HU.

p. 31 SONG ("What cruel pains Corinna takes")

TEXT. Copy-text: A-1680-HU, p. 65, and the Yale MS., p. 140, which are verbally identical. Other texts consulted: Portland MS. PwV 40, p. 56, and Gyldenstolpe MS., p. 174. For additional early texts, see *ARP*, pp. 420–21.

Departures from copy-text: 3 one] a.

AUTHORSHIP. See *ARP*, pp. 420–21.

DATE. The exact date of composition is unknown. The poem was first published in A-1680-HU.

p. 32 SONG ("Phyllis, be gentler, I advise")

TEXT. Copy-text: A-1680-HU, p. 65, Yale MS., p. 139, Edinburgh MS. DC.1.3, p. 67, and Victoria and Albert Museum MS. Dyce 43, p. 107, which are

verbally identical. Portland MS. PwV 40, p. 62, and
Gyldenstolpe MS., p. 176, are verbally identical except for the heading. For other early texts, see *ARP*,
pp. 418–20.

AUTHORSHIP.   See *ARP*, pp. 418–20.

DATE.   The exact date of composition is unknown.
The poem was first published in A-1680-HU.

p. 33   EPISTLE ("Could I but make my wishes insolent")

TEXT.   Copy-text: Portland MS. PwV 31 in Rochester's own hand, fols. 7ʳ–7ᵛ. The original has no
heading. At the beginning of l. 19, "That not the
humble" has been scored out and "Regardless of
my" written above it; then "my" has been scored
out and "A" written after it. Later in the same line,
"of" has been scored out and "soe" written above it.
In l. 21, "from" has been scored out and "in" written
above it.

For further information on the text, authorship,
and other aspects of this poem, see *ARP*, Chapter 7,
pp. 204–30.

DATE.   The date of composition is unknown. The
poem was first published in *Welbeck Miscellany No.
2. A Collection of Poems by Several Hands*, ed.
Francis Needham (Bungay, Suffolk, R. Clay and
Sons, 1934), p. 52.

p. 34   SAB: LOST ("She yields, she yields! Pale Envy said
amen")

TEXT.   Copy-text: Portland MS. PwV 31 in Rochester's own hand, fol. 6ʳ. For further information on

the text, authorship, and circumstances surrounding the composition of this fragment, see *ARP*, Chapter 7, pp. 204–30, especially pp. 223–24.

DATE. The date of composition is unknown. The poem was first published by Vivian de Sola Pinto in *Rochester: Portrait of a Restoration Poet* (London, John Lane the Bodley Head, 1935), p. 49.

p. 34   TWO TRANSLATIONS FROM LUCRETIUS. 1. ("Great Mother of Aeneas, and of Love")

TEXT. Copy-text: Portland MS. PwV 31 in Rochester's own hand, fol. 5^r. The original has no heading. In l. 2 the fifth word, "those," has the last two letters scored out and the "o" overwritten "e." In l. 5, "orbiting" is scored out and "vast regions of" written above it. In l. 6, what was originally the second word, "borrow'd," is scored out, and "of shipps" is written above the space between "groves" and "on."

For further information on the text and authorship of the poem, see *ARP*, Chapter 7, pp. 204–30.

DATE. The date of composition is unknown. This fragment was first published by Vivian de Sola Pinto in *Poems by John Wilmot, Earl of Rochester* (London, Routledge and Kegan Paul, 1953), p. 50.

p. 35   ———. 2. ("The gods, by right of nature, must possess")

TEXT. Copy-text: B-1691, p. 109, from which all other known texts apparently descend.

Departures from copy-text: *Heading*] Lucretius

in his first Book has these Lines. [Quotation of *De Rerum Natura*, I.1–6.] Thus Translated.

AUTHORSHIP.   Attributed to Rochester in B-1691.

DATE.   The date of composition is unknown. The poem was first published in B-1691.

p. 35   TO LOVE ("O Love! how cold and slow to take my part")

TEXT.   Copy-text: Yale MS., p. 67. Other texts consulted: A-1680-HU, p. 30; A-1680-PF, p. 30; *Miscellany Poems*, 1684 (Case 172-1-a), p. [1]135; Harvard MS. Eng. 636F, p. 58; University of Illinois MS. (uncatalogued), no page number; Cambridge MS. Add. 6339, fol. 20^r; Portland MS. PwV 40, p. 53; Gyldenstolpe MS., p. 159. For additional early texts, see *ARP*, pp. 382–84, and *Gyldenstolpe*, pp. 334–35.
   Departures from copy-text: *Heading*] To Love. By ye E: of R: O! Nunquam pro me satis indignate Cupido. 7 generously] certainly. 11 thine] thy. 18 else] or. 30 mischiefs] devils. 36 By sudden blasts are snatched] Are snatched by sudden blasts. 52 led] in.

AUTHORSHIP.   See *ARP*, pp. 382–84.

DATE.   The exact date of composition is unknown. The poem was first published in A-1680-HU.

p. 37   THE IMPERFECT ENJOYMENT ("Naked she lay, clasped in my longing arms")

TEXT. Copy-text: A-1680-HU, p. 28. Other texts consulted: A-1680-PF, p. 28; Yale MS., p. 62; Harvard MS. Eng. 636F, p. 114; B. M. Harl. MS. 7312, p. 85; Edinburgh MS. DC.1.3, p. 16; Gyldenstolpe MS., p. 53. For additional early texts, see *ARP*, pp. 381–82, and *Gyldenstolpe*, p. 325.

Departures from copy-text: 7 Her] The. 12 brinks] limbs. 22 bosom] breast, "And. 38 have] has. 42 man] boy. 48 Through] By. 55 Who] That. 55 justles] ruffles. 57 rakehell] rascal. 59 stew] stews. 60 when] if. 63 a common] the common. 65 gates] goats. 68 strangury] stranguries. 69 ne'er] *om.*

AUTHORSHIP. See *ARP*, pp. 381–82, and *Gyldenstolpe*, p. 325.

DATE. The exact date of composition is unknown. The poem was first published in A-1680-HU.

p. 40   A RAMBLE IN ST. JAMES'S PARK ("Much wine had passed, with grave discourse")

TEXT. Copy-text: Gyldenstolpe MS., p. 77, used without verbal alteration. For other early texts, see *ARP*, pp. 375–77, and *Gyldenstolpe*, p. 328.

AUTHORSHIP. See *ARP*, pp. 375–77.

DATE. Mentioned, evidently as a recent composition, in the letter of 20 March 1672/3 which also gives a date for "On the Women about Town" (see p. 188). The poem was first published in A-1680-HU, p. 14.

p. 46   ON THE WOMEN ABOUT TOWN ("Too long the wise Commons have been in debate")

TEXT.   Copy-text: Bodl. MS. Don. b. 8, p. 409. Other texts consulted: Victoria and Albert Museum MS. Dyce 43, p. 223; Edinburgh MS. DC.1.3, p. 77; Edinburgh MS. DC.1.3, p. 98; Vienna MS. 14090, fol. 119^r; Huntington MS. HA 12525; Taylor MS. 1, p. 112; Taylor MS. 3, p. 103; Osborn MS. Chest II, Number 3, p. 167; *Poems on Affairs of State*, 1704 (Case 211-3-a), p. 73; C-1707-a, p. ¹10. For additional early texts, see *ARP*, pp. 377–78.

Departures from copy-text: *Heading*] Lampoone by ye Earle of Rochester. (The heading "On the Women about Town," which probably possesses no authority, is taken from the text in C-1707-a.) 11 would] will. 13 who] which. 16 tarses] tails.

AUTHORSHIP.   See *ARP*, pp. 376, 377–78.

DATE.   The text in Huntington MS. HA 12525 occurs in a postscript to a letter dated 20 March 1672/3, written from London by Godfrey Thacker to his cousin, the Earl of Huntingdon. Preceding the poem, Thacker remarks that "I send your L^d-ship a copy of verses of my Ld Rochers makeing though inferiour to those of St James his Parke" (*ARP*, p. 376). Thus Rochester apparently composed these verses immediately before the date of the letter. They were first published in *Poems on Affairs of State*, 1704.

p. 48   SONG ("Quoth the Duchess of Cleveland to counselor Knight")

TEXT. Copy-text: A-1680-HU, p. 59. Other texts consulted: A-1680-PF, p. 59; Edinburgh MS. DC.1.3, p. 110; Edinburgh MS. La.II.89, fol. 229^r; Harvard MS. Eng. 636F, p. 277; Osborn MS. Chest II, Number 3, p. 110 (a piece of this page pinned to p. 108). For additional early texts, see *ARP*, pp. 410–11.

Departures from copy-text: 1 Cleveland to counselor Knight] Cl—— to Mrs. Kn——. 2 knew I] but. 6 Where] There. 9 Aye] Ah. 12 Churchill and Jermyn] C—— and G——.

AUTHORSHIP. See *ARP*, pp. 87, 410–11.

DATE. This lampoon must have been written after 3 August 1670, when Barbara Palmer, Countess of Castlemaine, was created Duchess of Cleveland. Also, since it does not refer to her as the King's mistress, it was apparently written after October 1671, when she was supplanted in Charles's favor by the Duchess of Portsmouth. Probably the poem was in existence before Cleveland moved her residence to Paris about April 1676, after which she returned to England only occasionally. It was first published in A-1680-HU.

p. 49 THE SECOND PROLOGUE AT COURT TO "THE EMPRESS OF MOROCCO" . . . ("Wit has of late took up a trick t' appear")

TEXT. Copy-text: *The Empress of Morocco. A Tragedy . . . by Elkanah Settle*, London, 1673, sig. A3^r.
Departures from copy-text: *Heading*] The second Prologue at Court spoken by the Lady Elizabeth

Howard. 22 *The stage direction after this line,* To the King, *has been inserted from the reprinting of the poem in B-1691, p. 134.*

AUTHORSHIP. Attributed to Rochester in the 1673 quarto of the play.

DATE. Rochester's prologue was almost certainly written just prior to the Court production of the play, for the tentative dating of which see Eleanore Boswell, *The Restoration Court Stage (1660–1702)* (Cambridge, Harvard University Press, 1932), pp. 131–33. The poem was twice printed in 1673, once in the first quarto of the play and again in *A Collection of Poems Written upon several Occasions By several Persons,* 1673 (Case 151-b), p. 172.

p. 51   SONG ("Love a woman? You're an ass")

TEXT. Copy-text: A-1680-HU, p. 60. Other texts consulted: Portland MS. PwV 40, p. 66; Gyldenstolpe MS., p. 182; Harvard MS. Eng. 636F, p. 247 (misnumbered 147); B-1691, p. 44, with leaf D7 in the uncanceled state (on which see my note, "An Unsuspected Cancel in Tonson's 1691 'Rochester,'" *Papers of the Bibliographical Society of America,* 55 [1961], 130–33). For additional early texts, see *ARP,* pp. 412–13.

Departures from copy-text: 4 silliest] idlest.

AUTHORSHIP. See *ARP,* pp. 412–13.

DATE. The exact date of composition is unknown. The poem was first published in A-1680-HU.

p. 52　UPON HIS DRINKING A BOWL ("Vulcan, contrive me such a cup")

>　TEXT.　Copy-text: A-1680-HU, p. 56. Other texts consulted: Harvard MS. Eng. 636F, p. 62; Portland MS. PwV 40, p. 12; Gyldenstolpe MS., p. 87. For additional early texts, see *ARP*, pp. 405–07, and *Gyldenstolpe*, pp. 328–29.
>　　Departures from copy-text: 9 no] not.

>　AUTHORSHIP.　See *ARP*, pp. 405–07.

>　DATE.　This song must have been written later than the two military operations of summer 1673 which are mentioned in ll. 11–12. The fact that Rochester selected two examples so close to one another in date suggests that his poem was composed not long afterward, probably before the end of the year. It was first published in A-1680-HU.

p. 53　GRECIAN KINDNESS ("The utmost grace the Greeks could show")

>　TEXT.　Copy-text: B-1691, p. 24, from which all other known texts apparently descend.
>　　Departures from copy-text: *Heading*] Gecian [*sic*] Kindness. A Song.

>　AUTHORSHIP.　Attributed to Rochester in B-1691.

>　DATE.　The date of composition is unknown. The poem was first published in B-1691.

p. 54　SIGNIOR DILDO ("You ladies all of merry England")

TEXT. Copy-text: Victoria and Albert Museum MS. Dyce 43, p. 119. Other texts consulted: B. M. Harl. MS. 7317, fol. 65^v; B. M. Harl. MS. 7319, fol. 4^r; Bodl. MS. Firth C. 15, p. 10; Bodl. MS. Don. b. 8, pp. 477, 480; Portland MS. PwV 42, p. 13; Vienna MS. 14090, fol. 66^v; Ohio MS., p. 10; Taylor MS. 2, p. 9; *Poems on Affairs of State*, 1703 (Case 211-2-a), p. 188.

Departures from copy-text: 1 all] *om.* 5 This] The. 17 My] By. 49 tall] call. 59 Borgo] Pergo.

AUTHORSHIP. The poem is attributed to Rochester in B. M. Harl. MS. 7319 (in "Catalogue," fol. 382^v), Bodl. MS. Firth C. 15, Victoria and Albert Museum MS. Dyce 43, Vienna MS. 14090, Ohio MS., Taylor MS. 2, and *Poems on Affairs of State*. This evidence outweighs the single ascription to "Lord Dorset & M^r: Shepperd" in Portland MS. PwV 42.

DATE. "Signior Dildo" must have been composed shortly after Mary of Modena's arrival in London on 26 November 1673. The poem is mentioned in a letter dated 26 January 1673/4 (*Letters Addressed from London to Sir Joseph Williamson*, ed. W. D. Christie, Camden Society, 1874, 2, 132). It was first published in *Poems on Affairs of State*, 1703.

p. 60 A SATYR ON CHARLES II ("'I' th' isle of Britain, long since famous grown")

TEXT. Copy-text: Bodl. MS. Rawl. D. 924, fol. 310^v. Other texts consulted: B. M. Add. MS. 23722, fol. 16^r; B. M. Harl. MS. 7315, fol. 83^v; B. M. Harl. MS. 7317, fol. 68^v; Bodl. MS. Don. b. 8, p. 585; All Souls College, Oxford, MS. Codrington 116, fol.

12ᵛ; Victoria and Albert Museum MS. Dyce 43, p. 110; Chetham MS. Mun. A. 4. 14, p. 25; Edinburgh MS. DC.1.3, p. 71; National Library of Scotland MS. Advocate 19.1.12, fol. 49ᵛ; Vienna MS. 14090, fol. 61ʳ; Harvard MS. Eng. 636F, p. 293; Princeton MS. AM 14401, p. 319; Osborn MS. Chest II, Number 1; Taylor MS. 1, p. 107; Taylor MS. 3, p. 241; *Poems on Affairs of State*, 1697 (Case 211-1-a), p. 181. For additional early texts, see my article, "Rochester's 'Scepter' Lampoon on Charles II," *Philological Quarterly*, 37 (1958), 424–32.

Departures from copy-text: *Heading*] Given by a Mistake to His Majesty. *Order of lines*] 1–13, 32–33, 20–21, 14–19, 22–31. 3 thrive] there. 6 that wanders] to wander. 9] That as his love is great, he swives as much. 16] 'Tis sure the swaucest that did ever swive. 17 peremptoriest] peremptory. 20 Restless he] Who restless. 21] Grown impotent and scandalously poor. 25] Which made her love too well, and yet so late. 27 ballocks] buttocks. 29 costs to] cost the. 32 All monarchs I hate] I hate all monarchs.

AUTHORSHIP. See my article, cited above.

DATE. The letter quoted in the headnote seems to imply that Rochester's lampoon was written not many weeks before 20 January 1673/4. For further evidence and arguments on the date of composition, see my article. The poem was first published in *Poems on Affairs of State*, 1697.

p. 65 TIMON ("What, Timon! does old age begin t' approach")

TEXT. Copy-text: A-1680-HU, p. 105. Other texts consulted: Yale MS., p. 227; Edinburgh MS. DC.1.3, p. 56; Gyldenstolpe MS., p. 37; Harvard MS. Eng. 623F, p. 52; Harvard MS. Eng. 636F, p. 228. For additional early texts, see *ARP*, pp. 453–54, and *Gyldenstolpe*, p. 323.

Departures from copy-text: *Heading*] Satyr. (On the heading "Timon," see *ARP*, p. 272.) 16 Shadwell's] S——. 29–30] *om.; lines supplied from Harvard MS. Eng. 623F.* 64 precedes] proceeds. 77 Mosely] M——. 88 up] *om.* 93 Blount] B——. 113 Orrery] O——. 122 Etherege] E——. 126 Huff] H——. 126 Settle] S——. 154 When] If.

AUTHORSHIP. See *ARP*, pp. 281–92.

DATE. Ll. 152–54 establish the date of composition as April, May, or early June of 1674 (*ARP*, pp. 274–75). "Timon" was first published in A-1680-HU.

p. 73   TUNBRIDGE WELLS ("At five this morn, when Phoebus raised his head")

TEXT. Copy-text: Yale MS., p. 251. Other texts consulted: B. M. Add. MS. 4456, fol. 201^r; B. M. Add. MS. 34362, fol. 22^r; B. M. Harl. MS. 7312, p. 5; B. M. Lansdowne MS. 936, fol. 50^r; Bodl. MS. Douce 357, fol. 136^r; Victoria and Albert Museum MS. Dyce 43, p. 234; Lambeth Codices Manuscripti Gibsoniani 941, item 115; Edinburgh MS. DC.1.3, p. 66; Vienna MS. 14090, fol. 124^r; Harvard MS. Eng. 636F, p. 131; Osborn MS. Chest II, Number 3, p. 123; Osborn MS. Chest II, Number 13, vol. 2, p. 164; Osborn MS. Box XXII, Number 3, p. 17;

Taylor MS. 3, p. 213; *Poems on Affairs of State*, 1697 (Case 211-1-c), p. [2]218; C-1707-a, p. [1]35. For additional early texts, see *ARP*, pp. 279–81.

Departures from copy-text: *Heading*] Tunbridge Wells, A Satyr. 7 that] it. 14 But] Yet. 18 *followed by:* Grant, ye unlucky stars! this o'ergrown boy / To purchase some inspiring pretty toy / That may his want of sense and wit supply, / As buxom crab-fish does his lechery. 24 has] have. 24 *followed by:* Thrice blessed be he who dildo did invent / To ram the neighboring hole to fundament, / Which may be lengthened, thickened in its measure, / And used at lecherous ugly Trulla's pleasure; / For ne'er was bulk or stomach given to tarses / Either to fill or smell such foggy arses. 30 For] So. 39 o' th' Ceremonies] of ceremony. 44 besides] beside. 49 t' complain] to 'plain. 55 beyond] above. 63 and] or. 69 *followed by:* Importance drank too, though she'd been no sinner, / To wash away some dregs he had spewed in her. 78 daughter] daughters. 83 sempstresses] and sempstresses. 93 Is] I. 95 his] its. 96 would] could. 115 girl] girls. 131 is] *om.* 158 their] the. 163 jackanapes] jackanape. 170 they] thy.

AUTHORSHIP. See *ARP*, pp. 278–81.

DATE. Ll. 58–69, alluding to the Marvell-Parker controversy, place the composition of "Tunbridge Wells" in the spring of 1674 (*ARP*, pp. 275–78, 293). The poem was first published in *Poems on Affairs of State*, 1697.

p. 81 UPON HIS LEAVING HIS MISTRESS (" 'Tis not that I am weary grown")

TEXT. Copy-text: A-1680-HU, p. 54, and Yale MS., p. 113, which are verbally identical. For other early texts, see *ARP*, pp. 403–04, and *Gyldenstolpe*, pp. 325–26.

AUTHORSHIP. See *ARP*, pp. 403–04.

DATE. There is no evidence of the date of composition except that this lyric seems to be a mature work. It was first published in A-1680-HU.

p. 82   AGAINST CONSTANCY ("Tell me no more of constancy")

TEXT. See my article, "A New Song by Rochester," *London Times Literary Supplement*, 6 November 1953, p. 716, and the subsequent commentary by J. L. Mackie, 19 February 1954, p. 121, and Macdonald Emslie, 26 February 1954, p. 137. These publications print the three known versions of the poem, found in B. M. Add. MS. 29396, fol. 107^v; Bodl. MS. Don. b. 8, p. 561; and *A New Collection of the Choicest Songs*, 1676 (Case 161), sig. A7^r. Proper procedure seems to call for the adoption of all readings shared by at least two of the three versions, an operation sufficient in itself to establish text. The heading is taken from *A New Collection*.

AUTHORSHIP. See my article, cited above.

DATE. This lyric was first published in *A New Collection*, which was licensed 28 April 1676 and advertised in the *Term Catalogues* on 12 June 1676. The skillful technique of the poem suggests that it was composed not much earlier.

p. 83   SONG ("How happy, Chloris, were they free")

p. 84   TO A LADY IN A LETTER ("Such perfect bliss, fair Chloris, we")

TEXT.   For both versions of this lyric, as well as the versions that intervene between them, see my article, "A Textual Paradox: Rochester's 'To a Lady in a Letter,'" *Papers of the Bibliographical Society of America*, 54 (1960), 147–62, and the sequel in the same journal, "An Unsuspected Cancel in Tonson's 1691 'Rochester,'" 55 (1961), 130–33.

AUTHORSHIP.   See *ARP*, pp. 209, 424–25.

DATE.   A variant text of the final version was published in *A New Collection of the Choicest Songs*, 1676 (Case 161), which was licensed 28 April 1676 and advertised in the *Term Catalogues* on 12 June 1676. Probably neither version of the poem was composed much earlier, for it is one of Rochester's most mature lyrics. The early version first reached print in A-1680-HU, p. 68.

p. 85   SONG ("Leave this gaudy gilded stage")

TEXT.   Copy-text: Portland MS. PwV 31 in Rochester's own hand, fol. 4ʳ. The original has no heading. In l. 9, before the word "difference," the word "this" has "s" deleted and "i" overwritten "e."
        For further information on the text and authorship of this lyric, see *ARP*, Chapter 7, pp. 204–30.

DATE.   The date of composition is unknown. The poem was first published by Vivian de Sola Pinto in

Rochester: Portrait of a Restoration Poet (London, John Lane the Bodley Head, 1935), p. 120.

p. 86   THE FALL ("How blest was the created state")

Text.   Copy-text: Harvard MS. Eng. 636F, p. 66. Other texts consulted: Portland MS. PwV 40, p. 64; Gyldenstolpe MS., p. 175; Yale MS., p. 149; A-1680-HU, p. 70. For additional early texts, see *ARP*, pp. 428–29.
   Departures from copy-text: 14 nobler] noble.

Authorship.   See *ARP*, pp. 428–29.

Date.   There is no evidence of the date of composition except that this song appears to be a mature work. It was first published in A-1680-HU.

p. 87   THE MISTRESS ("An age in her embraces passed")

Text.   Copy-text: B-1691, p. 25, from which all other known texts apparently descend.
   Departures from copy-text: *Heading*] The Mistress. A Song.

Authorship.   Attributed to Rochester in B-1691.

Date.   The date of composition is unknown. The poem was first published in B-1691.

p. 88   A SONG ("Absent from thee, I languish still")

Text.   Copy-text: B-1691, p. 28, from which all other known texts apparently descend.

Authorship.   Attributed to Rochester in B-1691.

Date.   The date of composition is unknown. The poem was first published in B-1691.

p. 89 A SONG OF A YOUNG LADY TO HER
ANCIENT LOVER ("Ancient person, for whom I")

TEXT. Copy-text: B-1691, p. 32, from which all other
known texts apparently descend.

Departures from copy-text: 10 heat] heart. 18 his]
their. In this poem I have ventured two conjectural
emendations. In l. 10, "heat" carries nearly the same
denotation as "heart" (vigor) but also sustains the
metaphor of the seasons which pervades the poem.
For similar figures, see l. 20 below and "The Imperfect Enjoyment," ll. 31–32 (p. 38). The in-
sertion of the letter *r* could easily have been an over-
sight of a copyist, or even of Rochester himself.

In l. 18, something is plainly wrong with the pro-
noun "their." Possibly this reading came about because the singular form "age's" in l. 17 was misunderstood as a plural "ages'." The original may have
read simply "ages," for in the late seventeenth century the apostrophe was used only sporadically to
designate possessives. Of the three singular pronouns
which might be substituted for "their," "her" is the
wrong gender whereas "its" in this context would be
unconvincingly cacophonous. "His" does double duty
as either a neuter or a masculine singular possessive,
in its latter sense reinforcing the latent personification
of "age" as an inimical old man.

AUTHORSHIP. Attributed to Rochester in B-1691.

DATE. The date of composition is unknown. The
poem was first published in B-1691.

p. 90 LOVE AND LIFE ("All my past life is mine no
more")

TEXT. Copy-text: Gyldenstolpe MS., p. 173, used without verbal alteration. A-1680-HU, p. 69, and Yale MS., p. 148, are verbally identical with the Gyldenstolpe text except for a minor difference in the heading. For other early texts, see *ARP*, pp. 425–28, and *Gyldenstolpe*, p. 337.

AUTHORSHIP. See *ARP*, pp. 425–28.

DATE. Evidence of the exact date of composition is lacking, but the poem is clearly a product of Rochester's literary maturity. It was first published in *Songs for 1 2 & 3 Voyces Composed by Henry Bowman*, [1677] (Day and Murrie 44), p. 9.

p. 91   EPILOGUE TO "LOVE IN THE DARK" . . .
("As charms are nonsense, nonsense seems a charm")

TEXT. Copy-text: *Love in the Dark, or The Man of Bus'ness . . . By Sir Francis Fane*, London, 1675, p. [95].
Departures from copy-text: *Heading* Epilogue to *Love in the Dark*] Epilogue.

AUTHORSHIP. Although the epilogue carries no attribution in the 1675 quarto of the play, it was reprinted as Rochester's in B-1691, p. 130.

DATE. Probably composed shortly before the acting of *Love in the Dark* on 10 May 1675, and certainly after the first performance of *Psyche* on 27 February 1674/5.

p. 94   A SATYR AGAINST REASON AND MANKIND
("Were I who to my cost already am")

TEXT.   Copy-text: A-1680-HU, p. 6 (for ll. 1-173), and Bodl. MS. Add. B. 106, fol. 20ᵛ (for heading and ll. 174–221). Other texts consulted: A-1680-PF, p. 6; *A Satyr against Mankind*, [1679]; C-1707-a, p. ¹1; B. M. Harl. MS. 7312, p. 11; B. M. Sloane MS. 1458, fol. 16ʳ; B. M. Add. MS. 4456, fol. 204ʳ; B. M. Add. MS. 14047, fol. 130ʳ; B. M. Burney MS. 390, fol. 6ʳ; B. M. Lansdowne MS. 936, fol. 63ʳ; Bodl. MS. Rawl. Poet. 81, fol. 23ʳ; Bodl. MS. Rawl. Poet. 123, p. 110; Bodl. MS. Eng. Poet. d. 152, fol. 70ʳ; Bodl. MS. Eng. Poet. e. 4, p. 181; Bodl. MS. Tanner 306, fol. 414ʳ; Bodl. MS. Don. b. 8, p. 495; Cambridge MS. Add. 6339, fol. 16ʳ; Edinburgh MS. DC.1.3, p. 19 and p. 25 (should be p. 27); National Library of Scotland MS. 2201, fol. 108ʳ; Gyldenstolpe MS., p. 21; Harvard MS. Eng. 623F, p. 12; Harvard MS. Eng. 636F, p. 80; Yale MS., p. 8; Illinois MS. (uncatalogued); Osborn MS. Chest II, Number 3, p. 124; Osborn MS. Chest II, Number 28. For additional early texts, see *ARP*, pp. 370–75, and *Gyldenstolpe*, pp. 322–23.

Departures from copy-text: 20 make] makes. 32 made him] makes him. 34 that] what. 45 heart] least. 74 Patrick's] P——. 74 Sibbes' soliloquies] S—— replies. 100 which] that. 120 Meres] M——. 135 friendship] friendships. 139 and] or. 143 passions] passion. 156 from] for. 176 vanity] vanities. 194 man] men. 202 own] very. 211 clothes] dress.

AUTHORSHIP.   See *ARP*, pp. 370–75.

DATE.   The poem is inscribed "Anno. 74" in Bodl. MS. Tanner 306 and is mentioned in a letter dated 23 March 1675/6 which may imply that it was a recent composition. It was first published in broadside in June 1679 (see *ARP*, pp. 293–95, 374, 497).

p. 102 FRAGMENT ("What vain, unnecessary things are men")

Text. Copy-text: Portland MS. PwV 31 in Rochester's own hand, fols. 9ʳ, 9ᵛ, 10ʳ. The original has no heading. In l. 2, "Why wee can" has been scored out and "How well we" written above it. Ll. 8–10, 33–34, 53–54, and the word "Then" in l. 31 are lightly scored out but are plainly necessary to the sense. In l. 8, where the second word was originally "the," the "e" is overwritten with an apostrophe; later in this line, "&" is written above the original word "nay." Before l. 21, a rejected version of the line, "E're I'de endure this scorne, I live," is scored out. In l. 28, "and" has been scored out and "to" written above it, but the original "gave" has not been altered to "give" as the sense requires. After l. 32 appears the apparently unnecessary word "a." In l. 33, above "wee dayly" are written two illegible words. In ll. 36, 37, 38, and 40, the concluding letters of the words "hereby," "suppose," "clothes," and "deserve" have been removed by trimming of the leaf. In l. 44, "hardly" has been scored out and "meanly" written above it. In l. 48, "honour'd" has been scored out and "worshipt" written above it. In l. 52, Rochester actually wrote "Atheist" rather than the plural form he obviously intended.

For further information on the text, authorship, and date of this satirical fragment, see *ARP*, Chapter 7, pp. 204–30.

DATE. The date of composition is unknown. The opening lines of the poem were first published by Vivian de Sola Pinto in *Rochester: Portrait of a Restoration Poet* (London, John Lane the Bodley Head, 1935), p. 144; the entire fragment was first printed by Pinto in *Poems by John Wilmot, Earl of Rochester* (London, Routledge and Kegan Paul, 1953), p. 116.

p. 104 A LETTER FROM ARTEMISIA IN THE TOWN TO CHLOE IN THE COUNTRY ("Chloe, in verse by your command I write")

TEXT. Copy-text: Bodl. MS. Don. b. 8, p. 490. Other texts consulted: B. M. Add. MS. 27408, fols. 8ᵛ, 10ᵛ; Bodl. MS. Rawl. Poet. 123, pp. 108–09, 116–23; Bodl. MS. Rawl. Poet. 152, fol. 50ʳ; Bodl. MS. North b. 24, fol. 60ʳ; Cambridge MS. Add. 29, fol. 33ʳ; Cambridge MS. Add. 6339, fol. 4ʳ; Victoria and Albert Museum MS. Dyce 43, p. 61; Portland MS. PwV 46, p. 11; Edinburgh MS. DC.1.3, p. 60; Vienna MS. 14090, fol. 35ᵛ; Gyldenstolpe MS., p. 5; Yale MS., p. 45; Harvard MS. Eng. 623F, p. 1; Harvard MS. Eng. 636F, p. 20; Folger MS. M. b. 12, fol. 10ᵛ; Huntington MS. Ellesmere 8793; *Artemisa to Cloe. A Letter from a Lady in the Town, to a Lady in the Country; Concerning The Loves of the Town: By a Person of Quality*, London, 1679; *A Letter From Artemiza in the Town, to Chloë in the Country. By a Person of Honour,* [1679]; A-1680-HU, p. 19; A-1680-PF, p. 19; B-1691, p. 65; *Poems on Affairs of State,* 1698 (Case 215), p. 25. For additional early texts, see *ARP*, pp. 378–81, and *Gyldenstolpe*, pp. 321–22.

Departures from copy-text: 19 you] you're. 25 convinced] convin'd. 28 Like . . . like] As . . . as. 29 'Cause 'tis the very worst thing] Because 'tis the worst thing that. 34 intrigues] intrigue. 76 his will] her will. 112 And] But. 112 hide our] hide their. 147 think] know. 173 interest] interesse. 196 looks] look. 196 bed] head. 200 away] his way *alternative reading*. 239 a love] alone. 254 contrived] provides.

AUTHORSHIP. See *ARP*, pp. 378–81.

DATE. On the date of composition, see *ARP*, pp. 293–94. The poem was twice published in broadside in 1679.

p. 113   A VERY HEROICAL EPISTLE IN ANSWER TO EPHELIA ("If you're deceived, it is not by my cheat")

TEXT. Copy-text: Yale MS., p. 344. Other texts consulted: B. M. Egerton MS. 2623, fol. 79^r; Bodl. MS. Don. b. 8, p. 602; Portland MS. PwV 40, p. 34; Edinburgh MS. DC.1.3, p. 23; Gyldenstolpe MS., p. 123; Huntington MS. Ellesmere 8736; Osborn MS. Chest II, Number 14, p. 1181; *A Very Heroical Epistle from My Lord All-Pride to Dol-Common*, 1679; A-1680-HU, p. 140. For additional early texts, see *ARP*, pp. 468–70, and *Gyldenstolpe*, p. 331.

Departures from copy-text: 38 canopies] canopy. 39 crouching] crowding. 50 dares] does.

AUTHORSHIP. See *ARP*, pp. 346–48.

DATE. Probably composed soon after Mulgrave's duel with Percy Kirke on 4 July 1675 (*ARP*, pp. 338–39). The poem was first published in the broadside of 1679.

p. 116 THE DISABLED DEBAUCHEE ("As some brave admiral, in former war")

TEXT. Copy-text: Yale MS., p. 71. Other texts consulted: A-1680-HU, p. 32; A-1680-PF, p. 32; B-1691, p. 100; B. M. Add. MS. 14047, fol. 130ᵛ; B. M. Add. MS. 23722, fol. 52ʳ; Bodl. MS. Rawl. Poet. 81, fol. 22ʳ; Bodl. MS. Eng. Poet. e. 4, p. 187; Bodl. MS. Don. b. 8, p. 409; Sackville (Knole) MSS. 79; Edinburgh MS. DC.1.3, p. 77; Gyldenstolpe MS., p. 47; Harvard MS. Eng. 636F, p. 1; Osborn MS. Chest II, Number 3, p. 178. For additional early texts, see *ARP*, pp. 384–85, and *Gyldenstolpe*, p. 324.

Departures from copy-text: *Heading*] Upon His Lying In and Could not Drink. 3] Soon as two rival fleets appear from far. 9 fire] ire. 11 Transported, thinks himself] Thinks at each sound he is. 19 When] While. 25 any] hopeful. 26 from his fair inviter meanly] meanly from his fair inviter. 30 night-] night's. 40 fucked] used. 46 action] danger.

AUTHORSHIP. See *ARP*, pp. 384–85, and *Gyldenstolpe*, p. 324.

DATE. The text in B. M. Add. MS. 23722 dates the poem 1675, which is plausible. It was first published in A-1680-HU.

p. 118 UPON NOTHING ("Nothing! thou elder brother even to Shade")

TEXT. Copy-text: Bodl. MS. Tanner 306, fol. 410^r. Other texts consulted: B. M. Add. MS. 4457, fol. 43^r; B. M. Add. MS. 29497, fol. 48^r; B. M. Add. MS. 30162, fol. 1^v; Bodl. MS. Rawl. Poet. 90, fol. 106^r; Bodl. MS. Add. B. 106, fol. 19^v; Bodl. MS. Don. b. 8, p. 654; Cambridge MS. Add. 6339, fol. 12^r; Lambeth Codices Manuscripti Gibsoniani 941, item 116; Portland MS. PwV 40, p. 51; Edinburgh MS. DC.1.3, p. 11; Gyldenstolpe MS., p. 153; Harvard MS. Eng. 623F (bound volume), p. 10; Harvard MS. Eng. 623F (loose sheet); Harvard MS. Eng. 636F, p. 55; Yale MS., p. 108; uncatalogued Illinois MS.; Osborn MS. Chest II, Number 4, p. 25; Osborn MS. Chest II, Number 13, vol. 2, p. 173; Osborn MS. Box LXXXIX, Number 13; *Upon Nothing. A Poem. By a Person of Honour*, [1679] ("Light" version); *Upon Nothing A Poem. By a Person of Honour*, [1679] ("Life" version); A-1680-HU, p. 51; *The Works Of His Grace, George Villiers, Late Duke of Buckingham*, London, 1715, *1*, 149. For additional early texts, see *ARP*, pp. 399–403, and *Gyldenstolpe*, pp. 333–34.

Departures from copy-text: 10 mighty] *om.* 16 Time] *word illegible.* 17 with] all. 17 these] *word partly illegible: probably* these *or* those. 40 weighty] mighty. 48 Spaniards'] Spanish.

AUTHORSHIP. See *ARP*, pp. 399–403.

DATE. Evidence of the exact date of composition is lacking, although a note appended to the text in

Osborn MS. Chest II, Number 13 shows that the poem was in existence by 14 May 1678. It was first published in the two broadsides of 1679.

p. 120 AN ALLUSION TO HORACE . . . ("Well, sir, 'tis granted I said Dryden's rhymes")

TEXT.   Copy-text: Yale MS., p. 87. Other texts consulted: B. M. Sloane MS. 655, fol. 51^r; B. M. Sloane MS. 1504, fol. 69^r; B. M. Add. MS. 18220, fol. 121^r; B. M. Add. MS. 34362, fol. 84^r; B. M. Harl. MS. 6947, fol. 199^r; Bodl. MS. Add. B. 106, fol. 5^r (heading and ll. 1–85 only); Cambridge MS. Add. 42, fol. 106^r; Cambridge MS. Add. 6339, fol. 13^r; Portland MS. PwV 40, p. 40; Gyldenstolpe MS., p. 145; Harvard MS. Eng. 623F, p. 28; Harvard MS. Eng. 636F, p. 40; Illinois MS. 30 Je 45 Stonehill, p. 209; Osborn MS. Chest II, Number 14, p. 974; A-1680-HU, p. 40; A-1680-PF, p. 40; C-1707-a, p. ^{1}18. For additional early texts, see *ARP*, pp. 386–90, and *Gyldenstolpe*, p. 333.

Departures from copy-text: *Heading and* 1–4] *removed by excision of a leaf. The missing lines are supplied from the other texts, eight of which agree with ll. 1–4 as printed; the heading follows the form which appears most frequently in these texts.* 14 assembling] assembled. 29 morosest] morosists. 35 Cowley imitates] imitates Cowley. 109 in] of. 117 censures] censure.

AUTHORSHIP.   See *ARP*, pp. 139–56, 386–90.

DATE.   Composed during the last few months of 1675 or the first few weeks of 1676 (*ARP*, pp. 156–59). The poem was first published in A-1680-HU.

p. 129 DIALOGUE ("When to the King I bid good morrow")

> TEXT. Copy-text: Victoria and Albert Museum MS. Dyce 43, p. 26, used without verbal alteration. For other early texts, see *ARP*, pp. 489–90.

> AUTHORSHIP. See *ARP*, pp. 489–90.

> DATE. Since l. 15 calls Mazarin "that new pretender," the poem must have been written soon after her arrival in England in December 1675.

p. 130 TO THE POSTBOY ("Son of a whore, God damn you! can you tell")

> TEXT. Copy-text: B. M. Harl. MS. 6914, fol. 21^r, and Vienna MS. 14090, fol. 128^r, which are verbally identical. For other early texts, see *ARP*, pp. 199–200.

> AUTHORSHIP. See *ARP*, pp. 199–203.

> DATE. Probably composed shortly after the death of Downs on 27 June 1676 (*ARP*, pp. 142–43, 200–01). For the publication history of the poem, see *ARP*, p. 201.

p. 132 ON THE SUPPOSED AUTHOR OF A LATE POEM IN DEFENCE OF SATYR ("To rack and torture thy unmeaning brain")

> TEXT. Copy-text: A-1680-HU, p. 49. Other texts consulted: Portland MS. PwV 40, p. 48; Portland MS. PwV 509; Edinburgh MS. DC.1.3, p. 13; Gyldenstolpe MS., p. 141; Harvard MS. Eng. 623F, p.

37; Harvard MS. Eng. 636F, p. 51; Yale MS., p. 102; Osborn MS. Chest II, Number 14, p. 1021; *A Collection of Poems By Several Hands,* 1693 (Case 151-c), p. 111; C-1707-a, p. [1]12. For additional early texts, see *ARP*, pp. 394–96, and *Gyldenstolpe*, p. 333.

Departures from copy-text: 7 are some] were some. 9 those] these.

AUTHORSHIP. See *ARP*, pp. 139–56, 394–96, and *Gyldenstolpe*, p. 333.

DATE. See *ARP*, pp. 160–63. The poem was first published in A-1680-HU.

p. 134 **IMPROMPTU ON CHARLES II** ("God bless our good and gracious King")

TEXT. Copy-text: B. M. Harl. MS. 6914, fol. 8[v], Victoria and Albert Museum MS. Dyce 43, p. 59, and Vienna MS. 14090, fol. 35[r], which are verbally identical; none of these three texts provides a heading. It seems impossible to determine which of the many surviving versions of this impromptu is most nearly authentic.

The heading "Posted on *White-Hall-Gate*" is from the text in C-1707-a, p. [3]135. Hearne's anecdote is in *Reliquiae Hearnianae*, ed. Philip Bliss, 2d ed. (London, 1869), *1,* 119–20. The third account, here given in modern spelling, introduces the text in the Vienna MS.; similar accounts precede the Harleian and Dyce texts.

AUTHORSHIP. Attributed to Rochester in C-1707-a and sources descended from it; *Reliquiae Hearnianae;*

Sepulchrorum Inscriptiones, 1727 (Case 346-2), p. 76; *The Agreeable Companion,* 1745 (Case 447), p. 354; Folger MS. 4108; C. Plumptre's commonplace book, in the Folger Library; and the three manuscripts used as copy-text. These sources may not all be independently descended.

DATE. The date of composition is unknown. The poem was first published in C-1707-a.

p. 135   IMPROMPTU ON THE ENGLISH COURT ("Here's Monmouth the witty")

TEXT. Copy-text: *The Agreeable Companion,* 1745 (Case 447), p. 341, used without verbal alteration; no heading is included. It seems impossible to determine which of the many surviving versions of this impromptu is most nearly authentic.

The quotation in the headnote introduces the text in *Reliquiae Hearnianae,* ed. Philip Bliss, 2d ed. (London, 1869), *1,* 119. A similar, though much more elaborate, account occurs in the copy-text.

AUTHORSHIP. Attributed to Rochester in *The Agreeable Companion,* 1745; *Reliquiae Hearnianae;* B.M. Add. MS. 29921, fol. 3^v; B. M. Harl. MS. 7316, fol. 18^r; Chetham MS. Mun. A. 4. 14, p. 127.

DATE. The text in Osborn MS. Chest II, Number 14, p. 873 (which carries no ascription) dates the poem 1676. It was apparently first published in *The Agreeable Companion,* 1745.

p. 136   THE MOCK SONG ("I swive as well as others do")

TEXT. Copy-text: A-1680-HU, p. 75, used without verbal alteration. For other early texts, see *ARP*, pp. 436–37, and *Gyldenstolpe*, pp. 331–32. The text of Scroope's lyric is taken from *Choice Ayres & Songs To Sing to the Theorbo-Lute or Bass-Viol*, 1679 (Day and Murrie 48), p. 8.

AUTHORSHIP AND DATE. For the authorship and date of composition of Scroope's lyric and Rochester's burlesque, see Chapter 8 of *ARP*, pp. 231–38. "The Mock Song" was first published in A-1680-HU.

p. 137 ON CARY FRAZIER ("Her father gave her dildoes six")

TEXT. Copy-text: Osborn MS. Chest II, Number 14, p. 1094, the only known text.
   Departures from copy-text: *Heading*] Upon Betty Frazer 1677.

AUTHORSHIP AND DATE. Ascribed to Rochester and dated 1677 in the Osborn manuscript. For a fuller discussion of this squib, see *ARP*, pp. 237–38, where it was published for the first time.

p. 137 ON MRS. WILLIS ("Against the charms our ballocks have")

TEXT. Copy-text: Gyldenstolpe MS., p. 157, used without verbal alteration. For other early texts, see *ARP*, pp. 433–34, and *Gyldenstolpe*, p. 334.

AUTHORSHIP. See *ARP*, pp. 433–34.

DATE. The exact date of composition is unknown. The poem was first published in A-1680-HU, p. 73.

p. 139   SONG ("By all love's soft, yet mighty powers")

TEXT.   Copy-text: A-1680-HU, p. 72. Other text consulted: Harvard MS. Eng. 636F, p. 69. For additional early texts, see *ARP*, p. 431.
    Departures from copy-text: 13 wise] kind.

AUTHORSHIP.   See *ARP*, p. 431.

DATE.   The exact date of composition is unknown.
The poem was first published in A-1680-HU.

p. 140   EPILOGUE TO "CIRCE" ("Some few, from wit,
have this true maxim got")

TEXT.   Copy-text: *Circe, a Tragedy . . . By Charles
D'Avenant,* London, 1677, p. [59].
    Departures from copy-text: *Heading*] The Epi-
logue, By the Earl of Rochester.

AUTHORSHIP.   Attributed to Rochester in the 1677
quarto of the play.

DATE.   Almost certainly written just prior to the first
performance of the play.

p. 141   ON POET NINNY ("Crushed by that just contempt
his follies bring")

TEXT.   Copy-text: Osborn MS. Chest II, Number 14,
p. 1182, and Huntington MS. Ellesmere 8737,
which are verbally identical. For other early texts,
see *ARP*, pp. 470–71, and *Gyldenstolpe*, p. 331.

AUTHORSHIP.   See *ARP*, pp. 348–49.

DATE.   For the conclusion that "On Poet Ninny" is
Rochester's "verses on Sir Car. Scroope at large"
mentioned in a letter of 25 April 1678 from John

Verney to Sir Ralph Verney, see *ARP*, pp. 348–49. The poem was first published in A-1680-HU, p. 143.

p. 142 MY LORD ALL-PRIDE ("Bursting with pride, the loathed impostume swells")

> TEXT.   Copy-text: Yale MS., p. 350. Other texts consulted: B. M. Egerton MS. 2623, fol. 80ᵛ; Portland MS. PwV 40, p. 37; Portland MS. PwV 513; Edinburgh MS. DC.1.3, p. 24; Gyldenstolpe MS., p. 129; Huntington MS. Ellesmere 8738; Osborn MS. Chest II, Number 14, p. 1183; *A Very Heroical Epistle from My Lord All-Pride to Dol-Common*, 1679; A-1680-HU, p. 144; A-1680-PF, p. 144. For additional early texts, see *ARP*, pp. 471–72, and *Gyldenstolpe*, p. 331.
>
> Departures from copy-text: 8 rake] take. 30 makes] make.

> AUTHORSHIP.   See *ARP*, pp. 348, 349–50.

> DATE.   Although "My Lord All-Pride" is possibly an answer to Mulgrave's "An Essay upon Satyr," the circumstances of its first publication in the broadside of 1679 argue that it antedates Mulgrave's lampoon, which was not put into circulation until shortly before 21 November 1679 (*ARP*, pp. 340–41). Its resemblances to "On Poet Ninny" in style and structure suggest that these two poems may have been written at the same time.

p. 144 AN EPISTOLARY ESSAY FROM M. G. TO O. B. . . . ("Dear friend, I hear this town does so abound")

> TEXT.   Copy-text: Yale MS., p. 1. Other texts consulted: Portland MS. PwV 40, p. 1; Gyldenstolpe

MS., p. 71; Harvard MS. Eng. 623F, p. 39; Harvard MS. Eng. 636F, p. 4; Osborn MS. Chest II, Number 28; A-1680-HU, p. 3; A-1680-PF, p. 3. For additional early texts, see *ARP*, pp. 369–70, and *Gyldenstolpe*, p. 327.

Departures from copy-text: *Heading* from M. G. to O. B.] Very Delightful and Solid from the Lord R. to the Lord M. 2 With] In. 5 spleen] spleens. 6 brow] brows. 13 hopes] hope. 20 critic] critics. 21 Those] These. 23 I'd] I'll. 40 though] if. 41 costive and] harsh. 50 But] Yet. 56 large] great. 64 munificent] magnificent. 66 is] are. 67 Who ever] For none e'er. 75 should . . . could] could . . . should. 76 be] were. 78 that's] there's. 82 will] shall. 84 of] on. 87 ten] two.

AUTHORSHIP. See *ARP*, pp. 369–70.

DATE. Probably composed soon after Rochester's letter of 21 November 1679. For further information on the subject and date of the "Epistolary Essay," see *ARP*, pp. 103–07, 119–36. The poem was first published in A-1680-HU.

p. 148 EPIGRAM ON THOMAS OTWAY ("To form a plot")

TEXT. Copy-text: Portland MS. PwV 31 in Rochester's own hand, fol. 8ʳ. The original has no heading.

For further information on the text, authorship, date, and subject of this epigram, see *ARP*, Chapter 7, pp. 204–30, especially pp. 214–19 and 224–25. It was first published by Vivian de Sola Pinto in *Poems by John Wilmot, Earl of Rochester* (London, Routledge and Kegan Paul, 1953), p. 118.

p. 149 ANSWER TO A PAPER OF VERSES . . .
("What strange surprise to meet such words as these")

TEXT. Copy-text: *A Collection of Poems By Several
Hands*, 1693 (Case 151-c), p. 127, the source of all
other known texts.

Departures from copy-text: *Heading*] The Earl
of Rochester's Answer, to a Paper of Verses, sent him
by L. B. Felton, and taken out of the Translation of
Ovid's Epistles, 1680.

AUTHORSHIP. The poem is attributed to Rochester in
the miscellany of 1693, which was published by
Francis Saunders. It is also specifically listed in the
edition of Rochester's poems that Saunders entered
in the *Stationers' Register* on 19 November 1690
but apparently never published.

DATE. If its heading is to be trusted, the poem must
have been written soon after the publication of *Ovid's
Epistles*, which was advertised in several newspapers
in February and March 1680 (Hugh Macdonald,
John Dryden: A Bibliography, Oxford, Clarendon
Press, 1939, p. 17).

p. 150 A TRANSLATION FROM SENECA'S
"TROADES," ACT II, CHORUS ("After death
nothing is, and nothing, death")

TEXT. Copy-text: Yale MS., p. 106. For other early
texts, see *ARP*, pp. 397–99, and *Gyldenstolpe*, p.
324.

Departures from copy-text: *Heading*] Seneca's
Troas, Act 2d, Chorus.

AUTHORSHIP. See *ARP*, pp. 31, 397–99, and *Gyldenstolpe*, p. 324.

DATE.   Evidently the poem was composed just before
the date of Charles Blount's letter (see headnote).
It was first published in A-1680-HU, p. 50.

p. 155   TO HIS SACRED MAJESTY . . . ("Virtue's triumphant shrine! who dost engage")

TEXT.   Copy-text: *Britannia Rediviva*, 1660 (Case
124), sig. Aa1ʳ.
   Departures from copy-text: *Heading* on His Restoration in the Year 1660] *added as in the text in
B-1691, p. 121.*

AUTHORSHIP AND DATE.   See headnote.

p. 156   IN OBITUM SERENISSIMAE MARIAE PRIN-
CIPIS ARAUSIONENSIS ("Impia blasphemi si-
leant convitia vulgi")

TEXT.   Copy-text: *Epicedia Academiae Oxoniensis, in
Obitum Serenissimae Mariae Principis Arausionensis,*
1660 (Case 126), sig. A2ᵛ.
   Departures from copy-text: *Heading*] *lacking;
supplied from the title of the volume.* 8 nequat] *corrected from* nequit.

AUTHORSHIP AND DATE.   See headnote.

p. 157   TO HER SACRED MAJESTY, THE QUEEN
MOTHER . . . ("Respite, great Queen, your just
and hasty fears")

TEXT.   Copy-text: *Epicedia Academiae Oxoniensis, in
Obitum Serenissimae Mariae Principis Arausionensis,*
1660 (Case 126), sig. G1ʳ.

Departures from copy-text: *Heading* on the Death of Mary, Princess of Orange] *added as in the text in B-1691, p. 124.* 31 curses] *corrected from* cures, *an obvious misprint.*

AUTHORSHIP AND DATE. See headnote.

p. 159 A RODOMONTADE ON HIS CRUEL MISTRESS ("Trust not that thing called woman: she is worse")

TEXT. Copy-text: Merton College, Oxford, MS. P.3.1. Other texts consulted: *Westminster Drollery*, 1671 (Case 151-1-a), reprint ed. J. Woodfall Ebsworth (Boston, Lincolnshire, 1875), *1*, 14; B. M. Add. MS. 18220, fol. 103ʳ, which is verbally identical with *Westminster Drollery* except for the heading.

Departures from copy-text: *Heading*] *lacking; supplied from "Westminster Drollery."* 6 she but] *that she.* 7 worse] *far worse.*

AUTHORSHIP. Attributed to Rochester in the copy-text. Headed "Lᵈ Buckhursts Rodomondado upon his Mistris" in B. M. Add. MS. 18220—which may, however, have been copied from *Westminster Drollery*. The verse style resembles Rochester's, but the ascription to Buckhurst (Dorset) cannot be discounted. See Brice Harris, *Charles Sackville, Sixth Earl of Dorset* (Urbana, University of Illinois Press, 1940), p. 37.

DATE. The exact date of composition is unknown. The poem was first published in *Westminster Drollery*, 1671, which was advertised in the *Term Cata-*

logues on 30 May 1671. The copy in B. M. Add.
MS. 18220 is subscribed "Cõmunic: á Mrs Sam: Nay-
lour Aug: 14. 1672."

p. 159   AGAINST MARRIAGE ("Out of mere love and arrant devotion")

> Text.   Copy-text: B. M. Add. MS. 23722, fol. 51^v.
> Other text consulted: Edinburgh MS. DC.1.3, p.
> 67.
> Departures from copy-text: *Heading*] By ye E. of
> Rochester. 6 That] It. 6 peep] peeps. 11 say] you.

> Authorship.   Ascribed to Rochester in the copy-text.

> Date.   Evidence of the exact date of composition is
> lacking. In *Mock Songs and Joking Poems*, 1675
> (Case 158), p. 134, is printed "A Mock to that
> against Marriage, Called out of pure, and arrant De-
> votion" ("'Tis the end of debauchery, the beginning
> of pleasure").

p. 160   A SONG ("Injurious charmer of my vanquished
heart")

> Text.   Copy-text: *Valentinian: a Tragedy. As 'tis
> Alter'd by the late Earl of Rochester*, London, 1685,
> p. 42, used without verbal alteration.

> Authorship.   This song is printed in *Valentinian*,
> 1685—some five years after Rochester's death—
> without being attributed explicitly to Rochester or
> to anyone else. In the absence of other testimony,
> the situation remains inconclusive.

> Date.   The date of composition is unknown. A trun-
> cated version of the poem appears in *Female Poems*

> *On Several Occasions. Written by Ephelia*, 2d ed., London, 1682, p. 125.

p. 161   **EPIGRAM ON SAMUEL PORDAGE** ("Poet, whoe'er thou art, God damn thee")

> TEXT AND AUTHORSHIP. See *The Dramatic Works of Roger Boyle, Earl of Orrery*, ed. William Smith Clark, Cambridge (Mass.), Harvard University Press, 1937, 2, 951–52. Orrery's anecdote is given in less detail in *The History of Herod and Mariamne; Collected and Compil'd from the best Historians, and serving to illustrate the Fable of Mr. Fenton's Tragedy of that Name*, London, 1723, Preface, sigs. A4ʳ-A4ᵛ. The distich appears in slightly different form:

>> Poet, whoe'er thou art, I say God damn thee;
>> Take my advice, and burn thy *Mariamne*.

> DATE. Pordage's *Herod and Mariamne* was acted on 28 October 1673 and published later in that year with a dedication (written by Elkanah Settle) to the Duchess of Newcastle, but it may have been written and produced several years earlier (Allardyce Nicoll, *A History of English Drama 1660–1900:* vol. *1, Restoration Drama*, 4th ed., Cambridge University Press, 1955, p. 424). The distich attributed to Rochester was apparently first published in *The History of Herod and Mariamne*, 1723.

p. 161   **ON ROME'S PARDONS** ("If Rome can pardon sins, as Romans hold")

> TEXT. Copy-text: A-1680-HU, p. 151, used without verbal alteration. For other early texts, see *ARP*, pp. 474–77.

AUTHORSHIP. The arguments for and against Rochester's authorship seem about equally strong. See *ARP*, Chapter 14, pp. 353–62.

DATE. The date of composition is unknown. The poem was first published in A-1680-HU.

*First-Line List of Poems
Omitted from This Edition*

A fellow in fear of eternal damnation
    Attributed to Rochester only in D-1761, p. 8.

A knight delights in deeds of arms
    Attributed to Rochester only in C-1707-a, p. [3]136, and sources descended from it.

A load of guts, wrapped in a sallow skin
    Attributed to Rochester only in D-1718, p. 38, and sources descended from it.

A lovely face and charming mien
    Attributed to Rochester only in D-1761, p. 34

A worthy woman lies here-under
    Attributed to Rochester only in D-1761, p. 61.

All the world can't afford
    Attributed to Rochester only in D-1718, p. 39, and sources descended from it.

All things fair, we find, are cold
    Attributed to Rochester only in D-1761, p. 105.

An honest, ancient, homebred clown
    Attributed to Rochester only in D-1761, p. 14.

Apollo, shining god of verse
    Attributed to Rochester only in D-1761, p. 34.

As Aaron and his priestly sons
    Attributed to Rochester only in D-1761, p. 80.

As Colin drove his sheep along
    Probably by Charles Sackville, Earl of Dorset. See *ARP*, p. 488, and *Gyldenstolpe*, pp. 348–50.

As crafty harlots use to shrink
    By George Etherege. See *ARP*, pp. 85, 88, 239–48, 439–40, and *Gyldenstolpe*, pp. 329–30.

As in the days of yore was odds
    Attributed to Rochester only in Harvard MS. Eng. 636F, p. 264. See Lord, *POAS*, *1*, 263.

As Margery by the fire sat
    Attributed to Rochester only in D-1761, p. 35.

As Menelaus, watchful, lay tossing in bed
    Attributed to Rochester only in D-1761, p. 190.

As wanton Cupid idly lay
    Attributed to Rochester only in D-1761, p. 39.

As when a bully draws his sword
    By Edmund Ashton. See *ARP*, pp. 75, 85, 250–51, 253–54, 257, 445–46.

At the sight of my Phyllis, from every part
   Attributed to Rochester only in C-1707-a, p. [1]8, and sources descended
   from it.
Baldwin, another Maccabee for might
   Attributed to Rochester only in D-1761, p. 59.
Base-mettled hanger by thy master's thigh
   Ascribed to Rochester in Bodl. MS. Eng. Poet. d. 152, fol. 9[r]; Victoria
   and Albert Museum MS. Dyce 43, p. 243; Chetham MS. Mun. A. 4.
   14, p. 75; Edinburgh MS. DC.1.3, p. 54; Vienna MS. 14090, fol.
   129[r]; Taylor MS. 3, p. 240. This unimaginative attempt at pornography
   is amateurish in its versification.
Before by death you newer knowledge gain
   By Sir William Davenant. See V. de Sola Pinto, "An Unpublished
   Poem Attributed to Rochester," *London Times Literary Supplement*,
   22 November 1934, p. 824; "A Poem Attributed to Rochester," 6
   December 1934, p. 875; and "Rochester and the Deists," 13 De-
   cember 1934, p. 895.
Behold these woods, and mark, my sweet
   By Thomas Randolph; see J. H. Wilson, "Two Poems Ascribed to
   Rochester," *Modern Language Notes*, 54 (1939), 458–60. Attributed
   to Rochester only in A-1685, p. 115, and sources descended from it.
Bella fugis, bellas sequeris, belloque repugnas
   These four lines of punning Latin are attributed to Rochester only in
   Bodl. MS. Add. B. 105, p. 62.
Betwixt Father Patrick and His Highness of late
   Attributed to Rochester in *A Third Collection of The Newest and
   Most Ingenious Poems, Satyrs, Songs, &c. against Popery and Tyranny*,
   1689 (Case 189-3), p. 31, and sources descended from it; also in National Library of Scotland MS. Advocate 19.1.12, fol. 82[r], whose text
   is closely related to that in *A Third Collection*. Rochester's authorship
   is seemingly doubted in a well-informed letter dated 15 April 1673,
   only a few days after the poem was written; see Lord, *POAS, 1*, 211.
Bless me, you stars! for sure some sad portent
   Ascribed to Rochester in Victoria and Albert Museum MS. Dyce 43, p.
   245, and Vienna MS. 14090, fol. 130[r]. This is a very ordinary piece
   of pornography, mediocre in its poetical technique.
By heavens! 'twas bravely done
   Attributed to Rochester only in C-1707-a, p. [3]135, and sources de-
   scended from it.
Can gold or gems diffuse the charm
   Attributed to Rochester only in D-1761, p. 59.

Chaste, pious, prudent Charles the Second

By John Freke; see Frank H. Ellis, "John Freke and *The History of Insipids*," *Philological Quarterly*, *44* (1965), 472–83. Attributed to Rochester in *Poems on Affairs of State*, 1697 (Case 211-1-a), p. 157, and sources descended from it; the 1697 text, however, was printed from *A Second Collection of The Newest and Most Ingenious Poems, Satyrs, Songs, &c. against Popery and Tyranny*, 1689 (Case 189-2), p. 9, which gives no ascription. In Bodl. MS. Douce 357, fol. 103ʳ, where the text is independent of printed sources, the ascription "By the E. of Rochester. Printed" was obviously added at a later date. A version ascribed "By yᵉ E: of R." in an uncatalogued manuscript in the University of Illinois Library, though independently descended, presents a seriously corrupt text transcribed not earlier than 1680 by a copyist who was ill-informed about the events mentioned in the poem.

See Lord, *POAS*, *1*, 243.

Chloris, to love without return

By Rochester's wife. See *ARP*, Chapter 7, pp. 204–30, especially pp. 208, 209–12.

Clarendon had law and sense

Probably by Charles Sackville, Earl of Dorset; see Mengel, *POAS*, *2*, 339. Attributed to Rochester only in *A New Collection of Poems Relating to State Affairs*, 1705 (Case 237), p. 129, and sources descended from it; this text was printed from some edition of *Poems on Affairs of State*, 1697 (Case 211-1-a), p. 173, which attributes the poem to Dryden.

Come on, ye critics! find one fault who dare

By Charles Sackville, Earl of Dorset. See *ARP*, pp. 75, 85, 250–53, 442–45.

Conquered with soft and pleasing charms

See my article "Poems by 'My Lord R.': Rochester versus Radclyffe," *PMLA*, *72* (1957), 612–19, especially p. 616.

Continue still ingrate

By Rochester's wife. See *ARP*, Chapter 7, pp. 204–30, especially pp. 208, 209–12.

Corinna, vainly I pretend

By Rochester's wife. See *ARP*, Chapter 7, pp. 204–30, especially pp. 208, 209–12.

Dear Nancy, you've made such a hole in my heart

Attributed to Rochester only in D-1761, p. 63.

Dearest Armilla, could you once but guess

By Rochester's wife. See *ARP*, Chapter 7, pp. 204–30, especially pp. 208–12.

Deep in an unctuous vale, 'twixt swelling hills
Apparently by Sir Francis Fane. Ascribed to Rochester only in Harvard MS. Eng. 636F, p. 32. Ascribed to Fane in B. M. Harl. MS. 7319, fol. 11ᵛ; Victoria and Albert Museum MS. Dyce 43, p. 248; and Vienna MS. 14090, fol. 131ᵛ.

Descend, O muse, and let me write
Attributed to Rochester only in D-1761, p. 100.

Disgraced, undone, forlorn, made fortune's sport
See *Gyldenstolpe*, pp. 357–59.

Dreaming last night on Mistress Farley
By Charles Sackville, Earl of Dorset. See *ARP*, pp. 85, 88, 239–48, 438–39, and *Gyldenstolpe*, pp. 329–30.

Enough! enough! thou damned eternal scold
Attributed to Rochester only in D-1761, p. 53.

Farewell, false woman! Know, I'll ever be
Attributed to Rochester only in C-1707-a, p. ¹31, and sources descended from it.

For standing tarses we kind nature thank
Probably by Charles Sackville, Earl of Dorset. See *ARP*, pp. 88, 437–38.

For that presumptuous fault of mine
Attributed to Rochester only in D-1761, p. 1.

Foulest of Furies, Stygian maid
Attributed to Rochester only in D-1761, p. 75.

Fruition was the question in debate
Attributed to Rochester only in C-1707-a, p. ¹15, and sources descended from it. Rochester's authorship is rejected by J. H. Wilson, "Two Poems Ascribed to Rochester," *Modern Language Notes*, 54 (1939), 458–60.

Fucksters, you that will be happy
See *ARP*, p. 489.

Gentle reproofs have long been tried in vain
By Edmund Ashton. See *ARP*, pp. 266–68, and *Gyldenstolpe*, p. 321.

Great Charles, who, full of mercy, wouldst command
Attributed to Rochester only in B. M. Add. MS. 34109, fol. 2ʳ. These verses are the envoy to Henry Savile's *Advice to a Painter to Draw the Duke by*; see Lord, *POAS*, 1, 213.

Had I been Jove, and mortals made
Attributed to Rochester only in D-1761, p. 60.

Have you heard of a lord of noble descent

Attributed to Rochester only in D-1718, p. 79, and sources descended from it. Internal evidence shows that this lampoon was written after Rochester's death on 26 July 1680.

Have you not in a chimney seen

Attributed to Rochester only in Chetham MS. Mun. A. 4. 14, p. 55, and in *Familiar Letters: Vol. I. Written by the Right Honourable John, late Earl of Rochester*, etc., 4th ed., London, 1705, p. 224, and sources descended from it. Attributed to Milton in *Oxford and Cambridge Miscellany Poems*, 1708 (Case 248), p. 286.

Have you seen the raging, stormy main

See *ARP*, pp. 88, 452.

Here lies a fruitful, loving wife

Attributed to Rochester only in D-1761, p. 97.

Hold fast thy sword and scepter, Charles

Attributed to Rochester only in Osborn MS. Box 55.

How far are they deceived who hope in vain

Probably by George Etherege. See *ARP*, pp. 88, 322–52, 465–67, and *Gyldenstolpe*, pp. 330–31.

How happy a state does the bridegroom possess

Attributed to Rochester only in D-1761, p. 62.

How now, brave swain, why art thou thus cast down

Attributed to Rochester only in A-1685, p. 53.

How sweet and pleasing are thy charms

Attributed to Rochester only in D-1761, p. 7.

Husband, thou dull, unpitied miscreant

Attributed to Rochester in *Poems on Affairs of State*, 1697 (Case 211-1-a), p. 26, and sources descended from it; B. M. Add. MS. 14047, fol. 111^r; Cambridge MS. Add. 6339, fol. 11^r; Chetham MS. Mun. A. 4. 14, p. 70. This is a doctrinaire libertine satire, skillful in its way but employing heavily end-stopped lines which are distinctively different from Rochester's usual manner of writing pentameter couplets (see *ARP*, pp. 291–92).

I cannot change as others do

Probably by Sir Carr Scroope. See *ARP*, pp. 84–86, 231–38, 434–36, and *Gyldenstolpe*, pp. 331–32. (For a text of this lyric, see p. 136.)

I know by this time you expect

Attributed to Rochester only in D-1761, p. 83.

I promised Sylvia to be true

Attributed to Rochester only in *Examen Miscellaneum*, 1702 (Case 228), p. 9.

I rise at eleven, I dine about two

Probably by Charles Sackville, Earl of Dorset. See *ARP*, pp. 86–87, 168–72, 411–12, and *Gyldenstolpe*, p. 323.

If I can guess, the Devil choke me
By Charles Sackville, Earl of Dorset. See *ARP*, pp. 85, 88, 239–48, 440–41, and *Gyldenstolpe*, pp. 329–30.

If, Nizy, what you write be true
Attributed to Rochester only in D-1761, p. 64.

In a dark, silent, shady grove
Attributed to Rochester only in C-1714-1, p. 113, and sources descended from it.

In a famous street near Whetstone's Park
See *Gyldenstolpe*, pp. 355–57.

In all humility we crave
These verses are part of a longer poem printed in 1662 and dating back to about 1642, before Rochester's birth. See Harold Brooks, "Attributions to Rochester," *London Times Literary Supplement*, 9 May 1935, p. 301.

In ancient days when William Rufus reigned
Attributed to Rochester only in D-1761, p. 9.

In ancient Greece in days of yore
Attributed to Rochester only in D-1761, p. 27.

In sixteen hundred seventy-eight
Attributed to Rochester only in D-1718, p. 37, and sources descended from it.

In the fields of Lincoln's Inn
Probably by Sir Charles Sedley. See *ARP*, pp. 87, 172–74, 404–05, and *Gyldenstolpe*, p. 339.

In this cold monument lies one
By Charles Cotton; see *Poems of Charles Cotton 1630–1687*, ed. John Beresford (New York, Boni and Liveright, 1923), p. 283. In Taylor MS. 3, p. 258, these verses were originally headed "On a Monument by ye E. R." At a later date, however, the ascription was crossed out and "Squire Cotton" and "In Print" were written in the margin.

Is there a man, ye gods, whom I do hate
By Abraham Cowley. See my communication, "Rochester and Cowley," *London Times Literary Supplement*, 12 October 1951, p. 645.

It was when the dark lantern of the night
Attributed to Rochester in C-1709, p. [2]106, and sources descended from it; B. M. Harl. MS. 6914, fol. 73^r; Victoria and Albert Museum MS. Dyce 43, p. 242; Chetham MS. Mun. A. 4. 14, p. 63; Edinburgh MS. DC.1.3, p. 71; Vienna MS. 14090, fol. 128^v; and Osborn

MS. Chest II, Number 1. Despite the many ascriptions to Rochester, the mediocre versification and conventional pornography of this piece cast doubt on its authenticity. The apparently early dates of several manuscript texts (especially those carrying no ascription), as well as the relatively old-fashioned diction of the poem, suggest that it originated in the early seventeenth century.

Julian, in verse to ease thy wants I write

Probably by Anthony Carey, fifth Viscount of Falkland. See *Gyldenstolpe*, pp. 340–43.

Kind friend, I have need

Attributed to Rochester only in D-1761, p. 94.

Let ancients boast no more

Attributed to Rochester only in *Poems on Affairs of State*, 1697 (Case 211-1-c), p. [2]239, and sources descended from it.

Let kings enjoy their formal state

Attributed to Rochester only in D-1761, p. 13.

Long time Plain Dealing in the haughty town

Attributed to Rochester only in A-1685, p. 54, and sources descended from it.

Marriage, thou state of jealousy and care

Attributed to Rochester only in *Examen Miscellaneum*, 1702 (Case 228), p. 7, and sources descended from it.

Methinks I see our mighty monarch stand

See *Gyldenstolpe*, pp. 368–71.

Methinks I see you newly risen

See *Gyldenstolpe*, pp. 366–67.

Must I with patience ever silent sit

See *Gyldenstolpe*, pp. 371–72.

My goddess Lydia, heavenly fair

By Edward Radclyffe, second Earl of Derwentwater. See my article "Poems by 'My Lord R.': Rochester versus Radclyffe," *PMLA*, 72 (1957), 612–19.

My part is done, and you'll, I hope, excuse

By John Oldham. See *ARP*, pp. 75, 461–63.

Nature, creation's law, is judged by sense

By Thomas Randolph; see J. H. Wilson, "Two Poems Ascribed to Rochester," *Modern Language Notes*, 54 (1939), 458–60. Attributed to Rochester only in A-1685, p. 113, and sources descended from it.

Nelly, my life, though now thou'rt full fifteen

Attributed to Rochester only in the undated (but probably eighteenth-century) pamphlet *A Genuine Letter from the Earl of Rochester to*

Nell Gwyn. Copied from an Original Manuscript in the French King's Library. On p. [20] appears an advertisement: "On the Sixth of June next will be published, A Satyr on the Court-Ladies. Written by the Earl of Rochester. Never printed before." This satire on the court ladies remains unidentified.

No longer blame those on the banks of Nile
    Attributed to Rochester only in C-1735, p. 120.

Not far from Woodstock, on a pleasant green
    Attributed to Rochester only in D-1761, p. 54.

Not Rome, in all its splendor, could compare
    See *Gyldenstolpe,* pp. 359–61.

Nothing adds to love's fond fire
    By Rochester's wife. See *ARP,* pp. 86, 209–12, 417–18, and *Gyldenstolpe,* p. 336. (For a text of this lyric, see p. 10.)

Now curses on ye all, ye virtuous fools
    By John Oldham. See *ARP,* pp. 75, 458–61, and *Gyldenstolpe,* p. 348.

O muse, in doleful ditty tell
    Attributed to Rochester only in D-1761, p. 95.

O muse, to whom the glory does belong
    By Edward Radclyffe, second Earl of Derwentwater. See my article "Poems by 'My Lord R.': Rochester versus Radclyffe," *PMLA,* 72 (1957), 612–19.

Of a great heroine I mean to tell
    Attributed to Rochester only in C-1707-a, p. ¹26, and sources descended from it. This lampoon on Nell Gwyn may have been written after Rochester's death; see Mengel, *POAS,* 2, 242.

Of all quality whores, modest Betty for me
    Attributed to Rochester only in D-1718, p. 53, and sources descended from it.

Of all the fools these fertile times produce
    Attributed to Rochester only in D-1718, p. 84.

Of all the plagues with which this world abounds
    Attributed to Rochester only in D-1718, p. 73, and sources descended from it.

Of all the wonders since the world began
    See *Gyldenstolpe,* pp. 352–53.

Of civil dudgeon many a bard
    Attributed to Rochester only in D-1718, p. 43, and sources descended from it. The poem alludes to the death of Samuel Butler on 25 September 1680, two months after Rochester's death. See Mengel, *POAS,* 2, 235.

Of villains, rebels, cuckolds, pimps, and spies

Attributed to Rochester only in D-1718, p. 90. Alludes to the death of Thomas Butler, Earl of Ossory, on 30 July 1680, four days after Rochester's death. See Mengel, *POAS*, 2, 228.

Oh, that I could by some chymic art
See *ARP*, pp. 33, 490.

Oh! what damned age do we live in
Ascribed to Rochester in B. M. Harl. MS. 6914, fol. 3^r; Bodl. MS. Firth C. 15, p. 26; Victoria and Albert Museum MS. Dyce 43, p. 26; and Vienna MS. 14090, fol. 20^v. This song is a dull, metrically inept piece of pornography.

Old Noll did late five friends invite
Attributed to Rochester only in D-1761, p. 13.

Old Thomas a Clarkibus lived in the fen
Attributed to Rochester only in D-1761, p. 81.

One day the amorous Lysander
By Aphra Behn. See *ARP*, pp. 85, 88–89, 448–50, and *Gyldenstolpe*, p. 329.

Opinion's a happiness everyone knows
Attributed to Rochester only in D-1761, p. 26.

Phyllis, misfortunes that can be expressed
By Rochester's wife. See *ARP*, Chapter 7, pp. 204–30, especially pp. 208, 209–12.

Pity, fair Sappho, one that dies
By Edward Radclyffe, second Earl of Derwentwater. See my article "Poems by 'My Lord R.': Rochester versus Radclyffe," *PMLA*, 72 (1957), 612–19.

Poscis ut omne meum soli tibi serviat aevum
See *ARP*, p. 427.

Preserved by wonder in the oak, O Charles
Probably by John Lacy, the actor, to whom it is ascribed in four manuscripts: B. M. Harl. MS. 7319, fol. 26^r; Victoria and Albert Museum MS. Dyce 43, p. 273; National Library of Scotland MS. Advocate 19.1.12, fol. 88^v; and Vienna MS. 14090, fol. 145^r. Attributed to Rochester in *Poems on Affairs of State*, 1703 (Case 211-2-a), p. 192, and sources descended from it; also in B. M. Harl. MS. 7312, p. 110, whose text is closely related to that in *Poems on Affairs of State* although apparently not derived from it. In Bodl. MS. Douce 357, fol. 101^v, where the text is independent of printed sources, the inscriptions "Printed" and "By the E. of Rochester" were obviously added at a later date. As a lesser-known author than Rochester, Lacy was less likely to be the recipient of false attributions. See Lord, *POAS*, *1*, 425.

Pride, lust, ambition, and the people's hate

Attributed to Rochester only in C-1709, p. [1]104, and sources descended from it. See Lord, *POAS*, *1*, 158.

Qualis ab exacto dux classis marte solutus

See *ARP*, p. 384.

Rail on, poor feeble scribbler, speak of me

By Sir Carr Scroope. See *ARP*, pp. 137–63, 396–97, and *Gyldenstolpe*, pp. 332–33. (For a text of this poem, see p. 132.)

Rat too, rat too, rat too, rat tat too, rat tat too

By Alexander Radcliffe. See *ARP*, pp. 88, 464–65.

Refrain, my friend, the baneful ebrious cup

Attributed to Rochester only in D-1761, p. 25.

Room, room for a blade of the town

By Thomas D'Urfey. See *ARP*, pp. 85, 86, 180–83, 432–33.

Say, heaven-born muse, for only thou canst tell

See *ARP*, pp. 86, 174–77, 385–86.

Shame of my life, disturber of my tomb

By Wentworth Dillon, Earl of Roscommon; see Mengel, *POAS*, *2*, 249. Attributed to Rochester only in *Poems on Affairs of State*, 1698 (Case 215), p. 167 and table of contents, and in sources descended from it.

She was so exquisite a whore

Attributed to Rochester in C-1718-1, p. 112, and sources descended from it. Subscribed "Authore D Rochester" in Chetham MS. Mun. A. 4. 14, p. 26. Subscribed "Duke of Buckingham" in Victoria and Albert Museum MS. Dyce 43, p. 262.

Silence! coeval with eternity

By Alexander Pope. Attributed to Rochester in one of the three editions of 1739 in the C series (2, 214), evidently because it is an imitation of "Upon Nothing."

Since death on all lays his impartial hand

Perhaps by Charles Blount; see *The Poems of Sir George Etherege*, ed. James Thorpe (Princeton University Press, 1963), pp. 134–36. Attributed to Rochester only in *Examen Miscellaneum*, 1702 (Case 228), p. 15.

Since now my Sylvia is as kind as fair

By John Sheffield, Earl of Mulgrave. See *ARP*, pp. 31–32, 85, 481–83, and *Gyldenstolpe*, p. 348.

Since the sons of the muses grew numerous and loud

Possibly by Elkanah Settle. See *ARP*, pp. 30, 75, 296–321, 455–58.

Six of the female sex, and purest sect

Attributed to Rochester only in D-1718, p. 1, and sources descended from it. An anti-Puritan satire evidently dating from the early seventeenth century, before Rochester's birth, it was printed without ascription in *Rump*, 1662 (Case 128-c), Pt. II, p. 158.

So soft and amorously you write

> By George Etherege. See *ARP*, pp. 85, 88, 239–48, 441, and *Gyldenstolpe*, pp. 329–30.

Stamford is her sex's glory

> Attributed to Rochester only in D-1718, p. 39, and sources descended from it.

Stamford's Countess led the van

> Attributed to Rochester only in D-1718, p. 17.

Sweet Hyacinth, my life, my joy

> By Edward Radclyffe, second Earl of Derwentwater. See my article "Poems by 'My Lord R.': Rochester versus Radclyffe," *PMLA*, 72 (1957), 612–19.

Sylvia, ne'er despise my love

> Attributed to Rochester only in *Chorus Poetarum*, 1694 (Case 202), p. 85, and sources descended from it.

Tell me, abandoned miscreant, prithee tell

> By John Oldham. See *ARP*, pp. 75, 463–64.

Tell me, Belinda, tell me why

> Attributed to Rochester only in D-1761, p. 26.

That you may know how I have spent

> Attributed to Rochester only in D-1761, p. 65.

The clog of all pleasure, the luggage of life

> See *Gyldenstolpe*, p. 325.

The earth of gold and silver veins hath store

> Attributed to Rochester only in D-1761, p. 207.

The glorious sun is not so bright

> Attributed to Rochester only in D-1761, p. 51.

The heaven drinks every day a cup

> Attributed to Rochester in *The Second Volume of Miscellaneous Works, Written by George, Late Duke of Buckingham*, 1705 (Case 232-2), p. [2]2, and sources descended from it; Victoria and Albert Museum MS. Dyce 43, p. 545; Portland MS. PwV 43, p. 38. Despite these ascriptions, the poem's clumsy syntax and imprecise diction and meaning cast doubt on its authenticity. In all three of the independently descended texts, one or more of the preceding or following poems are also ascribed to Rochester wrongly or improbably.

The husband's the pilot, the wife is the ocean

> By Tom Brown. Attributed to Rochester only in C-1735, p. 121.

The parson that preaches nor prays once a moon

> Attributed to Rochester only in D-1761, p. 7.

The parson to the people says
  Attributed to Rochester only in D-1761, p. 80.

The parsons all keep whores
  See *ARP*, p. 489.

The truth a thousand times denied
  Attributed to Rochester only in D-1761, p. 57.

There's no such thing as good or evil
  Ascribed to Rochester only in Harvard MS. Eng. 636F, p. 54. A variant
  version is ascribed to John, Lord Vaughan, in B. M. Harl. MS. 6914,
  fol. 3^v; Bodl. MS. Firth C. 15, p. 27; Victoria and Albert Museum MS.
  Dyce 43, p. 27; and Vienna MS. 14090, fol. 21^r.

Thou damned antipodes to common sense
  See *ARP*, pp. 75, 85, 250–51, 253, 446–48.

Thou mighty princess, lovely queen of holes
  Attributed to Rochester only in C-1707-a, p. [1]5, and sources descended from it. Dated 1684 in the text in National Library of Scotland MS. Advocate 19.1.12, fol. 38^v.

Though weaned from all those scandalous delights
  See *Gyldenstolpe*, pp. 353–54.

Tired with the noisome follies of the age
  Possibly by Charles Sackville, Earl of Dorset. See *Gyldenstolpe*, pp. 361–
  65.

'Tis the Arabian bird alone
  By Michael Drayton; these verses are ll. 149–52 of "King John to
  Matilda" in *Englands Heroicall Epistles*. Attributed to Rochester in
  Poems on Affairs of State, 1703 (Case 211-2-a), p. 191, and sources
  descended from it; *The Second Volume of Miscellaneous Works,
  Written by George, Late Duke of Buckingham*, 1705 (Case 232-2),
  p. [2]7, and sources descended from it; B. M. Add. MS. 21094, fol. 5^r,
  where the text seems to be independently descended but the ascription
  may have been copied later from a printed source; and Taylor MS. 2,
  p. 40.

'Tis thought tall Richard first possessed
  See *Gyldenstolpe*, p. 373.

To all young men that love to woo
  Attributed to Rochester in *Wit and Mirth*, 1700 (Day and Murrie
  188), p. 319, and sources descended from it, including *The Second Part
  of Penkethman's Jests*, London, 1721, p. 138.

To make myself for this employment fit
  See my communication "Rochester and 'A Young Gentleman,'" *London
  Times Literary Supplement*, 23 September 1955, p. 557; also V. de S.

Pinto, "A Poem Attributed to Rochester," *London Times Literary Supplement*, 5 November 1954, p. 705, and "Rochester and 'A Young Gentleman,'" 7 October 1955, p. 589.

T' th' honorable Court there lately came

Attributed to Rochester only in D-1718, p. 55, and sources descended from it.

To what intent or purpose was man made

By Alexander Radcliffe. Attributed to Rochester in A-1701, p. 110, and sources descended from it; also in a MS. note in a copy of the broadside of the poem published *c.* 30 January 1679/80 (*Poems by John Wilmot, Earl of Rochester*, ed. Vivian de Sola Pinto, 2d ed., London, Routledge and Kegan Paul, 1964, p. 220).

Virtue's my lawful prince, my tyrant love

By Rochester's wife. See *ARP*, Chapter 7, pp. 204–30, especially pp. 208, 209–12.

Was ever mortal man like me

Attributed to Rochester only in C-1718-2, p. 218, and sources descended from it.

Welcome, great prince, to life again at least

In Taylor MS. 3, p. 262, this poem is headed "To ye King by E. R."

What doleful cries are these that fright my sense

By Aphra Behn. See *ARP*, pp. 75, 85, 451–52, and *Gyldenstolpe*, p. 365.

What pleasures can the gaudy world afford

Attributed to Rochester only in A-1685, p. 66, and sources descended from it.

When jolly Bacchus first began

Attributed to Rochester only in D-1761, p. 3.

When rebels first pushed at the crown

Ascribed to Rochester only in Harvard MS. Eng. 636F, p. 54. Ascribed to Lord Buckhurst (Charles Sackville, Earl of Dorset) in B. M. Harl. MS. 6914, fol. 21ʳ; Victoria and Albert Museum MS. Dyce 43, p. 241; and Vienna MS. 14090, fol. 128ʳ.

When Shakespeare, Jonson, Fletcher ruled the stage

By Sir Carr Scroope. See *ARP*, pp. 137–63, 390–94, and *Gyldenstolpe*, pp. 332–33. (Part of the text of this poem is reproduced on p. 132.)

When weary time had spent a summer's day

Ascribed to Rochester only in Chetham MS. Mun. A. 4. 14, p. 54.

Where is he gone whom I adore

By Edward Radclyffe, second Earl of Derwentwater. See my article

"Poems by 'My Lord R.': Rochester versus Radclyffe," *PMLA*, 72 (1957), 612–19.

While I was monarch of your heart

By Edward Radclyffe, second Earl of Derwentwater. See my article, cited for the preceding poem.

While in divine Panthea's charming eyes

By Edward Radclyffe, second Earl of Derwentwater. See my article, cited for the two preceding poems.

Whilst duns were knocking at my door

By Alexander Radcliffe. See *ARP*, pp. 74–75, 473–74.

Whilst happy I triumphant stood

By Aphra Behn. See *ARP*, pp. 75, 450–51.

Why am I doomed to follow you

Attributed to Rochester only in D-1761, p. 2.

Why dost thou shade thy lovely face? Oh, why

Attributed to Rochester only in C-1707-a, p. [1]32, and sources descended from it. This poem is merely an adaptation of Francis Quarles, *Emblemes*, 1635, Book III, No. VII, with the last stanza taken from No. XII.

Within this place a bed's appointed

In a letter of 4 July 1951, Professor John Harold Wilson, of Ohio State University, informs me that in *Francelia*, 1734, a part-fictional, part-fact life of the Duchess of Portsmouth, the following couplet is attributed to Rochester:

> Within this Place a Bed's appointed,
> For a F—ch B— and G—ds Anointed.

The couplet is reproduced in Wilson's *Nell Gwyn: Royal Mistress* (New York, Pellegrini and Cudahy, 1952), p. 180. A variant version appears without ascription in Bodl. MS. Don. b. 8, p. 212, as "Written over Nell Gwins doore":

> These Lodgings are ready lett, & appoynted
> For Nell y[e] Bitch, & y[e] Lords appoynted [*sic*].

Woman was made man's sovereignty to own

Attributed to Rochester in *The Second Volume of Miscellaneous Works, Written by George, Late Duke of Buckingham*, 1705 (Case 232-2), p. [2]4, and sources descended from it; also in Harvard MS. Eng. 623F, p. 50. This is a conventional antifeminist diatribe. Together with three similar satires, it was attributed to "a Person of Quality" in the pamphlet *Female Excellence: Or, Woman Display'd*, London, 1679,

p. 4; none of the other three poems, to my knowledge, has ever been ascribed to Rochester.

Would you send Kate to Portugal

In Taylor MS. 3, p. 262, this lampoon is headed "Rochesters advice to yᵉ Parliament." See Mengel, *POAS*, 2, 292.

Ye sacred nymphs of Lebethra, be by

Attributed to Rochester only in C-1707-a, p. ¹53, and sources descended from it.

Young Jenny the wanton, a miss of fifteen

Attributed to Rochester only in D-1761, p. 36.

Your glory, Phyllis, is in being loved

See *ARP*, Chapter 7, pp. 204–30, especially pp. 208, 212.

First-Line Index to the Poems

In the column of Notes, Etc. below, an initial figure in italics designates the principal entry in the Notes on the Texts, Authorship, and Dates of the Poems or in the First-Line List of Poems Omitted from This Edition.

	Text	Notes, Etc.
A fellow in fear of eternal damnation	—	223
A health to Kate	20	178
A knight delights in deeds of arms	—	223
A load of guts, wrapped in a sallow skin	—	223
A lovely face and charming mien	—	223
A worthy woman lies here-under	—	223
Absent from thee, I languish still	88	198
After death nothing is, and nothing, death	150	*215*; xxxii, xxxv, lviii
Against the charms our ballocks have	137	*211*; xxxvii
All my past life is mine no more	90	*199*; lxiii
All the world can't afford	—	223
All things fair, we find, are cold	—	223
All things submit themselves to your command	18	*177*; xxvi, xxxvii
An age in her embraces passed	87	*198*; xxxiv, lxiii
An honest, ancient, homebred clown	—	223
Ancient person, for whom I	89	*199*; xxxvii
And after singing Psalm the Twelfth	22	179
Apollo, shining god of verse	—	223
As Aaron and his priestly sons	—	223
As charms are nonsense, nonsense seems a charm	91	*200*; 122
As Chloris full of harmless thought	26	181
As Colin drove his sheep along	—	223
As crafty harlots use to shrink	—	223
As in the days of yore was odds	—	223
As Margery by the fire sat	—	223
As Menelaus, watchful, lay tossing in bed	—	223
As some brave admiral, in former war	116	*205*; xxxv, xli, 140
As wanton Cupid idly lay	—	223
As when a bully draws his sword	—	223
At five this morn, when Phoebus raised his head	73	*194*; xxviii, xxxvii, xxxix, xli, lxi

Index of Persons

Aaron, 223
Achilles, 35, 73
Aeneas, 34, 185
Alcock, Thomas, liii-liv
Allen, Don Cameron, lvi
Allison, Alexander Ward, xxxviii
Anacreon, 52
Aretino, Pietro, 41
Ashton, Edmund, 223, 226
Aubrey, John, xxvi, 76
Auffret, Jean, lvi

Babington, Percy L., lvi
Babler, O. F., lvi
Baine, Rodney M., lvi
Baldwin I, King of Jerusalem, 224
Balfour, Sir Andrew, xx
Barry, Elizabeth, xxiii, lix, 85
Barton, Margaret, 74
Baynton, Henry, of Bromham, Wiltshire, xxii-xxiii
Beaumont, Francis, lxiv, 103, 124, 143
Beesley, Alfred, 22
Behn, Aphra, 173; poems written by, lxiv, lxix, 231, 235, 236
Bendo, Alexander, xxvii, xlii, liii-liv, lxii
Beresford, John, 228
Berkshire, Thomas Howard, first Earl of, 57
Berman, Ronald, lvi
Bliss, Philip, 155, 209, 210
Blount, Charles, xxxi-xxxii, lvi, lxiv, 150, 216, 232
Boileau-Despréaux, Nicolas, xxxix, lvii, lxii, 65, 94, 146
Boswell, Eleanore. See Murrie
Bovey, Sir Ralph, 106
Bowman, Henry, 173, 200

Bragge, Benjamin, 165
Bridges, George, xxviii-xxix
Brooks, Harold F., xxxix, lvii, 228
Brown, Tom, 176, 233
Bruser, Fredelle, lvii
Buckhurst, Charles Sackville, Lord. See Dorset
Buckingham, George Villiers, second Duke of, xvii, xviii, xx, xxvii, xxxi, xliv, lxii, 75, 126, 206, 232, 233, 234, 236
Buckingham, John Sheffield, Duke of. See Mulgrave
Bulkeley, Henry, 126
Bullough, Geoffrey, lvii
Bunyan, John, 97
Burnet, Gilbert, xxvii, xxxii, xlii, 135
Burr, Thomas Benge, 78
Bury, Phineas, xix
Busby, Richard, 122
Butler, Lord John, xxi, 126
Butler, Samuel, xxxviii, 53, 58, 126, 230
Butler, Thomas. See Ossory

Caryll, John, 125
Case, Arthur E., 163
Catherine, Queen of England, 20, 24, 41, 55, 57, 58, 65, 123, 137, 178, 237
Cavendish, William. See Devonshire
Charles I, xviii, 157
Charles II, xvii-xxiv passim, xxvii, xxviii, xxxii, 20, 24, 39, 42, 46, 48, 49, 50, 55, 58, 65, 67, 69, 113, 121, 123, 126, 135, 137, 155-56, 157, 177, 189, 190, 216, 226, 227, 229, 231,